Laurence
Tristram Shandy

A CASEBOOK

DISCARD

CASEBOOKS IN CRITICISM
recent titles

Chinua Achebe's *Things Fall Apart*: A Casebook
Edited by Isidore Okpewho

William Faulkner's *Absalom, Absalom!*: A Casebook
Edited by Fred Hobson

Edith Wharton's *The House of Mirth*: A Casebook
Edited by Carol J. Singley

James Joyce's *Ulysses*: A Casebook
Edited by Derek Attridge

Joseph Conrad's *Heart of Darkness*: A Casebook
Edited by Gene M. Moore

Ralph Ellison's *Invisible Man*: A Casebook
Edited by John F. Callahan

Orson Welles's *Citizen Kane*: A Casebook
Edited by James Naremore

Alfred Hitchcock's *Psycho*: A Casebook
Edited by Robert Kolker

D. H. Lawrence's *Sons and Lovers*: A Casebook
Edited by John Worthen and Andrew Harrison

D. H. Lawrence's *Women in Love*: A Casebook
Edited by Richard Peace

Cervantes' *Don Quixote*: A Casebook
Edited by Roberto González Echevarría

Fyodor Dostoevsky's *Crime and Punishment*: A Casebook
Edited by Richard Peace

Charlotte Brontë's *Jane Eyre*: A Casebook
Edited by Elsie B. Michie

LAURENCE STERNE'S
Tristram Shandy

◆ ◆ ◆

A CASEBOOK

Edited by
Thomas Keymer

OXFORD
UNIVERSITY PRESS

2006

OXFORD
UNIVERSITY PRESS

Oxford University Press, Inc., publishes works that further
Oxford University's objective of excellence
in research, scholarship, and education.

Oxford   New York
Auckland   Cape Town   Dar es Salaam   Hong Kong   Karachi
Kuala Lumpur   Madrid   Melbourne   Mexico City   Nairobi
New Delhi   Shanghai   Taipei   Toronto

With offices in
Argentina   Austria   Brazil   Chile   Czech Republic   France   Greece
Guatemala   Hungary   Italy   Japan   Poland   Portugal   Singapore
South Korea   Switzerland   Thailand   Turkey   Ukraine   Vietnam

Published by Oxford University Press, Inc.
198 Madison Avenue, New York, New York 10016

www.oup.com

Oxford is a registered trademark of Oxford University Press

Library of Congress Cataloging-in-Publication Data

Laurence Sterne's Tristram Shandy : a casebook / edited by Thomas Keymer.
    p.   cm.—(Casebooks in criticism)
ISBN-13 978-0-19-517560-8; 978-0-19-517561-5 (pbk.)
ISBN 0-19-517560-3; 0-19-517561-1 (pbk.)
1. Sterne, Laurence, 1713–1768. Life and opinions of Tristram Shandy, gentleman.
2. Experimental fiction, English—History and criticism.   3. Narration (rhetoric)—
history—18th century.   4. Body, human, in literature.   5. Authorship in literature.
6. Infants in literature.   7. Fetus in literature.   I. Keymer, T. (Thomas).   II. Series.
PR3714.T73L385 2006
823'.6—dc22   2005022445

1 3 5 7 9 8 6 4 2

Printed in the United States of America
on acid-free paper

Credits

◆　◆　◆

The editor and publisher are grateful to the authors and publishers listed below for permission to reprint the essays in this volume. The cover image is from a private collection, by kind permission.

Peter M. Briggs, "Laurence Sterne and Literary Celebrity in 1760." *Age of Johnson* 4 (1991): 251–80. Copyright © 1991 by *The Age of Johnson: A Scholarly Annual*. Reprinted with permission.

Madeleine Descargues, "*Tristram Shandy* and the Appositeness of War." *Shandean* 12 (2001): 63–77. Copyright © 2001 by *The Shandean*. Reprinted with permission.

Peter J. de Voogd, "*Tristram Shandy* as Aesthetic Object." *Word & Image* 4 (1988): 383–92. Copyright © 1988 by *Word & Image*. Reprinted with permission.

Thomas Keymer, "Sterne and the 'New Species of Writing.'" In his *Sterne, the Moderns, and the Novel*. Oxford: Oxford University Press, 2002, pp. 15–36. Copyright © 2002 by Thomas Keymer. Reprinted with permission.

Ross King, "*Tristram Shandy* and the Wound of Language." *Studies in Philology* 92 (1995): 291–310. Copyright © 1995 by the University of North Carolina Press. Reprinted with permission.

Contents

◆　　◆　　◆

Abbreviations   ix

Introduction   3
THOMAS KEYMER

Part I   Genres, Traditions, Intertexts

Swift, Sterne, and the Skeptical Tradition   23
J. T. PARNELL

Sterne and the "New Species of Writing"   50
THOMAS KEYMER

Part II   Public Performance and Print Culture

Laurence Sterne and Literary Celebrity in 1760   79
PETER M. BRIGGS

Tristram Shandy as Aesthetic Object   108
PETER J. DE VOOGD

Part III   Language of the Body

Tristram Shandy and the Wound of Language   123
ROSS KING

Consuming Time: Narrative and Disease in *Tristram Shandy*   147
CLARK LAWLOR

Part IV   Narrative, Reading, and Meaning

Reader as Hobby-horse in *Tristram Shandy*   171
HELEN OSTOVICH

Sterne and the Narrative of Determinateness   191
MELVYN NEW

Part V   Politics and History

Sterne and Irregular Oratory   213
JONATHAN LAMB

Tristram Shandy and the Appositeness of War   240
MADELEINE DESCARGUES

Further Reading   259

Gallery of illustrations appears after page 118

Abbreviations

◆ ◆ ◆

CH   Alan B. Howes, ed. *Sterne: The Critical Heritage*. London: Routledge, 1974.

Letters   *Letters of Laurence Sterne*. Ed. Lewis Perry Curtis. Oxford: Clarendon Press, 1935.

Notes   Melvyn New, with Richard A. Davies and W. G. Day. *The Life and Opinions of Tristram Shandy, Gentleman: The Notes.* The Florida Edition of the Works of Laurence Sterne, vol. 3. Gainesville: University Presses of Florida, 1984.

Sermons   *The Sermons of Laurence Sterne*. The Florida Edition of the Works of Laurence Sterne, vols. 4–5. Ed. Melvyn New. Gainesville: University Press of Florida, 1996. References in the form: sermon number.page number (e.g., *Sermons*, 23.214).

SJ   *A Sentimental Journey through France and Italy and Continuation of the Bramine's Journal: The Text and Notes.* The Florida Edition of the Works of Laurence Sterne, vol. 6. Ed. Melvyn New and W. G. Day. Gainesville: University Press of Florida, 2002.

TS   *The Life and Opinions of Tristram Shandy, Gentleman: The Text.*
          The Florida Edition of the Works of Laurence Sterne,
          vols. 1–2. Ed. Melvyn New and Joan New. Gainesville:
          University Presses of Florida, 1978. References in the
          form: original volume number.original chapter num-
          ber.Florida page number (e.g., *TS,* 5.16.446).

Laurence Sterne's
Tristram Shandy

A CASEBOOK

Introduction

THOMAS KEYMER

✦ ✦ ✦

THE HOSPITALITY OF *TRISTRAM SHANDY* to different approaches and divergent readings is not a discovery of modern criticism. Within this relentlessly self-conscious work, Tristram defines writing as an act of conversation or work of imagination in which a creative role is exercised by readers as well as by authors. An unruly cast of inscribed readers lurks in the margins of his text, differentiated by gender, rank, or profession, and dramatizing the openness of the work to varying modes of response. Sometimes Tristram breaks off to address these readers directly, berating "Madam" for mistaking his meaning, appealing against the judgment of "Sir Critick," or licensing "your Worships" to interpret at will. A similar blend of irritation and glee marks Sterne's comments as author. "It is too much to write books and find heads to understand them," he laments, or affects to lament, in a letter of thanks to an admirer who had sent him a curiosity from Wilmington, North Carolina: an elaborately carved walking stick that branched into multiple handles. To Sterne's obsessive, self-absorbed mind, the gift provided a metaphor for the profusion of interpre-

3

tations already generated in practice by *Tristram Shandy*. Just as walkers have a choice of handle and will grasp the one most suitable to their body or gait, so among his diverse readers "the handle is taken which suits their passions, their ignorance or sensibility." Characteristically, Sterne ends in a perception that looks forward to modern theories of meaning, in particular the idea that interpretation depends more on the subjective desire of the reader than on the objective words on the page: "His own ideas are only call'd forth by what he reads, and . . . 'tis like reading *himself* and not the *book*" (*Letters,* 411).

Sterne wrote this celebrated letter on 9 February 1768, by which time many of the competing approaches and emphases that now dominate criticism of *Tristram Shandy* had already emerged in embryonic form. Typically, the handles seized by early readers, consciously or otherwise, were intertextual. That is to say, Sterne's contemporaries sought to get to grips with his elusive masterpiece by assigning it, or by locating it in serious or satirical relation, to a particular tradition or genre. Many saw *Tristram Shandy* as supremely modern and of its moment, and read the narrative as a playful or parodic exercise in the ascendant genre of the day, the novel itself. In the hands of Richardson, Fielding, and other innovators, prose fiction had now established a formidable repertoire of techniques and conventions for representing inward experience and outward action, which Sterne was seen as simultaneously exploiting and dismantling. This was the approach guardedly adopted by Horace Walpole in a letter of 4 April 1760, when (somewhat simplifying Sterne's virtuoso games with narrative time) he described *Tristram Shandy* as "a kind of novel . . . the great humour of which consists in the whole narration always going backwards" (*CH,* 55). Jobbing critics of the breed satirized in the text itself, whose bread and butter was reviewing fashionable new fiction, approached from a similar angle, and a rash of imitatively disrupted novels was produced, the most brilliant example being Diderot's posthumously published *Jacques le fataliste* (1796). A comic narrative of domestic life that also wittily subverted its enabling procedures, *Tristram Shandy* was both novel and antinovel at once.

Yet this was only one among many interpretive handles fur-

nished by the text. Showy allusions to Rabelais and Cervantes in
Tristram Shandy indicated a different and much earlier mode of fiction, characterized by mock erudition, linguistic exuberance, teasing bawdry, and inventive play on the discourses of the professions,
from law to medicine to theology. Sterne was soon widely hailed
as the English Rabelais, and in the decades that followed, awareness
grew of his debt to a tradition of Renaissance learned wit that also
encompassed the ludic, skeptical essays of Michel de Montaigne
and the encyclopedic satire of Robert Burton's *Anatomy of Melancholy*
(1621–51). Indeed, Sterne's place in the learned wit tradition is
inherent in his meditation on the walking stick, which was not
the spontaneous reaction it might appear but a clever reformula-
tion of Renaissance satire about the limits of determinate knowledge. " 'Tis a Pot with two Ears, that a Man may take by the Right
or Left," as Montaigne describes the capacity of reason to interpret
any fact in opposite ways. Or, as Burton phrases a similar proposition, "Every thing saith *Epictetus* hath two handles, the one to be
held by, the other not, 'tis in our choice to take & leave whether
we will."[1]

The effect of hidden depths at this point is typical of *Tristram
Shandy,* though early excavations such as John Ferriar's *Illustrations of
Sterne* (1798) became bogged down in the issue of plagiarism and
tended to miss the creative surplus in Sterne's appropriations and
transformations. Shrewder than Ferriar in this respect was the annotator of a 1771 copy of *Tristram Shandy,* now preserved in the British
Library in London, who seems to have sensed the ironic, performative wit at work where Sterne plagiarizes Burton's attack on
plagiarism, just as he elsewhere quotes Montaigne about quotation:
"Plagiarisms on the subject of Plagiarism (V5) p 175 of this book!"[2]
At such points, Sterne's writing had little or nothing to do with
the modernity of the novel genre; it was learned wit satire, rooted
in the cornucopian energies of Renaissance prose.

The prior author most frequently named in *Tristram Shandy,* however, was neither the satirical Rabelais nor the skeptical Montaigne
but instead the rationalist philosopher John Locke. Here, in a series
of comic allusions to Locke's influential and wide-ranging *Essay
Concerning Human Understanding* (1690), was another of Sterne's han-

dles. It was not until the mid-twentieth century that philosophical readings of *Tristram Shandy* came to be worked out in print, with reference to key Lockean themes, such as the location in consciousness of personal identity, the distinction between subjective duration and objective time, the inveterate ambiguity of human language, and the disruption of mental processes by habitual association. Yet early readers were not blind to these issues, and to Jean-Baptiste Suard, a Parisian journalist who reviewed *Tristram Shandy* and discussed the role of Locke with Sterne in person, Lockean thought was "that philosophy which those who are able to recognize it explicitly and implicitly will discover or sense in all his pages, in all his lines, in the choice of all his expressions" (*CH,* 414). According to Suard, Sterne also attributed his originality as a writer to the influence of his biblical sources and religious convictions. This claim would not have impressed the many readers scandalized by Sterne's decision to publish his collected sermons under the frivolous, jesting pseudonym of Parson Yorick, but the religious reading of *Tristram Shandy* was taken seriously by others at the time and has recently returned to prominence in modern debates.

Another category of readers looked to politics and current affairs, responding to *Tristram Shandy* as an exercise in topical satire. In the public context of the Seven Years War (1756–63), a struggle for European and colonial ascendancy that is teasingly burlesqued in the war-gaming antics of Toby and Trim, this was "a smart satyrical piece on the vices of the age," according to a writer in *Lloyd's Evening Post* for 4–6 June 1760: an age in which "arms and military atchievements engross the attention" (*CH,* 85). Sterne reacted by placing a deadpan denial in Tristram's mouth—"I had no thoughts . . . in the character of my uncle *Toby*—of characterizing the militiating spirits of my country" (*TS,* 4.22.360)—but at the same time he also inserted further hints to strengthen just this impression.

Other contemporaries reached for the handle of sensibility, and toward the end of the century frequent reprints of a mawkish compilation entitled *The Beauties of Sterne . . . Selected for the Heart of Sensibility* (1782) filleted Sterne's writing and mediated it to the public as a straightforward celebration of sentimental ethics and human benevolence. This cloying abridgment was in its twelfth edition by 1793 and in the last years of the century may have found more readers than the original text. In the same period, though in stark contrast, a rigorously cerebral interpretation of *Tristram Shandy* grew up within German Romanticism, which found in Sterne's fragmented text a luminous expression of Romantic irony: a response to the ineffability of infinity that insisted at every turn on the impossibility of true representation. This reading returned to England in Coleridge's austere account of Sterne's humor, in a lecture of 1818, as a mode in which "the little is made great, and the great little, in order to destroy both, because all is equal in contrast with the infinite" (*CH,* 354).

With the exception of this somewhat abstracted example, there was nothing systematic about eighteenth-century responses to *Tristram Shandy,* and we should not forget the many other readers who either ignored or consciously refused the interpretive challenge of the text. Some approached the book as simply a source of comic pleasure or obscene wit, whereas others dismissed it as an impudent hoax, a farrago of nonsensical shocks. No meaning at all underlay Sterne's parade of profundity, snapped one exasperated reviewer in 1765, and *Tristram Shandy* was "a *riddle,* without an *object*" (*CH,* 169). Even here, however, early reception heralds recognizable lines of modern criticism, and readings of *Tristram Shandy* as pure disinterested comedy, as a book about sexuality and the body, and as chaos or nihilistic play have all been worked out at length. Although the informal letters, marginalia, and reviews in which eighteenth-century reactions survive come nowhere near the complex positions and arguments that subsequently developed in formal criticism, the convergence on common themes is fascinating to observe. Whether approaching Sterne's writing through its narrative reflexiveness, its learned wit satire, or its invocations of Lockean philosophy, Christian theology, sentimental ethics, or current affairs, early reception clearly indicates the multiple interpretive opportunities on which criticism continues to seize. The lively diversity of these responses also demonstrates the cogency of the classic statement about meaning in Sterne: that of Friedrich

Nietzsche, for whom the formal disruption and enigmatic style of *Tristram Shandy* made signification multiple and uncertain throughout, and Sterne himself "the great master of *ambiguity*."[3]

If the protean character of *Tristram Shandy* goes beyond the richness of meaning and openness to interpretation that are central to our idea of any classic, it is worth posing a basic question: why? For Nietzsche, the answer was to be found in the mysteries of the authorial soul, a unique and individual identity that made Sterne, in his characteristic transcendence of determinate meaning, "the most liberated spirit of all time." A more material explanation might lie in the intermittent, haphazard, improvisatory nature of *Tristram Shandy*'s composition.

Today we usually encounter Sterne's masterpiece in a single volume, fixed and unified as a physical object, and it is easy to forget that it was originally written and published in five long installments over more than seven years, beginning with a pair of volumes in late 1759 and closing with a stand-alone ninth volume in 1767. Debate still surrounds the question of whether this "final" volume marks a genuine conclusion or instead a more arbitrary point of abandonment or terminal interruption: Sterne died in March 1768, leaving characteristically mixed messages both inside and outside the text. Nor is it clear to what extent the work as a whole was composed according to a preconceived plan. Submerged structures and symmetries make clear that *Tristram Shandy* is far less formless than its bungling narrator suggests, and several painstaking analyses have identified beneath the jerks and reversals of Tristram's story line a systematic time scheme of almost flawless coherence. But the work is also unmistakably improvised in some of its most interesting turns and incorporates material that could not have been predicted when composition began (including, in volume 7, a comic reworking of a voyage to France that Sterne was only able to undertake with his earnings from earlier volumes). Built into the very mode of publication was an openness to chance and change, and this fundamental plasticity in *Tristram Shandy* was intensified by Sterne's determination to maximize his profile and sales among the broadest possible constituency of readers. The heterogeneous text he developed could cater to all tastes: "read by the clergy, approved of by the wits, studyed by the merchants, gazed at by the ladies, and . . . the pocket-companion of the nation," as one uninvited rider on Sterne's bandwagon described the work's reach and appeal.[4] "Tristram is the fashion," as Sterne more succinctly put it in March 1760 (*Letters,* 102), and it could remain the fashion through the mechanisms of serialization, recurrently rekeying itself to the shifting trends of its ongoing cultural moment.

Even before publication began, *Tristram Shandy* was a melting pot of competing discourses and traditions. A Yorkshire cleric in his mid-forties, born in a garrison town in Ireland and educated at Cambridge, Sterne was steeped in the literature of Anglican divinity, his main literary activity to date being the production of conventional, not to say derivative, weekly sermons. Two of these, including *Tristram Shandy*'s sermon on the abuses of conscience, were separately published as pamphlets in 1747 and 1750. As Sterne's borrowings from York Minster Library record, he read extensively in history, geography, and general encyclopedias of knowledge, and the posthumous sale catalog of his library includes (with other items that the bookseller may have added) the standard philosophical, legal, and medical textbooks of the day. During this period Sterne also wrote an unknown quantity of political journalism in the Whig interest, including the pamphlet *Query upon Query* (1741), and was rewarded with modest preferment in the diocese of York. By the later 1750s, however, his ecclesiastical career was in the doldrums, and the more riotous, subversive aspect of his taste and reading welled up in *A Political Romance,* a jeering lampoon of diocesan rivals that was heavily indebted, with its allegories, keys, and layers of bogus commentary, to the Scriblerian satirical techniques of Pope and Swift. *A Political Romance* was printed in York in January 1759 and almost immediately was suppressed at the order of the archbishop, "and it was to this disappointment," according to an acquaintance, "that the world is indebted for Tristram Shandy" (*CH,* 60).

Tantalizing evidence allows us to glimpse the emergence of *Tristram Shandy* as Sterne regrouped and redirected his newfound energies as a writer. These include an unpublished "Fragment in the

Manner of Rabelais" (an exuberant and somewhat self-implicating satire on plagiarism in sermon writing); a report that Sterne had composed an allegorical send-up of theological controversy about the Book of Job; and two self-promotional letters to prospective publishers in London. The first of these prepublication pitches describes the work in progress as a universal satire, "taking in, not only, the Weak part of the Sciences . . . but every Thing else, which I find Laugh-at-able in my way." In the second, Sterne reports that all local or parochial elements have now been removed from the text and proposes bringing out two test volumes "to feel the pulse of the world" (*Letters*, 74, 80).

As published in York in December 1759 and London the following month, the first installment of *Tristram Shandy* not only reflects these origins in a collision between traditional Anglicanism and Rabelaisian or Scriblerian satire. It also reads as much more novelistic in approach than Sterne's satirical forays of the previous year, creating a vividly represented fictional world even as it throws in question the efficacy of fictional representation. In tension with the generic belatedness of its learned wit elements, moreover, *Tristram Shandy* lodged an appeal to fashionable metropolitan taste that both dramatized and enabled Sterne's leap from provincial obscurity to international celebrity status. Hogarthian aesthetics, Voltaire's best-selling *Candide* (1759), and war-inspired novels like the anonymous *Life and Memoirs of Mr. Ephraim Tristram Bates, A Broken-Hearted Soldier* (1756) are among the installment's more obviously voguish touchstones. Novelty is the identity flaunted above all in the narrative's every move, the structural, rhetorical, and typographical peculiarities of the text combining to proclaim its double freshness as a novel exercise in the novel form. Sterne reinforced the effect in practice by publicly performing the dual self engineered in his text, writing letters as Tristram and frequenting pleasure gardens as Yorick, conspicuously consorting all the while with the A-list of cultural and political life: leading parliamentarians such as William Pitt and John Wilkes, the star actor David Garrick, the society portraitist Joshua Reynolds, the controversialist and pundit William Warburton.

In subsequent installments of January 1761, December 1761, January 1765, and January 1767, serialization enabled Sterne to subject the fashionableness of his text to ongoing refreshment and renewal. As his work took shape in the intervals of publication, it could move with the times, ever responsive to new developments in public culture as well as in personal experience. Sterne was slowly dying of pulmonary tuberculosis, and at one level the protracted dynamic of serialization allowed him to dramatize two of his great intertwined themes: the evanescence of human life and the resistance of human experience to verbal or textual capture. As each new installment of *Tristram Shandy* appeared, the basic plot no further ahead and the narrator more obviously consumptive, Sterne used the publishing process to stage an extended, tragicomic performance of digressive writing and progressive disease, with Tristram struggling to record his life while watching it waste away. At the same time, Sterne's philosophical games with time and duration, consciousness and memory, could take on a practical dimension through the delays and interruptions to the reading experience enforced by publication in parts.

But it was above all by facilitating improvisation, flexibility, and responsiveness to external opportunities and pressures that serialization could work to Sterne's creative advantage. By reemerging at irregular intervals on the publishing scene, absorbing or addressing the latest literary productions, cultural trends, and topical events, Sterne made available to himself an inexhaustible repertoire of possibilities, intertextual and contextual, on which his writing could play. *Tristram Shandy* could evolve or mutate as it went along, imbibing fresh innovatory characteristics from other new texts as they emerged over the years, such as the "Nonsense Club" verse of Churchill and Lloyd, James Macpherson's Ossianic fragments, and concurrently serialized fiction by Smollett and others. It could interact with Sterne's own concurrent publication, *The Sermons of Mr. Yorick* (volumes of which appeared after the first and fourth installments of *Tristram Shandy* and again after Sterne's death), enriching the brew with elements of the religious doctrine and moral sense philosophy that permeated these sermons. It could register and track political change: the ministerial roller coaster that sees Pitt allegorically expelled from office in volume 5 and restored with new honors in volume 9; the progress of the war in Europe, at its bloodiest as Toby and Trim campaign in volumes 3 and 4, nearing its end with Toby's "apologetical oration" in defense of warfare in volume 6, and at last resolved when Tristram whimsically claims credit for the Treaty of Paris in volume 7.

Most ingeniously of all, *Tristram Shandy* could respond to its own reception, and so make something more than merely theoretical of its proposition that writing is an act of conversation between author and readers. When enterprising hacks cashed in on Sterne's early volumes by recycling his ideas in Shandean imitations of their own, Sterne gleefully imitated his imitators, extending the intertextual loop by stealing back from the thieves. A free-wheeling text that could generate its own continuation from audience responses to past installments, as well as from other ongoing texts and events, *Tristram Shandy* is indebted to the Grub Street industry that sprang up around it in ways that remain to be fully explored. As one aggrieved pamphleteer put it on behalf of his brethren when six of Sterne's volumes were in print, "you have now turned the Tables upon them, and in more Places than one, have taken and pursued Hints that were chalked out by your Parodists."[5] *Tristram Shandy* could also incorporate or react to private suggestion, as when Sterne gave a new, though typically enigmatic, twist to the political implications of his writing in volume 9, which responds to the appeal of an African reader, Ignatius Sancho, to incorporate a critique of slavery resembling a passage that Sancho had already found in one of the sermons.

The classic case of this conversational dynamic is the dialogue between *Tristram Shandy* and the *Monthly Review,* the first and most influential reviewing periodical of the day. This dialogue not only leaves its trace in Tristram's various explicit appeals, challenges, and answers to reviewers and critics but also influenced the whole trajectory of the work as successive installments moved steadily away from the tradition of learned wit satire and toward the modern literature of sensibility. The growing emphasis on sympathy and pathos in later volumes, and Sterne's eventual suspension of *Tristram Shandy* to write his last work, *A Sentimental Journey* (1768), are generally recognized as responding to intervention from the

Monthly Review as sales appeared to be waning. Philanthropic sentimentalism was Sterne's most effective mode, the *Monthly* publicly
urged, and also an area of growing market demand. In acting on
this advice, however, Sterne did so with all his usual ambivalence,
and continued to write in ways that could cater to opposing tastes
at one and the same time. The sentimental vignettes of *Tristram
Shandy*'s later volumes, and *A Sentimental Journey* as a whole, are del-
icately poised between sincerity and satire, and have been read as
ironic or parodic critiques of the fashionable ideology they seem
to uphold. Always alert to the diversity of readerships and the
multiplicity of interpretations, Sterne now offers his audience a
text in which sentimental tastes are simultaneously fed and
mocked. When he assures his bookseller that *A Sentimental Journey* is
"likely to take in all Kinds of Readers" (*Letters,* 393), the local ambiguity of "take in" catches the effect to perfection. Accommodat-
ing all readers, and perhaps fooling most, Sterne provides the dev-
otees of sentiment and the aficionados of satire with a work
available to be understood in contrary ways, just like *Tristram Shandy*
before it. There could be no more fitting conclusion to a body of
writing that resists single or totalizing explanation, while massively
enabling the plenitude of interpretations generated by it ever since.

Throughout the nineteenth century, critical debate about
Sterne foundered on persistent allegations of plagiarism, indecency,
and hypocrisy, and it was in the creative practice of poets and
novelists that *Tristram Shandy* generated its most insightful responses.
Three of the key works of Romantic autobiography—Wordsworth's posthumously published *The Prelude* (1850), Coleridge's *Bio-
graphia Literaria* (1817), and De Quincey's *Confessions of an English Opium-
Eater* (1821)—are all haunted by a Shandean ghost as they fashion
their narrative selves, and Byron was explicit in calling *Don Juan*
(1818–23) "a poetical T Shandy."[6] Nineteenth-century novelists as
different from one another as Balzac, Dickens, Tolstoy, and Bra-
zilian author Machado de Assis looked to Sterne for various kinds
of release from realist convention, and *Tristram Shandy* was even
enlisted by George Eliot as a model—rather too closely, as her
schedule began to slip—for the serialization of *Middlemarch* (1871–
72) in book-length parts.

It was with the advent of modernism in the early to mid-twentieth century, however, that Sterne's innovatory literary practice came into its own. *Tristram Shandy* was a natural touchstone for James Joyce as he explained his attempt "to build many planes of narrative with a single esthetic purpose" in *Finnegans Wake* (1939),[7] and Virginia Woolf found in *A Sentimental Journey* an experimental prototype of stream-of-consciousness narration. Sterne's dazzling repertoire of metafictional devices continues to be exploited by writers of postmodern fiction, and his global reach is apparent in the work of Carlos Fuentes, Milan Kundera, and Salman Rushdie, to name just three conspicuous cases.

Accompanying this creative interest in Sterne's technical innovations and disruptions, influential works of narratology such as Viktor Shklovsky's *Theory of Prose* (1921), Wayne C. Booth's *The Rhetoric of Fiction* (1961), and Wolfgang Iser's *The Implied Reader* (1974) have been explicitly informed by *Tristram Shandy*. It is above all as a novelist that Sterne's twentieth-century revival was achieved, and the predominance of the novel-centered approach in postwar criticism is admirably illustrated by John Traugott's volume of 1968 in the Twentieth-Century Views series, for years the defining casebook of essays on Sterne and still a valuable repository of landmark readings.[8] Traugott included Shklovsky's account of *Tristram Shandy* as a parody of realist convention, and essays on other aspects of narrative technique, including the manipulation of plot, time, and first person, occupy the bulk of his casebook. But Traugott also represented other perspectives, including his own influential account of *Tristram Shandy* (in his 1954 monograph *Tristram Shandy's World*) as a work that was indeed permeated by Lockean thought, but in an irreverent mode of burlesque, resistance, and critique. For Traugott, *Tristram Shandy*'s relation to the *Essay Concerning Human Understanding* was above all adversarial, a heady mix of witty subversion and metaphysical interrogation that pushes Locke's skeptical method to the point of collapsing his system. The Sterne who emerged from this analysis—a secular modern, preoccupied by absurdity and alienation, but finding redemptive connection to the world through sentiment and sympathy—has provoked a wealth of subsequent debate. The fashion for reading *Tristram Shandy* as a proleptic demonstration of modern intellectual systems—existentialism, phenomenology, chaos theory—has now receded; in its place, a rigorously historicized body of criticism has reassessed Sterne's relationship to eighteenth-century sentimentalism in its diverse aspects, philosophical, physiological, and philanthropic.

Over the past two or three decades, much of the most significant research activity on Sterne has been editorial, and all the major works—*Tristram Shandy, The Sermons of Mr. Yorick,* and *A Sentimental Journey*—have now appeared in a standard scholarly edition. One important feature of the Florida edition of the works of Laurence Sterne (1978–present) is its establishment of a reliable and rigorous text, true to the visual as well as verbal features of Sterne's art, and in its wake most trade editions now do a greatly improved job of registering the role of typographical play, *mise en page,* and other material features of *Tristram Shandy*. Editorial work is never without interpretive implications, however, and in this case the implications have been pronounced. By richly documenting the key sources, analogs, and intertexts of *Tristram Shandy,* with particular emphasis on learned wit sources, the annotations to the Florida edition magisterially reassert the centrality of the satirical tradition. As the principal editor, Melvyn New, points out, the simple fact of their bulk—separately published in 1984, the annotations occupy 500 closely printed pages—distinguishes *Tristram Shandy* from the novel tradition, where referential transparency is usually at a premium, and intensive explication is rarely needed. Instead, the volume of notes underscores the prevalence of satirical features requiring heavy annotation, such as parody, burlesque, allusion, cross-reference, and imitation.

In this respect, the Florida edition reiterates the robust insistence of New's critical writing since his revisionist monograph of 1969, *Laurence Sterne as Satirist,* on reading Sterne as a belated exponent of Renaissance satire, albeit an exponent who reapplies this tradition in part to his own time and place. A key strand of New's argument, inherent in his original monograph and subsequently developed by others, is further reinforced by the prominence given in the Florida edition to the sermons (their flippant original title tactfully adjusted to read *The Sermons of Laurence Sterne*). Not only was Sterne a learned wit satirist, steeped in the complex literariness and playful skepticism of Rabelais, Montaigne, and Burton; he also turned the resources of this tradition against Enlightenment system building and the pretensions of modern knowledge, thereby implying a consistently Pauline emphasis on the limits of understanding in a fallen world and on the primacy of faith. The satirical play emanates, in other words, from a stable religious position: Sterne was neither Shklovsky's novelist nor Traugott's absurdist but a Christian satirist, and one whose revelry in disorder and opacity did not oppose but instead upheld the need for conventional faith. In 1992 New used a casebook of his own, in the Contemporary Critical Essays series, to foreground and promote, in this approach through satire and religion, "an alternative reading of *Tristram Shandy* to that which has dominated the past forty years." Rebuking Traugott for his tendentious editorial selections while mischievously repeating the trick, New concludes that "a new Sterne is emerging, separated from novel-centred discussions, from reliance upon Locke as the key to some esoteric coding, and, most importantly perhaps, free from the need to see him as 'one of us', as a secular sceptic or existentialist."[9]

Over the same period and alongside the Florida edition, *Tristram Shandy* criticism has also been transformed by a more general factor: the rise of theory in the discipline as a whole. Beyond the formalist, narratological, and reader-response approaches that were already established by the late 1970s, however, the application to Sterne's writing of new methodologies has not been unproblematic. With its focus on questions of reading and interpretation, language and meaning, textuality and fragmentation, and with its playful exploration of human subjectivity and the performance of identity and gender, *Tristram Shandy* seems an obvious host for some of the other strands of theory that came to prominence at about this time: poststructuralist, deconstructive, historical materialist, feminist, psychoanalytic. Yet in practice Sterne's work proved too slippery and evasive to be clamped under the rigid theoretical apparatuses that were first deployed, or even perhaps immune to kinds of interrogation and critique anticipated within its text. The earliest full-scale deconstructive readings of eighteenth-century literature turned on works that seemed confident in their ability to represent authentic experience and convey determinate meaning: works such as Boswell's *Life of Johnson* and Richardson's *Clarissa,* in which clear assumptions were there to be deconstructed, rather than the quizzical, opaque *Tristram Shandy.* By the same token, historical materialist and feminist criticism of the early 1980s chose targets that looked fixed and stable. Aim was taken at the rhetorical confidence and ideological certainty of Pope, mutinous subtexts were exposed beneath the conformist surface of Burney, but Sterne was left relatively untouched.

The letter in which Sterne writes that *"Tristram Shandy . . .* was made and formed to baffle all criticism," first published in *Original Letters of the Late Reverend Mr. Laurence Sterne* (1788), is almost certainly a forgery,[10] but there remains a sense in which the work has subsequently seemed to baffle all theory. Alongside its disarming overall instability, and its local mockeries of "the cant of criticism" (*TS,* 3.12.214), *Tristram Shandy* satirically expresses its resistance to theory in the character of Walter, whose subordination of fluid experience to rigid systems is ridiculed throughout. As Marcus Walsh shrewdly notes in his contribution to a series of casebooks devoted to theorized readings: "In Walter above all we see how a flight from the urgencies and hard edges of the real world, the particularities of events and objects, the compromises of day to day understanding, into an exclusive obsession with theory—into the dedicated riding of hobby horses—results in confused names, damaged children and a bloody nose."[11] The result is that the most successful essays in Walsh's volume are the least doctrinaire: not brash superimpositions of preconceived models but readings answering his call for a flexible combination of theoretical awareness, scholarly contextualization, and vigilant close analysis.

These two main developments in the last quarter of the twentieth century—the emphasis of the Florida annotations on determinate knowledge, and the emphasis of poststructuralist theories on the play of readerly desire—have not always worked in harmony. As Jonathan Lamb protests in a now somewhat notorious passage, "an unhappy result of [the Florida annotations] has been to re-position Sterne in a grid of borrowings, quotations and allusions that considerably restricts the freedom to read beyond the annotated pale."[12] Yet the best readings of *Tristram Shandy* to have been published within the past two decades, including books by Lamb and New themselves, have brilliantly married the theorized agenda of the modern academy with scholarly and historical understanding. In this context, the aim of the present volume is to represent the range and diversity of *Tristram Shandy* criticism since the appearance of the Florida annotations and the permeation of mainstream criticism by modern theory.[13] Essays are presented in pairs, whether complementary or adversarial in relation, each pair exhibiting the responsiveness of Sterne scholarship to key trends and themes in the academy at large. The opening pair of essays, by J. T. Parnell and Thomas Keymer, represents the present state of the debate about generic identities; the second pair approaches through the optic of print culture, reading *Tristram Shandy* as an early episode in book-trade celebrity (Peter M. Briggs) and as a text that creates meaning through material features of typography and physical format (Peter J. de Voogd). Essays by Ross King and Clark Lawlor reread *Tristram Shandy* in light of eighteenth-century theories of the body and language, and King's essay takes on additional interest as the response of a practicing novelist. The final two pairs of essays represent the ongoing importance of narrative, reading, and meaning in *Tristram Shandy* criticism, and the more recent turn to questions of politics and history. Helen Ostovich examines Sterne's dialogue with the reader from a feminist perspective, and Melvyn New addresses the fundamental question of indeterminacy in Sterne. The volume concludes with incisive attempts by Jonathan Lamb and Madeleine Descargues to locate the pervasive but recalcitrant political identity of the text.

Notes

1. *Montaigne's Essays in Three Books,* trans. Charles Cotton, 3rd ed., 3 vols. (1743), 2:293; Robert Burton, *The Anatomy of Melancholy,* ed. Thomas C. Faulkner et al., 6 vols. (Oxford: Clarendon Press, 1989–2000), 2:169 (part 2, sect. 3, memb. 3, subs. 1).

2. Annotation in the so-called Greville copy of *Tristram Shandy* (9 vols. in 3, 1771, BL shelfmark G. 13443–5), endpapers to volume 2. The author of these marginalia is identified by Antony Coleman as Edmund Ferrers (1749–1825), a Hampshire clergyman ("Sterne's Use of the Motteux-Ozell Rabelais," *Notes and Queries* 223 [1978], 55).

3. Friedrich Nietzsche, *Human, All Too Human: A Book for Free Spirits,* trans. R. J. Hollingdale, intro. Erich Heller (Cambridge: Cambridge University Press, 1986), 238.

4. "Christopher Flagellan," *A Funeral Discourse, Occasioned by the Much Lamented Death of Mr. Yorick* (1761), 20–21.

5. *An Admonitary Letter to the Rev. Mr. S———. Upon the Publication of His Fifth and Sixth Volumes* (1761), 5.

6. *Byron's Letters and Journals,* ed. Leslie A. Marchand, 12 vols. (London: John Murray, 1973–82), 10:150 (14 April 1823).

7. Eugene Jolas, "My Friend James Joyce," in Seon Givens (ed.), *James Joyce: Two Decades of Criticism* (New York: Vanguard, 1948), 12.

8. John Traugott (ed.), *Laurence Sterne: A Collection of Critical Essays* (Englewood Cliffs, N.J.: Prentice Hall, 1969).

9. Melvyn New, "Introduction," in New (ed.), *Tristram Shandy,* New Casebooks (New York: St. Martin's Press, 1992), 7–8; see also New's broader and more recent selection in *Critical Essays on Laurence Sterne* (New York: G. K. Hall, 1998).

10. *Original Letters of the Late Reverend Mr. Laurence Sterne* (1788), 86. On the status of this publication, see Harlan W. Hamilton, "William Combe and the *Original Letters of the Late Reverend Mr. Laurence Sterne* (1788)," *PMLA* 82 (1967), 420–29.

11. Marcus Walsh, "Introduction," in Walsh (ed.), *Laurence Sterne,* Longman Critical Readers (Harlow: Longman, 2002), 3.

12. Jonathan Lamb, *Sterne's Fiction and the Double Principle* (Cambridge: Cambridge University Press, 1989), 2.

13. The earliest essay in the present volume dates from 1988. References are standardized to the Florida editions of the *Sermons* and *A Sentimental Journey* where publication predates these editions, and in two cases contributors (de Voogd and New) have updated footnotes in light of subsequent research.

PART I

Genres, Traditions, Intertexts

Swift, Sterne, and the Skeptical Tradition

J. T. PARNELL

◆ ◆ ◆

IN A RECENT ESSAY Donald Wehrs suggests that the tradition of fideistic skepticism offers a meaningful context for Laurence Sterne's narrative and thematic concerns.[1] In so doing he highlights the most significant, and hitherto overlooked, legacy of the Renaissance humanists with whom Sterne's name is so frequently linked. It has long been a commonplace to see *Tristram Shandy* in the tradition of learned wit, but the late flowering of the tradition in Sterne's fiction has never been adequately explained. Similarly, the epithet "skeptic" occurs regularly in discussions of Sterne, from John Traugott's influential *Tristram Shandy's World* in the 1950s to Jonathan Lamb's recent *Sterne's Fiction and the Double Principle.* Until Donald Wehrs's article, however, skeptic had been used in its modern sense, denoting at worst universal doubt, or at best the kind of philosophical—and, more or less, secular—skepticism associated with Locke and Hume. Awareness of the tradition of fideistic skepticism allows us, for the first time, to understand more fully Sterne's "skepticism" and his relationship to those writers to whom, in his fiction and correspondence, he consistently draws his readers' attention.

It is no coincidence that Erasmus, Rabelais, and Cervantes were as highly prized by Swift as by Sterne or that the Scriblerians and Sterne were equally familiar with the skeptical writings of Montaigne and Charron.[2] The Renaissance legacy was, of course, pervasive in the eighteenth century, but the far-reaching influence of the skeptical branch of the Christian-humanist literary tradition on Sterne and Swift in particular has yet to be explored. For Swift and Sterne, as ministers of the Church of England during periods when Anglicanism was coming under increasing threat, Erasmus, Rabelais and Burton offered obvious role models. All five writers found a literary arena in which they could display their exuberant wit while attempting to sustain the belief system to which they adhered. It is too rarely stressed that the literary tradition represented by these writers is massively informed by their religious beliefs. In *The Praise of Folly, Gargantua and Pantagruel,* and *The Anatomy of Melancholy* "belief" is apparent in more than the shadowy presence of religious norms behind the exuberance of discrete artistic creations. In these works and the fiction of Swift and Sterne, form and content reflect and enact a skepticism which is closely allied to a defence of hard-pressed Christian ideology. In their favorite writers Swift and Sterne found formal techniques which were seized upon as the best means of addressing epistemological issues which had far-reaching implications for Anglican hegemony. The issues may have been born in the Reformation crisis, but they were far from moribund in the eighteenth century. An investigation of Sterne's and Swift's relationship to Christian-humanist fideism helps us to understand Sterne's professed admiration for the Dean of St. Patrick's, and suggests that a reassessment of critical commonplaces about the relationship might be in order.[3] In particular, the notion—which has become a critical fiat since Traugott first pronounced it—that Sterne's "comic vision" diverges from Swift's in "an odd synthesis of the satiric method of the Scriblerians with Locke's philosophical skepticism"[4] needs to be reexamined.

If *Tristram Shandy* remains an anachronism for many critics, it is because Sterne is too often viewed as a freak, a prophet of modernity, or even postmodernity. To be sure, if we look for evidence of "pre-Romanticism," existentialist angst or postmodern relativity, *Tristram Shandy* will offer comforting glimmers of confirmation, but the more difficult task is to face a less congenial anachronism. If Sterne remains hard to place, it is precisely because of his adherence to a much older worldview—a worldview which he found best suited to his plan of "taking in . . . the Weak part of the Sciences . . . [and] every Thing else, which [he found] Laugh-at-able." (*Letters*, 74). Blithely unaware of the alleged decline of satire and the conditions which produce it, Sterne discovered in Erasmus, Rabelais, Montaigne, and the Scriblerians, not just formal techniques but a credo fully in keeping with his role as a clergyman. The potential problems raised by exchanging one anachronism for another can be forestalled by a fuller understanding of why, as Donald Wehrs puts it, "Sterne transposes into narrative the rhetorical techniques of classical skepticism."[5] Such an understanding will also enhance our awareness of the affinities between Swift and Sterne—affinities which recent scholarship has mistakenly ignored in a rather narrow insistence on the perceived gap between the poisonous Augustan satirist and the amiable sentimentalist.

Without wishing to rehearse a full summary of the tenets of fideistic skepticism, it is necessary to outline the history of the tradition in order to understand its impact on Sterne and Swift. For our purposes it is essential to look at the philosophical underpinnings of classical skepticism *and* the remarkable uses to which such skepticism was put by Christian apologists from the sixteenth century onward. The methods of the classical skeptics were employed in the sixteenth century, chiefly by Catholic writers, as a defense against the central arguments of the Protestant reformers. As Richard Popkin puts it in *The History of Scepticism from Erasmus to Spinoza,* "the dispute over the proper standard of religious knowledge . . . raised one of the classical problems of the Greek Pyrrhonists, the problem of the criterion of truth." Luther's assertion that conscience was an infallible guide to correct biblical exegesis led to doubt in the whole field of epistemology and hermeneutics. This was not a localized debate but one which, according to Popkin, "was to have the most far reaching consequences, not just in theology but throughout man's entire intellectual realm."[6] Indeed, for Pierre Bayle—whose *Dictionary* was a source for Sterne and the Scriblerians—the rediscovery of Sextus Empiricus' *Outlines of Pyrrhonism* was seen as the beginning of modern philosophy. From the rediscovery of classical skepticism in the sixteenth century, the skeptical stance became one of the key weapons of philosophical and theological debate. Having been employed in the battle against the reformers, skepticism was leveled next against Scholastic and Platonic modes of thought before evolving in the late seventeenth century as a foil to Cartesian rationalism. In fact skepticism was a philosophical system capable of countering any and every system, including its own—its end being suspense rather than certainty. It is worth remembering that the legacy of the Schoolmen was such that its influence on the English universities was still felt late in the eighteenth century. That the satire of Sterne and the Scriblerians is consistently anti-Scholastic confirms the pervasiveness of the legacy. That both should attack Cartesian rationalism with the very skeptical strategies that Descartes had sought to discredit confirms Swift's and Sterne's keen awareness of the epistemological debate. Descartes joins the Schoolmen as a builder of "edifices in the air."

It was Erasmus, whose influence on *A Tale of a Tub* and *Tristram Shandy* has long been acknowledged,[7] who in the *Praise of Folly* first exploited the possibilities of a union of the characteristic strategies of the discourse of philosophical skepticism with the literary discourse of the paradoxical encomium. Indeed, Erasmus and his heirs clearly demonstrate what such nineteenth- and twentieth-century skeptics as Nietzsche and Derrida are so keen to stress—the untenable nature of neat distinctions between literary and philosophical discourse. But in the face of the burgeoning *crise pyrrhonienne,* Erasmus sought a solution to dogmatic wrangling and religious faction—behind which the faintest tones of the death knell of religious certainty could be heard. In the use of a form capable of demonstrating the complexity of sublunary truth, he sought to clear the way for an acceptance of God's even more vexed truths. While Erasmus did not have access to Sextus Empiricus' *Outlines of Pyrrhonism,* he was familiar with Cicero's less thorough accounts of Academic skepticism and Diogenes Laertes' summary of Pyrrhon-

ian skepticism. In addition, the recent experience of translating
Lucian's seriocomic dialogues offered Erasmus a literary form
which, through its exploitation of the comic, its love of paradox,
its extravagant foregrounding of intertextuality, and its "dialogue
without closure,"[8] presented a perfect vehicle for satire on opposition voices which could at the same time endorse the wisdom of
Christian "folly."

Just how close Erasmus is to Sterne and Swift can be seen from
the passage where Folly aligns herself with a blend of stoic and
skeptical thought:

> But it's sad, people say, to be deceived. Not at all, it's far
> sadder *not* to be deceived. They're quite wrong if they think
> man's happiness depends on actual facts; it depends on his
> opinions. For human affairs are so complex and obscure that
> nothing can be known of them for certain, as has rightly
> been stated by my Academicians, the least assuming of the
> philosophers.[9]

Echoes of the *Praise of Folly* in the *Tale* have been well documented.[10] But the possibility that Swift's debt extends beyond a
general concurrence of worldviews and shared rhetorical strategies
to a fideism which informs narrative structure has never been
articulated. Swift's much debated skepticism can, in fact, be better
understood when the nature of the skeptical tradition is grasped.
For readers of *Tristram Shandy,* Folly can be seen as anticipating Tristram's endorsement of the benefits of *philautia* which finds a parallel
in *A Tale of a Tub* in the Hack's delight in the "sublime and refined
point of felicity, called *the possession of being well deceived*."[11] More significantly, the passage contains the stoic maxim which Sterne chose
as his epigraph to the first installment of *Tristram* and would have
found in two texts which are central to his satire's intertextual
fabric—Montaigne's *Essays* and Shakespeare's *Hamlet*.[12] Further, the
final sentence not only encapsulates the skeptical stance, but parallels one of Sterne's most repeated borrowings from Locke:

> we live amongst riddles and mysteries—the most obvious
> things, which come in our way, have dark sides, which the

quickest sight cannot penetrate into; and even the clearest and most exalted understandings amongst us find ourselves puzzled and at a loss in almost every cranny of nature's works; so that this, like a thousand other things, falls out for us in a way, which tho' we cannot reason upon it,—yet we find the good of it . . . and that's enough for us. (*TS*, 4.17.350)

Given Sterne's familiarity with Erasmus, it is hard to imagine that he was unaware of the allusive resonance of his own use of Epictetus and Locke. In this light, the lifting of the phrasing from Locke seems less a confirmation of Sterne's much discussed debt to the *Essay Concerning Human Understanding,* and more a confirmation of a commonplace Christian sentiment.[13] Sterne delighted in a well-turned phrase and it is characteristic of his practice to alight on the most eloquent expression of a fideistic saw. The stress on the inadequacy of *reason* in the face of Nature's complexity is hardly new to the eighteenth century, but is rather typical of a fideistic view that is traceable to St. Paul and which came into particular prominence in the *crise pyrrhonienne* precipitated by the Reformation. Folly's words confirm also, if confirmation were necessary, that Sterne did not need Locke, still less Hume, to direct him to the skeptical high road.

The influence of Erasmus's thought and his use of the rhetoric of fideism was profound. The extent of the legacy is such that in the fiction of those who come after him it is sometimes difficult to ascertain whether the influence is direct or whether it has been picked up at second hand. Rabelais and Cervantes absorb much of Erasmus, but take his formal strategies much further by extending them into the realms of narrative satire.[14] But behind the marvelous complexities and skeptical nuances of *Gargantua and Pantagruel* and *Don Quixote* lies a fideism that is closer to the conservative skepticism of St. Paul then the "radical" skepticism of modernity. In this light we should beware of seizing upon Swift's and Sterne's much debated skepticism as evidence of the crumbling of conservative Anglican ideology. Nor in Sterne's case should we be too quick to celebrate a modern voice that breaks out from the supposed shackles of an imagined neoclassicism. Valerie Grosvenor

Myer's claim that we should consider Sterne "in relation to the dissolution of Augustan values into relativism and subjectivity in the wake of Locke,"[15] while typical of much criticism of *Tristram Shandy,* is quite untenable. In this account Locke's "wake" has washed over (or under?) Swift, Pope and Addison and hit Sterne full in the face seventy years after the *Essay*'s publication. Without question, Locke's influence on eighteenth-century thought was profound, but he can hardly be held responsible for the dissolution of Augustan values. Locke possibly had a greater influence on the Scriblerians than on Sterne, since they respond to his ideas while they are still fresh.[16] Furthermore, we have to be extremely wary of any simplistic conception of Augustan values. The formulation may be comforting, but it too readily falsifies literary history because of its tendency to turn what is disparate into a forced whole. Sterne found numerous examples of subjectivity and relativism of a different order in a tradition that long predates Locke.

Too much of the criticism that has dealt with the Locke/Sterne nexus has privileged the philosopher's influence without a sufficient investigation of the history of skeptical thought. One result is that Locke's skepticism is seen as more radically modern than it actually is. The nature of fideism is that it is a mitigated form of skepticism, so that for all the signs of "modern" preoccupations in Erasmus, Rabelais, Cervantes, Swift and Sterne, the underpinning certainty of belief in the Christian deity qualifies any celebration, such as Bakhtin's, of the writers' debt to the kind of joyful relativity exemplified in the carnivalesque.

That the skepticism of these writers is mitigated is crucial to our understanding of their texts. Far from embracing the conclusions of Pyrrhonian skepticism, they adopt its rhetoric for radically different ends. As Terence Penelhum has argued, Erasmus *uses* skepticism in defense "of one dogmatic solution—namely a middle-of-the-road theology."[17] Similarly, all of the writers under consideration use a bewildering range of weapons from the skeptic arsenal to serve satiric, and consequently dogmatic, ends. Erasmus is unrelenting in his satire on "false" learning, but is finally more interested in discrediting his religious opponents.

From Erasmus onward, the alliance of fideism and Menippean

form became almost exclusively associated with a skeptical interrogation of the human-based search for truth in the sciences and the arts and with satire on "abuses" in religion.[18] In the seventeenth century Anglican apologists usurped the form to counter both the Jesuits and the Puritans. Burton's *Anatomy*—beloved of Swift and Sterne—and More's *Enthusiasmus Triumphatus* are the most enduring examples of the characteristic blend of satire on religious opponents and skeptical rhetoric in the service of Anglican fideism. Again Swift's and Sterne's acknowledged debt to Burton becomes more significant with a fuller historical overview of the skeptical tradition.[19]

Scriblerian and Sternean satire should be seen in the context of this tradition of skeptical, antidogmatic arguments of the sixteenth and seventeenth centuries. The satiric reduction of system builders in Burton, Swift and Sterne is more than a conflict between the comic and the scientific; it is a product of, and a response to, an intellectual movement that had its birth in the crisis of the Reformation. Swift and Sterne employ the rhetoric of fideism—at some risk of undermining the very ground they seek to preserve—and seize on narrative strategies calculated to deflect readers from the search for *rational* grounds for truth toward acceptance of Anglican orthodoxy. The skeptical method of perplexing the adversary with an exuberant heaping up of pros and cons at the extreme poles of debate on vexed issues gives their satire a seldom rivaled edge.

Donald Wehrs has rightly noted the "interpretative 'suspense' " that Sterne brings about by breaking off the narrative of the Widow Wadman's and Toby's amours at the very moment when the extent of Toby's wound is to be revealed. Expected resolution is denied and the reader is left in suspense. This strategy—typical of Sterne's narrative techique throughout *Tristram Shandy*—comes *close* to genuine skeptical suspense, but should not blind us to the fact of Sternean certainties. These certainties are central to proper understanding of the skeptical tradition in which, paradoxically, skeptical rhetoric is made to serve dogmatic ends. For the reader, at least, the nature of Toby's wound does not "remain uncertain."[20] At the end of the preceding chapter Tristram resolves this particular ambiguity in his discussion of Toby's "fitness for the married state." Nature had not only made Toby "gentle, generous, and humane," but

> she had moreover considered the other causes for which matrimony was ordained——
>
> And accordingly   *   *   *   *   *   *
> *   *   *   *   *   *   *   *   *   *   *
> *   *   *   *   *   *   *   *   *   *   *
> *   *   *   *   *   *   * .
>
> The DONATION was not defeated by my uncle Toby's wound. (*TS*, 9.22.777)

In spite of the preceding lacuna, the final sentence is unequivocal.[21] Within six short chapters, just to make certain that the *facts* are known, and in order to extract the greatest humor from his "choicest morsel," Sterne has Trim apprise Bridget of the same information. The Trim/Bridget scene of chapter 28 beautifully parallels the Toby/Widow Wadman scene in chapter 26, in such a way as to recall the doubleness of truth that we may see as characteristic of Sterne's skeptical strategies. The contrast between master and man is stark. In response to the Widow's "whereabouts?" the hopelessly deluded Toby calls upon documentary evidence in the shape of a map of Namur. By contrast, Trim first responds to Bridget's enquiry by indicating, on his own body, the exact place where Toby received his wound, "*here*—In pronouncing which he slightly press'd the back of her hand towards the part he felt for—and let it fall" (*TS*, 9.28.796). Bridget's doubts cause Trim to denounce vehemently the rumors as "false as hell" before the chapter ends in a mass of equivocal lacunae in which the one certainty is that whatever *is* happening is the "unfortunate" result of Bridget's having "begun the attack with her manual exercise" (*TS*, 9.28.797). Suspense here is not all that it might be. There is no doubt that Sterne exploits the skeptical form as a means of demonstrating the nonlinear, labyrinthine nature of the paths to truth, but that does not prevent him, as a satirist, from demonstrating quite clearly that there *are* some truths.

In the second of his *Crazy Tales* ("My Cousin's Tale of a Cock and a Bull"), John Hall-Stevenson is insightful about Sterne's view of knowledge. Impersonating his friend's voice, Hall-Stevenson describes the quadrangle at Jesus College in which undergraduates were "taught to wrangle," under the shade of the "Tree of Knowledge":

It overshadowed ev'ry room,
   And consequently, more or less,
Forc'd ev'ry brain, in such a gloom,
   To grope its way, and go by guess.

For ever going round about;
   For that which lies before your nose,
And when you come to find it out,
   It is not like you suppose.[22]

Bereft of any other merit, the verses neatly encapsulate the basis of Sterne's skepticism with regard to knowledge. Toby, the seeker after the arcane "truths" of fortification, is so blinded by his hobbyhorse and his sensibility that he is unable to *understand* the obvious denotation of the Widow's question. By contrast, Trim—whose artlessness is clearly approved of by Sterne in other contexts—understands completely the drift of the question and quickly turns Bridget's curiosity into another sexual encounter. As William J. Farrell has demonstrated, "Nature" and "Art" do constant battle in *Tristram Shandy,* and Sterne, like his skeptical forebears, consistently endorses the superior claims of nature.[23] Similarly, Charron in *Of Wisdom* (which is heavily dependent upon Montaigne's *Essays*) recommends that, given the impossibility of discovering truth other than by revelation, our moral lives should be guided by following nature. Hence, in the contrasting courtship scenes the "truths" of Nature are firmly set against the arid "truths" of the science of fortification. Here—their functions constantly shift—Trim and Toby are the means by which Sterne is able, quite clearly, to recommend an uncomplicated sexuality as against the naive confusions of a soldier/sentimentalist who has forgotten that war involves death and that marriage involves sexual pleasure.

Another of Tristram's favorite skeptical strategies is to offer two or more possible explanations for a given happening and to refuse to "determine" anything from the opposing possibilities. Tristram's comments on his father's response to Susannah's unhelpfully brief relation of Elizabeth Shandy's condition is fairly typical:

> Pish! said my father, the button of his breeches slipping out of the button-hole—So that whether the interjection was levelled at Susannah, or the button-hole,—whether pish was an interjection of contempt or an interjection of modesty, is a doubt, and must be a doubt till I shall have time to write the three following favorite chapters. (*TS*, 4.14.345)

The discourse is characteristically equivocal and is typical of many passages in which Tristram uses the device that classical rhetoric termed *aporia*.[24] On one level Sterne is satirizing the pointless human obsession with causality, but on another he is demonstrating the "riddles and mysteries" of interpretation at the most fundamental, and seemingly trivial level. In an earlier passage Tristram explains his strategy:

> My way is ever to point out to the curious, different tracts of investigation, to come at the first springs of the events I tell;—not with a pedantic *Fescue*,—or in the decisive Manner of *Tacitus*, who outwits himself and his reader;—but with the officious humility of a heart devoted to the assistance merely of the inquisitive;—to them I write,———and by them I shall be read. (*TS*, 1.19.74)

There is, of course, more than a hint of irony in Tristram's claim, but given Sterne's awareness of skeptical fideism and its characteristic rhetoric, it can also be taken seriously.

Interestingly, Tristram's skeptical method is defined in opposition to pedantry and Tacitus's "decisive" manner. The Florida edition of Sterne's work notes Tacitus's reputation for "excessive subtlety," but "decisive" suggests a conviction of certainty which is anathema to Tristram and his creator. Furthermore, Bayle's entry on Tacitus in the *Dictionary* suggests another reason for Tristram's rejection of the historian's methods. Bayle endorses Tacitus's reputation as a historian, but comments that "he may be censured for the affectation of his language, and for his inquiring into the secret motives of actions, and construing them to be criminal."[25] It is precisely the dogmatic conclusions of the enquirer into "the secret motivations of actions" that Tristram is rejecting in favor of a skeptical approach to human motivation. Thus Tacitus's method represents a combination of dogmatism with regard to character and obfuscation of style. For an eighteenth-century perception of pedantry Addison's definition is apropos: "a Man who has been brought up among Books, and is able to talk of nothing else, is . . . what we call a Pedant. But, methinks, we should enlarge the Title, and give it to every one that does not know how to think out of his Profession and particular way of Life."[26] In this light the hobby-horsical Shandy males are all guilty of pedantry.

Pierre Charron, to whom Sterne, significantly, alludes in the first and last chapters of *Tristram Shandy,* offers an equally suggestive definition of the "Pedante" as the antithesis of the wise man. "Pedanticall Science," pictured in the emblematic frontispiece as one of Wisdom's four slaves, is described as having a "sullen visage, her eye-lids elevated reading in a Booke, where was written, *Yea, No.*"[27] The curious reader is freed from the mind-numbing choice between affirmation and negation that so plagues Walter Shandy. Thus, Tristram's constant use of the favorite device of *aporia* represents a deliberate rejection of dogmatic assertion. Given the qualities that Tristram defines his method against, the epithets applied to the ideal reader are doubly significant. In opposition to dogmatists and pedants Tristram hopes for "curious" and "inquisitive" readers. Tristram's characterisation of his readers quite clearly recalls the Greek derivation of "skeptic," signifying "inquiring" or "reflective."[28]

Neither Sterne nor Swift needs to have been deeply read in esoteric works to have been familiar with skeptical methods of argumentation nor the intellectual and theological debates in which they were employed. The intellectual map had itself been irreversibly changed by the Reformation and the *crise pyrrhonienne* it was to generate. Quite apart from the literary models, both writers were familiar with the philosophical tenets of fideistic skepticism from a number of sources. As well as the comic and somewhat reductive account of Pyrrhonian skepticism in book 3 of *Gargantua and Pantagruel,* and Diogenes Laertes's "life" of Pyrrho, Swift and Sterne could have read the first English translation of Sextus Empiricus' *Outlines of Pyrrhonism* in Stanley's *History of Philosophy.*[29] But by far the most influential treatment of fideism is to be found in Montaigne's *Apology for Raimond de Sebonde.* Again, we would be ill advised simply to abstract philosophical content from Montaigne's discourse since, as in the essays of Sir Thomas Browne, form and rhetoric are inseparable from the skeptical ideas conveyed. Thus the acknowledged influence of the essayists on Sterne's narrative techniques also has a skeptical lineage. That said, it is worth reminding ourselves of Montaigne's defense of fideism in the *Apology* in order to correct our tendency to view him as something of a whimsical banterer, a view which profoundly affects our notion of his influence on Sterne and Swift. The *Apology* demonstrates how close Montaigne's fideism is to Swift's and Sterne's Anglican orthodoxy, and to their stance as satirists. Montaigne is important not just because of Swift's and Sterne's familiarity with the *Essays,* but because of the immense impact of his articulation of the skeptical position for fideistic ends.[30]

Unlike Sterne, Swift may seem an odd bedfellow for Montaigne. Montaigne's supposed geniality has been seen to have more in common with Sterne's tone than the satiric rage of Swift. Here, as elsewhere, critical pigeonholing can prevent us from understanding what these writers share. Montaigne's avowed purpose in the *Apology* suggests Sterne might have gleaned more from the *Essays* than what Fluchère has called "amused tolerance."[31] Montaigne aims to "crush and spurn under Foot Pride and human Fierceness; to make them sensible of the Inanity, Vanity and Vileness of Man: To wrest the wretched Arms of their Reason out of their Hands, to make them bow down and bite the Ground under the Authority and Reverence of the Divine *Majesty*" (*Essays,* 2:128–29).

The language and tone might seem closer to received readings of Swift than Sterne, but the purpose is surely one that all three share. It is also worth remembering that it is this assault on human

self-sufficiency and the limitations of human reason that lies behind Montaigne's account of pyrrhonian skepticism in the *Apology*.
Skepticism itself is seen as a check to human pride. It cannot be
overstressed that for the Christian, skepticism, far from undermining faith, becomes the key reason for relying on faith above everything else. The fact that such skepticism often results in negative
dogmatism, rather than the suspense that classical skepticism required, is one of the main reasons why the conclusions of the
Christian differ radically from those of the secular skeptic. Humility in the face of God's "riddles and mysteries" leads, according
to Montaigne, to "a peaceable condition of Life, temperate and
exempt from the Agitations we receive by the Impression of Opinion and knowledge that we think we have of things" (*Essays*, 2:195).

It is evident from the *Apology* that Montaigne has moved further
than Erasmus in his anti-intellectualism. The desire to put an end
to religious sectarianism is common to both writers, but, as Terence
Penelhum argues, "by being as explicit . . . about the impotence of
reason . . . [Montaigne] is shifting away from a strict Pyrrhonism
toward the very sort of negative dogmatism he says he follows
Sextus in rejecting."[32] A similar negative dogmatism is evident in
the artfully dialogic satiric discourse of the *Tale* and *Tristram Shandy*.
The undermining of the sufficiency of human reason is, of course,
continued by the Scriblerians and Sterne in such arid rationalists
as Cornelius Scriblerus and Walter Shandy. The assault on blind
faith in the reasoning faculty is relentless in *Gulliver's Travels*, and
in *Tristram Shandy* the antithesis between "truths" of the head and
heart constantly undermines the claims of the former. Anti-
intellectualism and the satiric reduction of the *philosophus gloriosus*
can, of course, be traced back to Aristophanes, but the employment
of skeptical strategies and their intimate relationship with religious
apologetics is peculiar to the skeptical tradition.[33]

Since Philip Harth has aligned Swift's religious thought with
"Anglican rationalism"[34]—in direct opposition to the "heresy" of
fideism—it may be well to remind ourselves of the nature of late
seventeenth-century Anglican theology. South, Stillingfleet, and
Tillotson, who did so much to form Anglican thought of the suc-
ceeding century, were themselves forced into countering the cen-

tral problem raised by the Reformation crisis, the problem of the criterion of truth. Without, of course, adopting skeptical strategies, the Anglican divines of the seventeenth century had to provide reliable grounds for scriptural interpretation in opposition to the perceived dangers of Puritan subjectivity. Thus they attempted to explain the Christian "mysteries" in an intellectually satisfying manner without having recourse to the potentially subversive escape clause of private conviction. Much has been made of the fact that the divines resolved the problem by calling upon the shining light of "Reason," but, as Gerard Reedy argues in *The Bible and Reason*, the "scriptural apologetics of the divines must rank very low in any hierarchy of rationalisms one might construct out of late seventeenth-century thought." In the end the gap between the theology of the seventeenth-century divines and the fideism of some of their Catholic predecessors may not be so great. As Reedy demonstrates, the divines were forced into a "wider" definition of reason:

> Reason in this wider sense thus holds, in its core, an abiding affection for a source of truth that is not rationally verifiable in all its operations; such a commitment is not the result of persuasion but of some deeper human act that has always been called, in spite of the divines' attempt to broaden the category, specifically religious faith.[35]

There is no suggestion that Stillingfleet and Tillotson embraced the skeptical tradition, but it is important to see that rational proof was inadequate to the task of closing what Richard Popkin has called the "Pandora's box that Luther had opened at Leipzig."[36] The skeptical strategies of Swift's and Sterne's fiction have the same *ends* in view as the more orthodox discourse of their sermons which owe much to Tillotson. Rather than adopting a dangerous heresy, they colonize skeptical discourse for the Anglican cause.

It is hard to escape the conclusion that reason is used only selectively by the divines because of the risk of undermining religion itself. There is, therefore, a vested interest at stake in Swift's and Sterne's adoption of the rhetoric of fideism, and more than a hint of a contrary dogmatism in their satire on Catholics and Enthusiasts. Hence the Christian skeptics' attitude to much scientific and philosophical enquiry is deeply conservative, since faith in the incomprehensible makes such enquiry fruitless. Beyond the sure knowledge of God, man can have nothing but the will-o'-the-wisp of opinion. One of Montaigne's repeated arguments against the sufficiency of human reason is that, characteristically, it is incapable of achieving certainty: "it finds Appearance for divers Effects. 'Tis a Pot with two Ears, that a Man may take by the Right or Left" (*Essays,* 2:293). Interestingly the enquiry into the seat of the soul and the debate between the ovists and animalculists are two of Montaigne's examples of the contradictory nature of scientific enquiry—debates which both the Scriblerians and Sterne were later to hold up to ridicule.

What is significant about the *Apology* for our purposes is that, as well as recommending skeptical suspense as an alternative to dogmatism, Montaigne offers a full and cogent manifesto for fideism. Not only does the *Apology* highlight the power of skeptical arguments to counter opponents, but it provides an intellectual foundation for satire on abuses in learning. The suggestion that "whoever should bundle up a lusty Faggot of the Fooleries of human Wisdom, would produce Wonders" (*Essays,* 2:248), is surely one which the Scriblerians and Sterne were to take up with a vengeance. The intimate relationship between satire on system builders and that on religious opponents in the *Tale* and *Tristram Shandy* becomes clearer in the context of Montaigne's arguments. By relentlessly ridiculing the inadequacies of human systems Swift and Sterne are better placed to recommend the haven of Anglican certainty. Thus the satirists were not motivated simply by the fact that the eighteenth century offered more numerous examples of misguided theorists than previous ages. Although Sterne and the Scriblerians are concerned to attack what they perceive to be "of disservice to sound learning," their attitude toward *all* system builders is the same as Montaigne's. When Gulliver learns from Aristotle in Glubbdubdrib that all "new Systems of Nature were but new Fashions, which would vary in every Age,"[37] Swift treats Gassendi, Descartes, and Newton with the same skeptical contempt. The blending of satire on contemporary intellectual folly together with that on already outmoded thinking is yet one more way of demonstrating the limitations of human reason. What John Ferriar failed to see when he accused Sterne of attacking "forsaken fooleries"[38] was the satiric impact of yoking together ancient and modern searchers after the truth. John Burton and Archbishop Warburton join the Schoolmen, Descartes, Obadiah Walker, and many more, as dangerously misguided seekers after certainty. The point is clear; if reason demonstrably fails to elucidate the sublunary world, how much more inadequate is it likely to be in achieving certainty with regard to the deity? All human systems are flawed because, in Montaigne's words: " 'Tis *Faith* alone, that livelily and certainly comprehends the deep Mysteries of our Religion." While we should strive to "accompany our faith with all the reason we have," we must beware of believing that "it is upon us that it depends . . . [or] that our arguments and Endeavours can arrive at so supernatural and Divine a knowledge" (*Essays,* 2:120).

The influence of Montaigne's *Apology* was far-reaching. Richard Popkin summarizes it thus: "throughout the 17th and 18th centuries, Montaigne was not seen as a transitional figure, or a man off the main roads of thought, but as a founder of an important intellectual movement that continued to plague philosophers in their quest for certainty."[39] While it would be quite wrong to ignore what distinguishes Sterne and Swift by subsuming them into a falsely homogenous category, the fideistic tradition influences their literary discourse to such an extent that what they share is more pronounced than their differences. Although Melvyn New's thoroughgoing attempt to demonstrate that "*Tristram Shandy* can best be understood by locating it in the mainstream of the conservative, moralistic Augustan tradition" has proved unpopular with some critics, its thesis still stands. By understanding the skeptical heritage that Sterne and Swift drew upon, the claim that "*Tristram Shandy* joins works like *A Tale of a Tub* and *The Dunciad* as one further effort to stem the eighteenth century's ever increasing enthusiasm for human self-sufficiency" can, in fact, be substantiated.[40] Many of the problems associated with accepting that *Tristram Shandy* is a satire recede when the alliance of skeptical strategies and Christian dogmatism is understood.

Of all the works of the Scriblerians it is *A Tale of a Tub* which, for obvious reasons, has most invited comparison with Sterne's masterpiece. Critics, before emphasizing the differences, have acknowledged the formal resemblances between the two works. Max Byrd's assessment is typical: "from a common starting-point they tend to go racing in utterly different directions." For Byrd, as for many critics, the crucial difference is that "Swift is writing a satire, Sterne a novel." Ronald Paulson—who is prepared to go further than most in acknowledging the similarities between the Scriblerian project and Sterne's—distinguishes between the two writers' approach to the "chaotic" form. For Paulson, Sterne "does with the image of chaos almost the reverse of what Swift did, restoring the positive value it had for Rabelais and Erasmus."[41] Apart from the fact that Swift's and Sterne's use of form is anything but antithetical, Rabelais and Erasmus are clearly models for both. For all four writers the "image of chaos" is, in large part, a foil to the dogmatism that they seek to counter. Sterne, in fact, took more from Swift than a suggestion of the *comic* possibilities of the experimental form. Both *A Tale of a Tub* and *Tristram Shandy* engage in one of the central issues of post-Reformation intellectual enquiry— that of the proper criterion of *truth.* Both works are concerned with hermeneutics at textual and metaphysical levels, and both employ form as a rhetorical tool in order to endorse the arguments of the skeptical fideists against secular dogmatists and abstruse system building.

Everett Zimmerman has argued convincingly that Sterne extends "the critique of biblical and especially textual criticism to be found in Swift's *Tale of a Tub,*" and that he is concerned to show the impossibility of certainty based upon the kind of textual scholarship practised by the likes of Bentley and Warburton. In the same essay he offers an insightful explanation of Sterne's linking of *A Tale* and *The Divine Legation of Moses* with *Tristram Shandy:* Sterne links them, according to Zimmerman, "not only to suggest Swift's work as an ironic commentary on Warburton's but also to acknowledge the subversiveness of all three."[42] While Zimmerman is right to note the potential subversiveness of the works, the common factor is surely a concern with epistemology, and hermeneutics, and an exploitation of skeptical rhetoric to serve the Anglican cause. Sterne's treatment of the Job controversy, like Swift's of textual scholarship, is skeptical and commonsensical. What Sterne makes clear in *Tristram Shandy* and his sermon, "Search the Scriptures," is that questions of historical provenance or allegorical readings fly in the face of the "simplicity" of the Christian message. For Sterne, the Bible is quite simply "that grand charter of our eternal happiness" (*Sermons,* 42.396). In *Tristram Shandy,* for all of its formal complexity, Sterne endorses the "simple," Christian, "common sense" beliefs, expounded at critical moments by Toby, Trim and Yorick.

Since, as we have seen, the methods of the classical skeptics were resurrected in the sixteenth century to deal with arguments over the proper standard of religious knowledge, it should come as no surprise to find Swift and Sterne countering the same problems with the rhetoric of fideism. Swift ingeniously links the allegory of the brothers—dealing explicitly with the Reformation crisis—with the attempts of the Hack and various system builders to explain away the "riddles and mysteries" of God's universe. Swift's common sense endorsement of the Anglican *via media* is intimately linked with his satire on "new schemes in philosophy." The link is made not simply because an abuse at one level is symptomatic of a deeper malaise, but because they are all homocentric answers to epistemological and teleological issues. The Catholics, the Dissenters, and such textual scholars as Bentley are guilty of overrefining the simplicity of the Gospel in the same way as the philosophers who advance "new systems . . . in things impossible to be known" (*Tale,* 80). The allegory of the brothers treats the issue of biblical interpretation in deliberately reductive terms, warning of the dangers of the human propensity to distort Divine meaning. The *Tale* proper is also concerned with epistemology as it charts the attempts of the Hack, and more auspicious system builders, to achieve certainty by the most convoluted of means.

For Swift, as later for Sterne, these aberrations have a common source—the overzealous desire of the prideful dogmatist to make the self the measure of all things. The Hack himself attempts to disguise the inane and the vacuous under a cloak of pseudo-scholarship and mystification, but this becomes the means by which Swift, paradoxically, recommends an uncomplicated "belief in things invisible" (*Tale,* 82). The form of *A Tale of a Tub* is much more than the result of Swift's desire to parody the methods and style of the Grub Street hacks. While Swift is clearly concerned to highlight the shortcomings of the moderns, he did not need their digressive habits to shape the *Tale.* The writers of the skeptical tradition all employ nonlinear and "open" form as part of their assault on dogmatism. The *Tale* is a vivid example of just how easily the human imagination, when it "is at cuffs with the senses" (*Tale,* 82), can construct an abstruse framework to disguise emptiness. Like that of *Tristram Shandy,* the form of the *Tale* graphically illustrates the vanity of human-based attempts to achieve certainty without reference to God. In both works, the skeptical form demonstrates the labyrinthine paths into which seekers after truth are led. At the same time—and here we are reminded of the doubleness of truth in the *Praise of Folly*—the reader is being led into a comic celebration of skepticism in all matters *except* the divine "truths" of Anglicanism. The range of Swift's and Sterne's satire should not blind us to the fact that all of their targets are finally guilty of searching for truth everywhere but where it is to be found, not in man but in "received wisdom."

The complexity of Swift's vehicle, like Sterne's, can prevent us from seeing the one pervasive and dogmatic blind spot that underpins them. Swift and Sterne, like Rabelais before them, never tire of the joke that beneath the surface of their work lie hidden meanings and allegories, largely to check the readers' propensity for overreading. At the same time, we are constantly being urged to seek the Christian truths within. The metaphor of the Sileni central in Erasmus and Rabelais is quite deliberately echoed by Tristram and the Hack. The Hack simultaneously recommends deep delving and surface scratching just as Tristram insists that the marbled page ("motly emblem of my work"), like the black one, mystically hides "opinions, transactions, and truths" (*TS,* 3.36.268). On one level, all four writers are satirizing the dangerous ingenuity of scriptural exegetes, but on another they are insisting upon the opposing truth of the simplicity of the gospel message. As several critics have noted, there are dangers inherent in viewing the Hack or Tristram as consistent satiric butts; part of their function is to endorse Pauline Christian folly. Hence the narrators of the *Tale* and *Tristram Shandy* can at one moment appear as despicable egotists and at another as spokesmen—albeit foolish ones—for their authors. The effect is a quite deliberate perplexing of the reader which is further enhanced by the dialogic texture of the prose. Swift's and Sterne's pleasure in exercising the exuberance of their wit cannot be doubted and yet their suspicion of rhetoric and intellectual obfuscation is so pronounced as to validate their own methods only as a means to pious ends. The writers of the skeptical tradition, for all their own erudition and mastery of rhetoric, consistently derogate refinements in the arts and sciences because they represent a threat to the "illogical" message of the Gospels.

Behind the anti-intellectualism and praise of folly lies a favorite skeptical text—St. Paul's defense of the indefensible in 1 Corinthians. St. Paul, in the face of "contentions" among the church of Corinth, makes a virtue of his lack of eloquence in much the same way as Sterne recommends Trim's eloquent ineloquence in opposition to Walter's rhetoric. The eminently reasonable desire of the Jews for "a sign" and of the Greeks "to seek after wisdom" is swept aside with a sleight of hand consistent with all Christian apologetics and particularly prominent in the skeptical texts under consideration. For St. Paul, since earthly wisdom provides no access to God, the flaw *must* be in man: "God hath chosen the foolish things of the world to confound the wise" (1 Cor. 1:27). If Paul's words lack persuasion, it is *because* his discourse is not that of "the enticing words of man's wisdom" (1 Cor. 2:4). Finally, Paul trumps his opponents with a claim that validates Erasmus's, Rabelais's, Montaigne's, Swift's and Sterne's relentless satire on searchers after truth: "we speak the wisdom of God in a mystery, *even* the hidden *wisdom,* which God ordained before the world to our glory" (1 Cor. 2:7). We may be inclined to feel Walter's exasperation—after years of delving into the mysteries of nose sizes—with Toby for providing Grangousier's unanswerable solution to the problem, but St. Paul, Toby, and Grangousier have much in common. It is, in part, the very weakness of the case for the defense that leads Swift and Sterne to adopt skeptical strategies to silence their opponents.

The butts of Swift's and Sterne's satire are the same as Montaigne's targets in the *Apology*—those, in the Hack's words, "whose converting imaginations dispose them to reduce all things into *types*, who can make *shadows*, no thanks to the sun, and then mould them into substances, no thanks to philosophy," who refine "what is literal into figure and mystery" (*Tale*, 92). Swift's association of the Dissenters with the Aeolists and the Hack's work with the empty tub has the same rhetorical effect as the images of wind and smoke that Montaigne employs in his arguments to undermine dogmatism.

Laughter is, of course, the primary means by which the Scriblerians and Sterne attempt to discredit the vast range of dogmas which they perceive as pernicious. Despite the wealth of criticism that has concentrated on the fundamental differences between Swift's mordant satire and Sterne's amiable humor, there is basically very little difference in attitude or tone. As is well known, both writers claim that their works are "writ against the spleen,"[43] emphasizing the importance of laughter as purge. While this belief in the medicinal value of laughter found support in Burton and such works as William Stukeley's *Of the Spleen*, its source may be older and more significant than has previously been allowed. In the preface to the first modern translation of Sextus Empiricus' *Hypotyposes*, published in 1562, Henri Estienne explains how he discovered the work. Reading Sextus when he was sick made him laugh, and so helped bring about a cure. In Richard Popkin's summary, Estienne "saw how inane all learning was, and this cured him of his antagonism to scholarly matters by allowing him to take them less seriously."[44] Estienne's claim was itself an extension of Sextus' own metaphor for the ends of skeptical philosophy: the medical metaphor of skepticism as laxative or diuretic, administered to cure the mental disquietude caused by dogmatic wrangling. If Sterne and Swift had not come across the metaphor in Sextus, they could have found it in Montaigne's *Apology*. Laughter, then, for Sterne and Swift is much more than Hobbes's "sudden glory." It is a liberating and happiness-inducing activity that is calculated to purge the mind as preparation for the reception of God's grace. Shandean and Swiftean laughter, like Pantagruelism, is the

joyous response to the liberation of fideism which enables its ad-
herent to "remain in Suspense [rather] than to entangle himself
in the innumerable Errors that human Fancy has produc'd" (*Essays,*
2:196).

The relationship between Sterne and the Scriblerians needs to
be looked at anew. If this is undertaken without the prejudice of
received readings of Swift and Sterne, our understanding of both
writers can be enhanced. Of course, Sterne is much more than a
latter-day Swift, but by tracing the fideistic line of descent from
the Renaissance humanists through the Scriblerians to Sterne, we
are, perhaps, better able to understand both writers. Swift's skepticism no longer seems incompatible with religious belief, and *Tristram Shandy*'s much vaunted indeterminacy can be better understood
when it is seen as part of a consistent satiric strategy. Some well-
worn commonplaces of Sterne criticism may have to be put to
rest, but that is all to the good. We may, for example, have to
accept that Sterne's religious belief was no sham; that he may never
have read the "novelists," let alone contemplated a devastating
critique of the shortcomings of the emerging genre; and that Locke
is no more the interpretive "open sesame" than the doctors of the
Sorbonne or Tobias Smollett.[45] Sterne wrote late enough in the eighteenth century for many of his readers to be unaware of the full
implications of his explicit alignment with the writers of the
learned wit tradition. Consequently, then as now, *some* readers and
critics considered the work original and impious, but many contemporaries, including Lord Bathurst, familiar with less fashionable
writers like Burton and the Scriblerians, immediately understood
the significance of family resemblances. It may, in some ways, be
a hard pill to swallow to accept that such a marvelous book as
Tristram Shandy can have been written from a conservative, not to
say reactionary perspective, and that it is a satire (with all that the
generic distinction implies) and not a postmodernist novel. But if
there is a value in the lessons of literary history, the pill may not
be without beneficial effects. Of course, as different readers bring
different experiences and different interpretive models to bear on
Tristram Shandy, it will continue to yield new fruits. Quite clearly
literary discourse will always give the slip to the controls of au-

thorial intention and the neat closure implied by placing texts within traditions. But this does not invalidate a literary-historical perspective. Before our interpretive hobby-horses take us whither they will, it may be useful to remember that the insights gained from historical perspectives allow us to better understand our own habitual, and hence unconscious, ideological prejudices. The consistent privileging of the "plural" text in many recent theoretical treatments of the novel has led to some uncritical conclusions about *Tristram Shandy.* It is surely, in part, our desire to use texts to confirm current theoretical orthodoxies which prevents us from acknowledging them to be informed by worldviews uncongenial to our own.

Notes

1. Donald R. Wehrs, "Sterne, Cervantes, Montaigne: Fideistic Skepticism and the Rhetoric of Desire," *Comparative Literature Studies* 25 (1988): 127–51.

2. For a discussion of Sterne and Charron see Françoise Pellan, "Laurence Sterne's Indebtedness to Charron," *Modern Language Review* 67 (1972): 752–55, and *Notes,* 39–40, 549–50. Pope refers to Montaigne and Charron with approbation in the *Epistle to Lord Cobham* (line 87). Swift owned copies of the *Essays* and *Of Wisdom. Dean Swift's Library,* ed. Harold Williams (Cambridge: Cambridge University Press, 1932), items 21, 648.

3. The most notable dissenting voice in discussions of the relationship between Swift and Sterne is Melvyn New. Since 1969 New has consistently and persuasively argued the shared Anglican and satiric basis of the Swift/ Sterne nexus. I am not only indebted to Professor New's publications on Swift and Sterne but am also grateful for his useful comments at various stages of this essay's development.

4. John Traugott, *Tristram Shandy's World: Sterne's Philosophical Rhetoric* (Berkeley: University of California Press, 1954), 17.

5. Wehrs, "Sterne, Cervantes, Montaigne," 130.

6. Richard H. Popkin, *The History of Scepticism from Erasmus to Spinoza* (Berkeley: University of Califronia Press, 1979), 1, 4.

7. The most thorough consideration of Swift and Erasmus is Eugene R. Hammond, "In Praise of Wisdom and the Will of God: Erasmus' *Praise of Folly* and Swift's *A Tale of a Tub,*" *Studies in Philology* 80 (1983): 253–76.

Ronald Paulson also considers the relationship in *Theme and Structure in Swift's Tale of a Tub* (New Haven: Yale University Press, 1960). Sterne's relationship to Erasmus is discussed by John Traugott and John M. Stedmond, *The Comic Art of Laurence Sterne* (Toronto: University of Toronto Press, 1967) and Wehrs, "Sterne, Cervantes, Montaigne."

8. P. H. Holland, "Robert Burton's 'Anatomy of Melancholy' and Menippean Satire" (Ph.D. diss., University of London, 1979), 362. Holland applies the phrase to Menippean satires in general, but considers the *Tale* and *Tristram Shandy* as examples of the genre.

9. Erasmus, *Praise of Folly*, trans. Betty Radice (Harmondsworth: Penguin Books, 1971), 135.

10. See Hammond, "In Praise of Wisdom," and Paulson, *Theme and Structure*.

11. Jonathan Swift, *A Tale of a Tub*, ed. Angus Ross and David Woolley (Oxford: Oxford University Press, 1986), 84. Future references to this edition will be cited in the text.

12. Montaigne, *Essays*, trans. Charles Cotton, 5th ed., 3 vols. (1738), 1: 285. Future references to this edition will be cited in the text. Shakespeare, *Hamlet*, 2.2.249–50.

13. This is also the conclusion of the editors of *Notes*, 313.

14. For a discussion of Erasmus's influence on Rabelais see Radice's annotations to *Praise of Folly*. The Erasmian elements of *Don Quixote* are considered at length by Alban K. Forcione in *Cervantes and the Humanist Vision: A Study of Four Exemplary Novels* (Princeton: Princeton University Press, 1982).

15. Valerie Grosvenor Myer, ed., *Laurence Sterne: Riddles and Mysteries* (London and Totowa, N.J.: Vision and Barnes and Noble, 1984), 9.

16. For a stimulating discussion of Locke's impact on the Scriblerians see Christopher Fox, *Locke and the Scriblerians: Identity and Consciousness in Early Eighteenth-Century Britain* (Berkeley: University of California Press, 1988).

17. Terence Penelhum, "Skepticism and Fideism" in *The Skeptical Tradition*, ed. Myles Burnyeat (Berkeley: University of California Press, 1983), 294.

18. See Eugene Kirk, *Menippean Satire: An Annotated Catalogue of Texts and Criticism* (New York: Garland, 1980), especially ix–xxxiii.

19. For an insightful treatment of Burton's links with Sterne see Holland, *Robert Burton's "Anatomy of Melancholy,"* 411–15.

20. Donald Wehrs, "Sterne, Cervantes, Montaigne," 143.

21. For earlier discussions of the question of Toby's potency see Mark Sinfield, "Uncle Toby's Potency: Some Critical and Authorial Confusions in *Tristram Shandy*," *Notes & Queries* 223 (1978): 54–55 and Arthur H. Cash,

Laurence Sterne: The Later Years (London and New York: Methuen, 1986), 258 n. 16.

22. John Hall-Stevenson, *Crazy Tales* (1762), 17.

23. William J. Farrell, "Nature versus Art as a Comic Pattern in *Tristram Shandy*," *ELH* 30 (1963): 16–35.

24. See Richard Lanham, *A Handlist of Rhetorical Terms* (Berkeley: University of California Press, 1968), 126.

25. See *Notes*, 110; Pierre Bayle, *The Dictionary Historical and Critical*, 5 vols. (1734–38), s.v. *Tacitus*.

26. Joseph Addison, *Spectator* no. 105, cited by *Oxford English Dictionary*, s.v. "Pedant."

27. Pierre Charron, *Of Wisdom*, trans. Lennard (1608), ix. For Sterne and Charron see note 2, above.

28. Of course, "curious" and "inquisitive" also have negative connotations in Sterne and Swift. Just as Sterne rejects dogmatic treatments of character only to offer his own favored conception of the ruling passion, skeptical readers are only desirable to a limited extent. This paradox is typical of those generated by Sterne's and Swift's appropriation of skeptical rhetoric for dogmatic, satiric ends. For another possible implication of Tristram's construction of "curious" readers see *Notes*, 50.

29. Thomas Stanley, *History of Philosophy: Containing the Lives, Opinions, Actions, and Discourses of Every Sect*, 3rd ed. (London, 1701).

30. See Dominick Grundy, "Skepticism in Two Essays by Montaigne and Sir Thomas Browne," *Journal of the History of Ideas* 34 (1973): 530–42; Popkin, *History of Skepticism*, 42–86.

31. Henri Fluchère, *Laurence Sterne: From Tristram to Yorick. An Interpretation of "Tristam Shandy*," trans. and abridged by Barbara Bray (London: Oxford University Press, 1965), 178.

32. Penelhum, "Skepticism and Fideism," 295.

33. For a discussion of the relationship between Menippean satire and religious apologetics see Eugene P. Kirk's introduction to his *Menippean Satire*.

34. Philip Harth, *Swift and Anglican Rationalism: The Religious Background of a "Tale of a Tub"* (Chicago and London: University of Chicago Press, 1961), especially 21ff. Harth's conception of Anglican rationalism is, in fact, consistent with Popkin's definition of fideism. However, Harth rejects Kathleen Williams's suggestion that Swift can be viewed as a fideist on the grounds that such a distinction suggests that reason and supernatural religion are incompatible, and that fideism itself was associated with Puritanism.

35. Gerard Reedy, *The Bible and Reason: Anglicans and Scripture in Late Seventeenth-Century England* (Philadelphia: University of Pennsylvania Press, 1985), 62, 37.

36. Popkin, *History of Scepticism,* 4.

37. Sterne, *Letters,* 120; Jonathan Swift, *Gulliver's Travels,* ed. Paul Turner (Oxford: Oxford University Press, 1986), 198.

38. John Ferriar, *Illustrations of Sterne with other Essays and Verses* (London: 1798), 182.

39. Popkin, *History of Scepticism,* 54.

40. Melvyn New, *Laurence Sterne as Satirist: A Reading of "Tristram Shandy"* (Gainesville: University of Florida Press, 1970), 1, 2.

41. Max Byrd, *Tristram Shandy* (London: Unwin Hyman, 1988), 40; Ronald Paulson, *Satire and the Novel in Eighteenth-Century England* (New Haven, Conn.: Yale University Press, 1967), 256.

42. Everett Zimmerman, "*Tristram Shandy* and Narrative Representation," *Eighteenth Century* 28 (1987): 127–47, 138. For a different, but equally interesting, reading of the linkage see Melvyn New, "Sterne, Warburton, and the Burden of Exuberant Wit," *Eighteenth-Century Studies* 15 (1982): 245–74.

43. *TS,* 4.22.360; Swift, "The Author upon Himself," line 48.

44. See Michael DePorte, *Nightmares and Hobbyhorses: Swift, Sterne, and Augustan Ideas of Madness* (San Marino, Calif.: Huntington Library, 1974), 136; Popkin, *History of Skepticism,* 33–34.

45. For dissenting views of the Locke/Sterne relationship see Duke Maskell, "Locke and Sterne: Or Can Philosophy Influence Literature?" *Essays In Criticism* 23 (1973): 22–39, and W. G. Day, "*Tristram Shandy:* Locke May Not Be the Key," in Myer, *Laurence Sterne,* 75–83.

Sterne and the "New Species of Writing"

THOMAS KEYMER

◆　◆　◆

O F THE PLURALITY of discourses and traditions that bump up against one another in *Tristram Shandy,* two have dominated critical attempts to make generic (and hence interpretative) sense of Sterne's richly heteroglot text. One strain of criticism reads *Tristram Shandy* as a belated exercise in Renaissance learned wit; the other as a parody (or, if the implications of its parodic gestures are pursued, a deconstruction) of representational conventions in the modern novel. Each identity, all too often, is presented as exclusive of the other, and the critical dichotomy persists not least because its most evident point of stress—the overtly Cervantic aspect of *Tristram Shandy*—has been obscured by readings that present Cervantes himself as primarily an exponent of Erasmian satire, or of fideistic skepticism in the vein of Montaigne, rather than in his alternative guise as a proto-novelist.[1] The difficulty of grounding the novel-centered approach to Sterne in features equivalent to the close and direct allusiveness of his learned wit set pieces, moreover, has often left it stranded in anachronism or generality, so fueling the counterclaim that *Tristram Shandy*'s subversiveness of novelistic convention is nothing more than accidental or proleptic, or even a mere illusion. At best, in this view, the metafictional element in Sterne's writing is a chance by-product of his cooption, within a mock-autobiographical framework, of Scriblerian techniques of fragmentation and disruption, and lacks any solid connection to a genre in which he took little or no provable interest.

Yet it is not necessary for the novel-centered approach to *Tristram Shandy* to take refuge in classic poststructuralist theory, with its rationale for cutting relational meanings loose from inconvenient circumstances of chronology or intention. To acknowledge the prominence of the learned wit tradition in Sterne's writing need not be to deny the deliberacy of its engagement with newer forms. Instead we may find within it a cornucopia of textual relations in which Menippean satire and metafictional self-consciousness co-exist and unfold themselves in different intertextual modes, and display, as they do so, a hybridization of traditions and genres that in itself is typically novelistic. Here the satirical mode is characteristically determinate, involving necessary connections with specific precursors named, quoted, or otherwise verbally indicated in the text, and this applies even where (as in the instances of determinate intertextuality that fill the standing *Scriblerian* column of "scholia" to the Florida annotations) the verbal indications are so subtle, or the indicated sources so recondite, that they pass undetected for centuries. The novelistic mode, by contrast, is characteristically aleatory, gesturing toward a plurality of potential intertexts through its play on terms, tropes, or conventions that all of them hold in common, but necessarily specifying no single one.[2]

Although Sterne's engagement with the novel genre, I argue below, can occasionally be pinned down to concrete allusion, this fuzzier kind of intertextuality is its usual and appropriate mode for several reasons. The expectations inevitably generated by *Tristram Shandy*'s title and fictional content, coupled with the fashionable prominence of the "new species of writing" over the previous twenty years, made it unnecessary for Sterne to flag his entanglement with the genre with anything like the specificity needed to evoke historically more distant imbrications—imbrications that, as a result, have dominated the work of source-hunters since the time of John Ferriar's *Illustrations of Sterne* (1798). Sterne's primary interest, moreover, is with large questions about the novel and its mechanisms, not with the uniqueness of particular novels. Where a specific instantiation of the genre does help to clarify these larger generic conditions, the towering contemporary stature of certain key works—by Richardson and Fielding above all—acts as a natural check on the randomness of association otherwise generated by aleatory intertextuality, so that only the faintest of allusive touches can serve to bring to mind a specific reference point.

The coexistence with Sterne's noisy displays of learned wit of this quiet but no less pervasive engagement with the novel genre—an engagement that also seems, if we listen to the evidence of reception, to have been immediately accessible to early readers—takes several forms, and marks not only the "novelistic-sentimental" final volumes of *Tristram Shandy* but also its "satirical-Scriblerian" opening. *Tristram Shandy* absorbs and resumes the most vexed topics of experimentation and debate in novels such as *Clarissa* and *Tom Jones,* notably the mimetic efficacy (or otherwise) of narrative language, the dynamics of communication between narrator and reader, and the openness of narrative meaning to plural construction. Several years intervened, however, between the well-publicized retirements of Richardson and Fielding and the inaugural installment of *Tristram Shandy,* and in the interim novelists had made further innovatory gestures while explicitly registering the new (and in some respects newly adverse) conditions of authorship and publication in the later 1750s. In this respect, forgotten experimental novels of this decade such as John Kidgell's *The Card,* the anonymous *Life and Memoirs of Mr. Ephraim Tristram Bates,* Thomas Amory's *The Life of John Buncle, Esq.,* William Toldervy's *The History of Two Orphans,* and Edward Kimber's *The Juvenile Adventures of David Ranger, Esq.,* constitute an equally significant body of precursor texts. Sterne not only adopts the episodic repertoire and formal reflexiveness of the subgenre represented by these novels, ostentatiously trumping their prior deployment of both with elaborate displays of narrative involution and excess. He also digests and reworks the most innovative feature they share, which is their tendency to push a literary self-consciousness inherited from Fielding into a more directly practical self-consciousness about the mechanisms and institutions of print culture: specifically, about the relationship between authorial production and its materialization as a printed object, and about the overdetermination of both by the forces of literary commodification, consumer fashion, and regulatory reviewing. Sterne's systematic exploitation of this incompletely realized potentiality in the novels of the 1750s, like his parodies of circumstantial realism in Richardson or his Fielding-esque tropes of narrative as conversation or travel, is too capricious and ironic to be assimilated to a consistent thesis about the emerging genre. *Tristram Shandy* recurrently indicates, however, an explosive skepticism about the referential and rhetorical pretensions of novelistic discourse, specifically as these were developed and interrogated in the twenty years preceding its opening volumes of December 1759.

Tristram Shandy, Satire, and the Novel

The competing traditions of *Tristram Shandy* criticism reach back to the earliest reviews. At one extreme is a fatuous puff in the *London Magazine* for February 1760, which finds *Tristram Shandy* "rare" and "unaccountable," and asks: "what shall we call there?—Rabelais, Cervantes, What?" (*CH,* 52). The point is carried no further, but clearly heralds that modern approach to Sterne that finds its *locus classicus* in Jefferson's influential essay on "*Tristram Shandy* and the Tradition of Learned Wit," and its amplest expression in the rich intertextual annotations of the Florida edition: the idea that *Tristram Shandy,* inexplicable by the literary norms and conventions of its own day, can be understood only by analogy with Renaissance satire (and only then with reference to some idiosyncratic further element in the brew, an indefinable "What"). Here the *London* obligingly picks up a message that Sterne had carefully embedded in his opening volumes, and that his fashionable promoters were spreading about town. It is in the second installment that Sterne most pointedly stakes his claim (with Tristram's oath "by the ashes of my dear *Rabelais,* and dearer *Cervantes*" [3.19.225]) to be the true heir to these long-dead masters, a latter-day phoenix sprung from their embers; but the claim is hinted well enough in the opening volumes, with their pervasive Rabelaisian echoes and several overt allusions to *Don Quixote*. It gained resonance from the pontifications of Bishop Warburton, who, having previously published two genealogical accounts of the modern novel (one culminating with Richardson, the other with Fielding), presented Sterne as a case apart. Here was "the English Rabelais," Warburton was telling anyone who would listen, who had written "an original composition, and in the true Cervantic vein"[3]—praise that (with nice economy of contradiction) makes plain the advantage Sterne reaped by flagging such distant forebears as his primary models. At a time when Richardson's status as the very type of originality had been sealed by the dedication to him of Young's *Conjectures on Original Composition* (1759), and similar claims had been made for Fielding in commentaries like *An Essay on the New Species of Writing Founded by Mr. Fielding* (1751), it is as though the noise Sterne makes about Rabelais and Cervantes could preempt allegations of indebtedness to his immediate contemporaries, and so assist his standing, paradoxically, as an original himself.

A yet earlier reviewer, however, had been willing enough to accept the originality of *Tristram Shandy* while unhesitatingly associating it with the modern novel. Writing in the *Monthly Review,* which had been complaining for years about the staleness of the fiction churned out since the retirement of Richardson and Fielding ("those loads of trash, which are thrown in upon us under the denomination of *Lives, Adventures, Memoirs, Histories,* &c."[4]), William Kenrick praised Sterne's work for reconfiguring the hackneyed outlines of the genre. Sterne's title implied the whole process. "Of Lives and *Adventures* the public have had enough, and, perhaps, more than enough, long ago," Kenrick writes, with all the weariness of a jobbing reviewer: "A consideration that probably induced the droll Mr. Tristram Shandy to entitle the performance . . . his Life and *Opinions.*" *Life and Adventures* had indeed been a standard formula since the days of *Robinson Crusoe,* and Kenrick was right to imply that there had been no previous *Life and Opinions.* By creatively recasting the usual formula, and playing on its terms in the text itself, Sterne advertises his self-conscious preoccupation with discourse over story (or opinion over transaction, as Tristram would have it), and thereby flags his ironic relationship to the genre as a whole. Kenrick seems to understand as much when recommending him, in conclusion, "as a writer infinitely more ingenious and entertaining than any other of the present race of novelists" (*CH*, 47–48). In this usage it is the modern sense of "novelist" that clearly applies, though Kenrick's larger point is that Sterne himself is also a "novelist" in what then was the primary sense.[5] He is a novelist among novelists, an innovator among writers of fiction—a judgment that gains real weight from Kenrick's extensive recent experience of where the genre now stood. As a new recruit to the *Monthly,* Kenrick seems to have been allocated a disproportionate share of novels, and had reviewed at least twelve in the previous year—several of which, as he confesses in the case of William Guthrie's *The Mother; or, The Happy Distress,* were "so very little interesting, that we could not bear to read through them at all."[6]

Kenrick was not alone in his view of *Tristram Shandy*'s opening installment as essentially (though also eccentrically) novelistic. His diagnosis of the work as pointedly disrupting the norms of the genre was echoed by Horace Walpole, who wrote of it as "a kind of novel . . . the great humour of which consists in the whole narration always going backwards"—as though we might find in *Tristram Shandy* a precursor of much more recent narrative experiments like Martin Amis's novel in rewind, *Time's Arrow* (1991).[7] From here it is a simple step to that alternative line of interpretation advanced by modern commentators who, like Kenrick before them, approach *Tristram Shandy* via a specific professional interest in the novel as a genre: the view that this is not a belated exercise in learned wit satire but a modern novel about novel writing, which self-consciously stages (as Everett Zimmerman succinctly puts it) "a complex parody of conventional narrative procedures."[8]

But whose narrative procedures, and which ones? There is a telling evasiveness in Zimmerman's phrasing here, and specifically in "conventional," which haunts this whole approach. Sterne writes at a time when the conventions of fictional representation, such as they were, remained fluid, ill-defined, and keenly contested: Witness the Richardson–Fielding dispute of the 1740s, which was as much about competing narrative strategies as it was about religion and ethics, or ideologies of gender and class. Do we assume that *Tristram Shandy* is sending up the minute and massive particularizations of Richardsonian narrative, the magisterial manipulations of Fielding's, something else entirely—or all three at once? Or do we assume no relationship at all to any specific precursor, and read the antinovelistic element of *Tristram Shandy* as essentially fortuitous—a deconstructive potential inherent in the text, which illuminates, through strictly synchronic analysis and without any corresponding diachronic claim, the assumptions and mechanics of narrative realism in its classic (that is, later) phase? Michael McKeon elegantly conflates the diachronic and synchronic versions of this approach to Sterne when writing that the formal breakthroughs achieved by novelists of the 1740s were "pursued with such feverish intensity over the next two decades that after *Tristram Shandy,* it may be said, the young genre settles down to a more deliberate and studied recapitulation of the same ground, this time for the next two centuries."[9] Equations as deft as these have a powerful appeal, but they also reveal the extent to which a strictly formalist case about Sterne's affinity with postmodern narrative (McKeon's "next two centuries" take us, of course, to the 1960s) can slip, almost by default and without demonstration, into a historical assertion about his posture toward Richardson, Fielding, and the novelists who wrote in their wake. An implied analogy with writers of experimental metafiction like Barth, Burroughs, or B. S. Johnson, or with the French *nouveau roman* (a critique, overtly theorized as such by exponents like Robbe-Grillet, of nineteenth-century realism), is being used to support a proposition about Sterne's relationship toward his own precursors. This proposition is otherwise unsubstantiated—and has never, indeed, been argued through.

To review the rise of *Tristram Shandy*'s reputation as a work that counts Richardson and Fielding (as much as Warburton, say, or Locke) among its satirical butts—as a work in which the groaning conventions of mid-eighteenth-century fiction meet their parodic waterloo—is to see this slippage in action. The classic prewar readings of *Tristram Shandy* as parodic antinovel or sophisticated meta-novel are unabashedly ahistorical, and largely sidestep the question of Sterne's posture toward experiments with narrative, and debates about it, in the decades before he wrote. It is hardly surprising (given the resources available to him in 1920s Russia) that Viktor Shklovsky's celebration of Sterne as "a radical revolutionary as far as form is concerned" is based on little acquaintance with earlier novels, and Shklovsky's claim, though brilliantly substantiated through formal analysis, has no historical weight. Foils for his argument about the antithetical relationship "between the conventional novel and that of Sterne" are repeatedly found in the repertoire of the century to follow, and, although generalizations about prior conventions are occasionally ventured—"Sterne was writing against a background of the adventure novel with its extremely rigorous forms that demanded . . . that a novel end with a wedding" (which hardly touches the most prominent background novels, such as *Amelia* or *Clarissa*)—the overall case is synchronic.[10] In much the same period, though of course independently, Virginia Woolf remarked of Sterne that "no young writer could have dared to take such liberties with . . . the long-standing tradition of how a novel should be written," but did little to develop this instinctive sense of *Tristram Shandy*'s iconoclastic stance toward earlier fiction. Instead Woolf was mainly concerned with an ulterior motive in the present: that of coopting Sterne for her ongoing campaign against the bricks-and-mortar realism typified by Galsworthy and Bennett. Her deft reading of *A Sentimental Journey* converts it into a stream-of-consciousness novel *avant la lettre,* laudably indifferent to its material environment, and alert to the fluidity of perception: "no writing seems to flow more exactly into the very folds and creases of the individual mind, to express its changing moods, to answer its lightest whim and impulse."[11]

From influential analyses such as these—which finely adumbrate Sterne's proleptic unravelling of high-realist conventions, but fail to ground it in any demonstrable response to eighteenth-century fiction—flows the more or less unexamined assumption, in more recent criticism, that the narrative conventions unpicked by Sterne are specifically those of his immediate precursors: the novelists who, like Richardson and Fielding, self-consciously saw themselves as giving shape (or shapes) to "a New Species of Writing."[12] Literary historians of the postwar years made more targeted attempts to seal the connection, but even the most distinguished, Ian Watt, found his proposition that Sterne turns irony "against many of the narrative methods which the new genre had so lately developed" hard to substantiate in practice. Sometimes Watt simply flannels, as in his strained analogy with Defoe (whose "brilliant economy of suggestion" Sterne is held to absorb) or in his odd claim that "Fielding's criticism of Richardson is implicit in the way that Sterne's masculine embodiment of sexual virtue is pitted against the Widow Wadman's villainous Lovelace."[13] And, whereas other aspects of Watt's thesis have been valuably developed or contested by a second wave of rise-of-the-novel studies in the 1980s and 1990s, this particular part has stayed much where it is. McKeon's excellent *Origins of the English Novel* typifies the tendency of revisionist studies to cut out in midcentury, thereby confining Sterne's relationship to the tradition to passing reference (the sentence cited above being McKeon's only mention of *Tristram Shandy*). The most authoritative recent overview of the century as such, by John Richetti, guardedly sidesteps the issue by restating the Renaissance-satirical inheritance of *Tristram Shandy* and stressing its identity as "almost *sui generis,*" "not a novel in the customary sense." By confining Sterne to his chapter on sensibility, Richetti focuses his analysis instead on ethical rather than narratological aspects of *Tristram Shandy*'s contemporary resonance, and specifically its equivocal status as "a proleptic parody of the novel of sentimental education."[14]

One possible response at this point would be to say that Sterne's status as a witty parodist (and/or a sophisticated deconstructor) of the "new species of writing" and its underlying conventions is so self-evident that demonstration would be pointless. Watt has made the general point that "Sterne's narrative mode gives very careful attention to all the aspects of formal realism: to the particularisation of time, place and person; to a natural and lifelike sequence of action; and to the creation of a literary style which gives the most exact verbal and rhythmical equivalent possible of the object."[15] Add to this Watt's recognition that this attention is typically parodic in cast, and chapter-and-verse specification seems otiose. More recently, however, formidable questions have been posed that demand a direct answer. Why, in this most allusive of works (to say nothing of every other published or manuscript source from Sterne's pen), does Sterne never refer explicitly to Richardson or Fielding, and why has no modern editor of *Tristram Shandy* (including Watt himself, in the Riverside edition of 1965) caught Sterne reworking any specific passage from their fiction? As the Florida edition so richly documents, the embeddedness of *Tristram Shandy* in a learned wit tradition from Rabelais and Montaigne to Swift and the Scriblerians is not only close but also overt. Locke, Sterne's philosophical source-cum-stooge, is cited by name on fully seven occasions. Intertextual allusiveness is *Tristram Shandy*'s stock in trade, and from volume 1, which will be "no less read than the *Pilgrim's Progress* itself" (*TS*, 1.4.5), to volume 9, which will "swim down the gutter of Time" with Warburton's *Divine Legation* and *A Tale of a Tub* (*TS*, 9.8.754), Sterne's strategy is to highlight its operation—though his total silence about Robert Burton, incontestably a major source for *Tristram Shandy*, should make us pause before assuming that "Sterne's system of imitation," in Jonathan Lamb's phrase, always proclaims its own workings.[16]

One explanation—Melvyn New's—is that this absence should not surprise us: Sterne fails to cite the novelists for the simple reason that he takes no interest in them. The assumption that he has any such interest derives not from the text itself, but from an inherent bias in our institutional and pedagogic arrangements, in which casual juxtapositions slide inexorably into causal conclusions. As New puts it, "what might appear to us as innocent, neutral, or inevitable—the inclusion of *Tristram Shandy* in the eighteenth-century novels course, immediately following Fielding and Richardson—is in fact an interpretative act, one that preconceives the genre—and hence our expectations—of the work." Our sense of Sterne's responsiveness to the representational practices of *Clarissa* or *Tom Jones* is simply "the result of teleologically structured novels courses and the critical writing they generate," not of any concrete connection to works that (as New insists elsewhere)

Sterne "gives no sign anywhere of having read."[17] From this point of view, those features that seem to offer mileage for reading *Tristram Shandy* as directly responsive to earlier novels are better explained as accidental by-products of the learned wit tradition, solidly attributable to the disrupted forms and self-conscious literariness of genuine precursor texts like *The Anatomy of Melancholy* or *A Tale of a Tub*. Pursuing these same objections, J. T. Parnell identifies the formal techniques of Swift and Sterne as a satirical inheritance from Erasmus, Montaigne, Rabelais, and other writers of a fideistic-skeptical tradition, which both inheritors could redeploy in mockery of Enlightenment system building. The resulting effect of structural havoc and communicative impasse may retrospectively look like parody of novelistic discourse, but is something entirely other. "Some well-worn commonplaces of Sterne criticism may have to be put to rest," Parnell concludes: We must now accept "that he may never have read the 'novelists,' let alone contemplated a devastating critique of the shortcomings of the emerging genre."[18]

My argument here is that Sterne did indeed contemplate a critique of the emerging genre, and also that he achieved it. I do not mean, however, to deny the centrality of the Rabelaisian–Cervantic inheritance detected by some of *Tristram Shandy*'s earliest readers and emphasized in the formidable line of scholarship that culminates with New and Parnell. It is vital, moreover, to retain one telling part of New's objection to the novel-centered approach, which is that (in so far as it works at any such level of detail at all) the reading of *Tristram Shandy* as a sophisticated dismantling of mid-eighteenth-century narrative practices almost invariably works by caricaturing these practices as lumbering and epistemologically naive—"by turning Fielding and Richardson into dolts," as New robustly puts it.[19] Rather than seeing Sterne as engaged in mockery alone, I see him as alert and responsive to problems that Richardson and Fielding were themselves intelligently exploring, and as following up these explorations in a mode of exaggeration or *reductio ad absurdum* that, though certainly often parodic, is not necessarily dismissive. Sterne was indebted to both the Rabelaisian–Cervantic tradition and to the modern novel, and wholly rejected neither; in this respect the very plenitude of *Tristram Shandy*'s discursive entanglements intensifies its allegiances to the modern novel, this being the medium *par excellence* of generic hybridization and polyglossia.[20]

For this sense of creative coexistence between learned wit and novelism, as opposed to either/or competition between them, one may look back again to *Tristram Shandy's* earliest reception, and specifically to a third review, which appeared in the *Critical Review* immediately between the notices of the *Monthly* and the *London.* Like Kenrick's in the *Monthly,* it is a review that gains authority from its provenance in a periodical that, since its foundation in 1756, had extensively covered developments in the novel genre. Having voiced its uncertainties about the literary identity of this new work, the *Critical* moves implicitly toward a composite identity by calling Toby, Trim, and Slop "excellent imitations of certain characters in a modern truly Cervantic performance, which we avoid naming" (*CH,* 52). Alan B. Howes has convincingly identified this unnamed work as *Peregrine Pickle* (written, of course, by the editor of the *Critical,* Tobias Smollett, who was also *Don Quixote's* most recent translator); and by invoking this simultaneously modern yet Cervantic performance the *Critical* adroitly registers *Tristram Shandy's* double face. Backward-looking yet up to date, Sterne's work absorbs from Cervantes his sophisticated debunking of romance conventions (the aspect of *Don Quixote* that dominated the views of mid-eighteenth-century readers who, like Smollett, thought it written "with a view to ridicule and discredit" heroic romance[21]) but redirects this metafictional concern toward the species of fiction now generally held, as in Charlotte Lennox's recent *The Female Quixote,* to have rendered romance obsolete.

In later reviews the *Critical* pulled markedly away from the analogy with *Don Quixote:* Sterne's imitation was so botched as to leave "no more resemblance between his manner and that of Cervantes, than there is between the solemnity of a Foppington and the grimace of a Jack Pudding." But even as it did so the *Critical* continued to indicate the overlap between learned wit and novelism, stressing now the Rabelaisian inheritance of *Tristram Shandy* as seen in "the same sort of apostrophes to the reader, breaking in upon the narrative . . . the same whimsical digressions; and the same parade of learning."[22] In the broadest terms, *Tristram Shandy* draws from the learned wit tradition of which both Rabelais and Cervantes were part, up to and including *A Tale of a Tub,* an overall preoccupation with textuality, indeterminacy, and fragmentation of form, adding, once again, the new move of focusing this preoccupation on the novel—which by now had become the preferred genre, of course, of Swift's "freshest moderns." This redeployment on to new objects of traditional satirical moves is characterized, moreover, by the same ambivalence that had marked Swift's response to Grub Street half a century beforehand (an ambivalence also discernible, it might be added, in the increasingly complex attitude to romance that develops as *Don Quixote* progresses). Sophisticated aloofness mingles throughout with intense imaginative absorption, and for all its interludes of ridicule and hostility *Tristram Shandy* is better seen as wittily developing the rigorous self-consciousness of earlier novelists, rather than as magisterially revealing to these writers narratological cruxes that they had been pondering all along.

Imagining Dr. Slop

One way of establishing the groundedness of *Tristram Shandy* in mid-eighteenth-century fiction, yet also the resistance of this feature to single-source annotation, is through localized close reading. Consider a well-known passage from volume 2, in which, having self-consciously "prepared the reader's imagination for the enterance of Dr. *Slop* upon the stage" (2.8.120), Tristram introduces the physician and man-midwife in chapter 9. Then follows Slop's farcical unseating, in which, continuing his play in the novel with ill-matched durations of action and narration, Sterne brilliantly inverts the familiar comic technique of burlesque acceleration (the effect that predominates in Fielding's *Shamela,* for example, with its high-speed parodic rerun of *Pamela*'s plot). An entire chapter lingers here on the events of a few seconds, slowing down the frames of its narrative to particularize how the overweight Slop "left his pony to its destiny, tumbling off it diagonally, something in the stile and manner of a pack of wool" (2.9.122–123). Two chapters later, Tristram goes on to theorize about his own narrative practice, in ways prompted by his depiction of Slop.

The episode is famous not least because Sterne cites it himself as an instance of his comic technique. He specifies, indeed, the technique's source. Addressing a reader who had criticized the pre-publication version for its overload of ornamentation, he is ready, he says, to "reconsider Slops fall & my too Minute Account of it—but in general I am perswaded that the happiness of the Cervantic humour arises from this very thing—of describing silly and trifling Events, with the Circumstantial Pomp of great Ones" (*Letters*, 77; see also 79). Minutely particularized, and with a mock solemnity that lurches into comic bathos (the fussy redundancy of "stile and manner"; the crashingly inelegant—though also oddly evocative—"pack of wool"), the passage brings back to life the satirical repertoire of *Don Quixote*. It is as though the pompous elaboration is there to assert, purely at the level of style, the claim that Sterne was more explicitly making in other private and public identifications of *Tristram Shandy* as a work of "Cervantic Satyr" (*Letters*, 120)—as a work of ostentatiously literary mock-heroic, in other words, which in its seventeenth-century origins has little to do with more recent, trashier fiction.

Critics anxious to stress the Cervantic inheritance of *Tristram Shandy* have seized on this passage and Sterne's commentary to press their case, and this same sense of a text drenched in the traditions of Renaissance satire is richly substantiated by the Florida notes, which associate Slop's fall with similar equestrian mishaps in Montaigne and Scarron. One might even press further down this route, and invoke other, nonsatirical sources to locate Sterne's playfulness with material little different in kind from the diet of satirists such as Burton a century beforehand. In the relentless domino effect of Dr Slop's losses—first his whip, then his stirrup, then his seat, "and in the multitude of all these losses . . . the unfortunate Doctor lost his presence of mind" (2.9.122)—Sterne pirouettes around a proverbial sequence first imported from France in seventeenth-century collections such as George Herbert's *Outlandish Proverbs* (1640), and recently revived by Benjamin Franklin: "For want of a nail the shoe is lost; for want of a shoe the horse is lost; for want of a horse the rider lost."[23] Two chapters later, a reference back to "Dr. *Slop*'s sad overthrow" (2.11.126) is another mock-heroic touch, jokily enlisting the physician among the rebel angels who, in *Paradise Lost*, "rue the dire event, / That with sad overthrow and foul defeat / Hath lost us heaven."[24] Not only does Sterne's text spring a practical joke here on the critic who tries to locate it, luring him within range of its own satire on the scholarly equivalent of over-circumstantial narrative (or "writing like a Dutch commentator," as Tristram puts it elsewhere [9.13.763]). It also seems to disclose, as the outcome of any such commentary, a picture of provincial isolation in which the literary materials Sterne plays on are those of the minster library or the local great house, and not of the fashionable modern marketplace for new fiction.

But not exclusively so. The Florida annotations also record, at the very outset of the chapter, a striking parallel with Le Sage's picaresque novel, *Gil Blas*, specifically in Smollett's 1748 translation. "Imagine to yourself a little, squat, uncourtly figure of a Doctor *Slop*, of about four feet and a half perpendicular height," Tristram begins, setting up an intermittently anaphoric sequence of imperatives ("imagine . . . imagine . . . imagine") that culminates in his much-quoted resolution, two chapters later, to halve meanings with the reader and "leave him something to imagine . . . as well as yourself" (2.11.125). As the Florida editors note, the instruction bears comparison with Smollett's wording ("Figure to yourself a little fellow, three feet and a half high, as fat as you can conceive"), and it is possible that Sterne was elaborating its specific gestures. The more important general point, however, is that the "imagine to yourself"/"figure to yourself" formula was a standard trope in the fictional repertoire of the day, used in particular to herald set-piece exercises in the grotesque. "Imagine to yourself, a man rather past threescore, short and ill made, with a yellow cadaverous hue, great goggling eyes, that stared as if he was strangled," as Cleland introduces one of his heroine's less appetizing clients in *Memoirs of a Woman of Pleasure* (1748–149).[25] Specific suggestions about derivation become unnecessary here, and perhaps even misleading. By adopting what had become a cliché of modern novelistic discourse, and using it to build toward the famous writing-as-conversation passage, Sterne does much more than echo Smollett, Cleland, or any other source. He prepares his readers to understand this passage as addressing, in general, the stock rhetoric of fictional representation as practiced in the past two decades.

In the sentence following this "imagine to yourself" formula, Tristram's allusion to Hogarth's *Analysis of Beauty* adds to the effect in ways again partly registered by the Florida editors. Citing a set of instances from Fielding and Smollett (as first collated by William V. Holtz in his account of *Tristram Shandy*'s engagement with contemporary aesthetic theory), they identify "Sterne's evocation of Hogarth in relation to character-drawing" as a commonplace of the day.[26] It might be added that the reference here to Hogarth on how a figure may be "caracatur'd, and convey'd to the mind" (2.9.121) points, more directly than any of Holtz's four examples, to the Hogarth-centered discussion of character and caricature in the preface to *Joseph Andrews* (which Hogarth himself had prominently cited in his print of 1743, *Characters and Caricaturas,* "for a Farthar Explanation of this Difference").[27] Even in its opening sentences, Sterne's chapter is keying itself very firmly to the mimetic codes and conventions developed in fiction since the *Pamela* controversy, and specifically to the novel's self-consciousness about them.

And this is merely the tip of the iceberg. Episodic precedents for Slop's sad overthrow are easily as frequent in fiction of the 1740s and 1750s as in Montaigne or Scarron, and often much closer in detail. Banana skins were thin on the ground in eighteenth-century England, but of the alternative hazards to which comic novels of the period expose their characters, falling off a horse must be the surest. A conspicuous victim is Parson Adams, who nearly manages it twice in a single chapter, and then only "by good Luck, rather than by good Riding" (*JA,* 300). Closer to Slop's case is that of Dr. Zachary Heartley, a physician and man-midwife in William Toldervy's *The History of Two Orphans* (1756), who early in the narrative rides out into the country, having been "summoned to attend a woman in labour, four miles distant from the town where he lived." Like Sterne, this minor novelist derives the humor of his scene from a comic disproportion between action and narration. The difference is that, where Sterne lavishes too much detail on Slop's fall, Toldervy's offhand abruptness involves too little. Heartley rides full speed to his destination without mishap, and safely delivers the baby; "but, returning homewards on a gentle trot, the legs of his horse flew up, and the doctor pitching upon his head, died on the spot." The inevitable instruction ensues: "our readers may more easily figure to themselves the deplorable situation of Mrs. *Heartley,* on her receiving this terrible account, than we can describe."[28]

The likelihood that Sterne knew Toldervy's novel (which is prominently advertised in another he must surely have known, the anonymous *Life and Memoirs of Mr. Ephraim Tristram Bates*) is strengthened by other situational parallels, including the obsessive reminiscences of a half-pay soldier whose companions "can't take a nap after pudding" (as one of them complains) "but must be disturbed with your curs'd expeditions to *Flanders.*"[29] Whether or not he saw himself as stealthily reworking Toldervy's text, however, hardly matters. As with the "figure to yourself" instance from *Gil Blas,* the significant thing about Heartley's "sad catastrophe" (as Toldervy calls it in his chapter title) is that it typifies the repertoire of the genre. Whatever Sterne's relationship to any individual case, the underlying point is that he is playing ostentatiously here with some of the most hackneyed formulae, both verbal and episodic, of the modern novel in general. By calling to mind the standard clichés of the genre, he clearly identifies this genre as the subject of his theoretical and satirical play on representation and reading in the chapters to come, while displaying his virtuosity as a writer able to take its stalest gestures and render them fresh.

As the display goes on, Sterne continues to lift his ideas from the genre, even as he trumps it. His "Circumstantial Pomp" of narration may very loosely be thought of as Cervantic, but its particular distinguishing feature—pompous scientism—has a more immediate ancestry that the emphasis on Cervantes obscures. With its incongruous technical vocabulary, the mock-scientific account of Obadiah's speeding horse ("a phenomenon, with such a vortex of mud and water moving along with it, round its axis . . . to say nothing of the NUCLEUS . . . the MOMENTUM of the coach-horse") is less original than it might seem in applying the lexical resources of Cartesian physics to slapstick collisions and falls. (All these terms, of course, would originally have suggested a much more specialized register than they do today, a fact pointed up by Tristram's etymologically fussy spelling of "phenomenon" and the typographical emphasis of "nucleus" and "momentum.") In *Peregrine Pickle* (1751)—the novel identified by the *Critical Review* on other grounds as a proximate source for *Tristram Shandy*—Smollett exaggerates his distinctive effect of random violence and brutality by framing it, with amused detachment, in the language of scientific observation. Here, too, a speeding horse terrifies "a waggoner who . . . saw this phenomenon fly over his carriage"; a food-fight is observed by a witness "secure without the vortex of this tumult"; an assailant twists his victim's nose "with the momentum of a screw or peritrochium."[30] Anna Seward may or may not have been right to judge that Slop's fall, "so happily told, outweighs . . . all the writings of Smollett," but she was certainly right to sense the connection.[31] The difference is that Sterne distils and concentrates into a single chapter a comic resource that Smollett leaves scattered and latent.

This well-known episode of Slop's fall makes clear the groundedness of *Tristram Shandy* in modern fiction. Though identifying the passage as distinctively "Cervantic" in its mock-heroic elaboration of trivial matter, Sterne pursues this goal by reworking one of the most familiar plot devices in the mid-eighteenth-century repertoire, and doing so in terms that pick up and exaggerate verbal formulae and narrative tropes from identifiable recent novels. Nor should this convergence of Renaissance satire and modern fiction surprise us, given the extent to which Sterne's neo-Cervantic pose was anticipated by many eighteenth-century writers who saw Cervantes as first and foremost a novelist himself—as the pioneer, indeed, who "introduced novel writing," or founded a "Species of Fiction . . . of *Spanish* invention."[32] Ronald Paulson has documented the role of *Don Quixote* (with *Paradise Lost*) as "one of two books that profoundly shaped English writing of the eighteenth century,"[33] and here Sterne's identification with Cervantes binds him more rather than less closely with recent developments in the novel, the

genre in which this shaping was most actively felt. Fielding had
already won for himself the designation of "our *English Cervantes*,"[34]
and the title-page claim of *Joseph Andrews* to be "Written in Imitation
of the *Manner* of CERVANTES" is reminder enough that, in harking
back to *Don Quixote*, Sterne was not bypassing the work of recent
novelists, but drawing on a stock that Fielding had made common
to them all. The intensive Cervantic gestures of *Roderick Random* and
Peregrine Pickle were among the more prominent results, and by the
1750s minor writers were queueing up to associate their novels
with this tradition. *The Juvenile Adventures of David Ranger* (in which
Edward Kimber asks the "inspirer of the inimitable *Cervantes*, of the
facetious *Scarron*, of the thrice renowned *Sage* . . . to shed thy influence on thy humble votary") typifies the trend, while also indicating the impossibility of disentangling it, now, from the medi-
ating influence of Fielding and Smollet: more directly
over-shadowing his text, Kimber acknowledges, are "the multilo-
quacious *Henry F———*, or that poetical, critical, physical, political
novelist Dr. ———".[36] Clearly enough, to be Cervantic by now
was to be in the mainstream of novelistic production, in which
responsiveness to *Don Quixote* (even via conduits such as the Motteux–Ozell translation of 1700–1703, which Sterne appears to have
used) could no longer fail to be colored by the modern novels that
now defined and diffused the influence of Cervantes's text.

Nor is it any easier to disentangle from this strictly modern
hinterland to *Tristram Shandy* the other Renaissance satirical sources
that Sterne most clearly flags, who like Cervantes are standard
points of reference, too, in Fielding, Smollett, and their school.
Even the punctilious Pamela is a reader of Rabelais (though only
when decently married in Richardson's sequel), and Smollett's
scathing remarks about readers "who eagerly explore the jakes of
Rabelais" while primly castigating contemporary fiction make clear
his currency in a period when sanitizing translation and learned
annotation had brought Rabelaisian bawdry within the pale of politeness (or almost so).[36] The reference to Lucian, Rabelais, and
Cervantes in *Tristram Shandy* (3.19.225) has an obvious precedent in
Tom Jones's invocation of "thy *Lucian*, thy *Cervantes*, thy *Rabelais*," and
this or similar invocations of tradition were regularly imitated in

between, in works ranging in distinction from *Ferdinand Count Fathom* (which throws in Scarron, Le Sage, and Swift for good measure) to Adolphus Bannac's *The Life and Surprizing Adventures of Crusoe Richard Davis* (which made the *Critical Review* scoff at its claim to be following "*Lucian, Rabelais* and *Swift*").[37] Fielding gets in first, too, when adopting from "the celebrated *Montagne,* who promises you one thing and gives you another" (*JA*, 77), the quintessentially Shandean idea—or so one might have thought it—of a chapter that fails to get round to its advertised content.[38]

To say all this, of course, is not to revive the tedious old scandal of Sterne the plagiarist, or to intensify it by alleging that in the very act of imitating Renaissance satire Sterne was also imitating the imitations of more recent novelists. By juxtaposing explicit references to Cervantes and others with implicit invocations of modern fiction, Sterne could present *Tristram Shandy* as doing to the "new species of writing" what *Don Quixote* had done to romance, which was to test, explore, and satirize its working assumptions. Though one of the defining features of the "new species" in general was its formal self-consciousness, *Tristram Shandy* brings new sophistication to bear on a primary area of narrative experimentation and narratological debate at the time: the question of how the novelist, addressing the unknown mass readership of the modern literary market, can simultaneously stimulate and control the responses of the distant, diversified audience that consumes his writing. It does so as intensively as anywhere else in the "Cervantic" passage concerning Slop's fall, above all as elaborated in the chapters that follow.

Varying a remark about drama that he will shortly attribute to Walter ("there is something in that way of writing, when skilfully managed, which catches the attention" [2.17.165]), Tristram similarly finds in oral media a recipe for circumventing the distancing effects of print. Writing, "when properly managed," should resemble conversation (2.11.125). Absence, in this now celebrated analogy, will turn into presence, and print become talk—not mere unstructured chat (conversation being an art), but a regulated transaction with interlocutors who will be given a reciprocal role. Fielding offers a relevant sense of the required balance between

rules and ease in an essay that defines as synonymous "*Good Breeding*
. . . or the *Art of pleasing in Conversation,*" and finds that art most
pleasurable when practised in egalitarian spirit. Conversation works
best, he writes, "in the Society of Persons whose Understanding is
pretty near on an Equality with our own," and must arise "from
every one's being admitted to his Share in the Discourse."[39] This is
very much the spirit in which Tristram applies the conversation
trope to his own narrative practice:

> As no one, who knows what he is about in good company,
> would venture to talk all;—so no author, who understands
> the just boundaries of decorum and good breeding, would
> presume to think all: The truest respect which you can pay
> to the reader's understanding, is to halve this matter ami-
> cably, and leave him something to imagine, in his turn, as
> well as yourself. (2.11.125)

The anonymity of print is dispelled, and perfect communication
prevails.

Or that is Tristram's theory. But in a novel where perfect or
even adequate communication is conspicuous by its absence, and
conversation as practiced by its characters the least auspicious way
of making it happen, a whiff of contextual irony is hard to dispel.
Nor is there any sense at this point (though the experience of
serialization would later provide it) that conversation in any gen-
uinely interactive sense is within the novel's reach. Tristram will
talk to his readers, and they will imaginatively respond; but there
the conversational flow of response and counterresponse must
come to a halt. Thereafter only Tristram's manic construction of
imaginary inscribed readers, including—notoriously in recent feminist criticism—the prurient, imperceptive "Madam," can simulate
a way round the impasse. At this point there is not even a hypos-
tasized reader of the "Madam" kind on show, and in the absence
of any audibly responsive voice it is not long before Tristram is
forced to contravene his own theory, in a welter of bossy imperatives. " 'Tis his turn now," he magnanimously tells his reader; but
then, far from bestowing on this reader the creative or proactive

role implied by the conversation model, he becomes increasingly directive.

> Let the reader imagine then, that Dr. *Slop* has told his tale;—
> —and in what words, and with what aggravations his fancy
> chooses:———Let him suppose that *Obadiah* has told his tale
> also, and with such rueful looks of affected concern, as he
> thinks will best contrast the two figures as they stand by each
> other: Let him imagine that my father has stepp'd up stairs
> to see my mother:—And, to conclude this work of imagi-
> nation,—let him imagine the Doctor wash'd,———rubb'd
> down,—condoled with,—felicitated,—got into a pair of *Oba-*
> *diah's* pumps. (2.11.126)

In the first flush of reader-response theory, commentators turned a blind eye to the fussy overdetermination of response at this point. But it is now a familiar observation that Tristram's mutualist narrative aesthetic has unceremoniously been dumped. Within a few sentences, the relaxed convenor of collaborative meanings has mutated into a control freak. Already we are on the way to an answering passage from volume 5, in which, with condescending mock solicitude, Tristram explicitly retracts the collaborative model. "It is in vain to leave this to the Reader's imagination," he now writes. The task is beyond his audience, whose brains should not be tortured: " 'Tis my own affair: I'll explain it myself" (5.18.450).

These instructions on how to view Dr. Slop brilliantly complete (and collapse) the discursive sequence that begins with Tristram making ready "the reader's imagination" for this character's appearance in chapter 8—a sequence we must recognize not only as a memorably vivid exercise in farce, but also as a sophisticated exploration of the dynamics of narrative communication. As such, it has become an almost compulsory reference point for the novel-centered approach to Sterne, whether in readings that take at face value Tristram's aesthetic of reader participation and equate it with Sterne's own, or in those that detect ironic space between these positions.[40] The advantage of this second option is that it lets us see the extent to which Sterne is playing skeptically not just with a narratological issue in the abstract but with an urgent and explicit area of debate in the fiction of the previous two decades.

Notes

1. On Cervantes and humanist satire, see Donald R. Wehrs, "Sterne, Cervantes, Montaigne: Fideistic Skepticism and the Rhetoric of Desire," *Comparative Literature Studies,* 25 (1988), 127–51; also J. T. Parnell, "Swift, Sterne, and the Skeptical Tradition," *Studies in Eighteenth-Century Culture,* 23 (1994), 220–42.

2. On the distinction between determinate and aleatory intertextuality (first formulated by Riffaterre), see Graham Allen, *Intertextuality* (London: Routledge, 2000), 130–31, 140. I use the term *aleatory* here in a strictly limited sense, to denote textual features that call to mind a genre in general but specify no single example, so that different readers, according to the contingencies of their individual reading experiences, will sense different particular hypotexts (i.e., earlier novels) beneath the hypertext of *Tristram Shandy.*

3. *CH,* 56: Warburton's widely repeated words are reported here by Horace Walpole, who notes the contradiction inherent in making *Tristram Shandy* "the only copy that ever was an original." For Warburton on the novel genre, see his preface to the first edition of *Clarissa* (1747–48), 3:iii, which he later adapted (shifting the compliment from Richardson to Fielding) as an extended note to Pope's *Epistle to Augustus* (*The Works of Alexander Pope,* 9 vols. [1751], 4:166–69). Warburton had earlier contributed an essay on romance (as "A Supplement to the Translator's Preface") to Charles Jarvis's translation of *Don Quixote* (1742).

4. *Monthly Review,* 11 (Dec. 1754), 470.

5. "Innovator; assertor of novelty" (Johnson, *A Dictionary of the English Language* [1755], s.v. Novelist). Johnson's secondary sense, "A writer of novels," had been current since the 1720s, though Johnson gives no illustration.

6. *Monthly Review,* 21 (Apr. 1759), 380. Kenrick joined the *Monthly* in February 1759, by which time novels were normally relegated to short notices in the "monthly catalogue" appendix (*Rasselas* and *Tristram Shandy* being the only works of fiction to win main-review billing in 1759). These notices are listed by number alone in Benjamin Christie Nangle, *The*

Monthly Review, First Series, 1749–1789: Indexes of Contributors and Articles (Oxford: Clarendon Press, 1934), 231–34: they correspond to entries about Sarah Fielding's *The Countess of Dellwyn,* Voltaire's *Candide,* and minor novels such as *The Campaign: A True Story, Abassai: An Eastern Novel,* and *The Auction: A Modern Novel.*

7. Walpole was writing in April 1760 (*CH,* 55), and of course later installments of *Tristram Shandy,* in their narrative loops and involutions, are far less straightforward (or straight-backward) than his comment suggests: see Samuel L. Macey, "The Linear and Circular Time Schemes in Sterne's *Tristram Shandy,*" *Notes and Queries,* 36 (1989), 477–79.

8. Everett Zimmerman, *The Boundaries of Fiction: History and the Eighteenth-Century British Novel* (Ithaca, N.Y.: Cornell University Press, 1996), 203.

9. Michael McKeon, *The Origins of the English Novel, 1600–1740* (Baltimore, Md.: Johns Hopkins University Press, 1987), 419.

10. Viktor Shklovsky, *Theory of Prose* (Elmwood Park, Ill.: Dalkey Archive Press, 1991), 147, 156.

11. Virginia Woolf, *The Common Reader, Second Series,* ed. Andrew McNeillie (London: Hogarth Press, 1986), 78, 79. Woolf's piece first appeared in 1928 (as an introduction to the World's Classics *Sentimental Journey*), four years after her famous essay on "Mr. Bennett and Mrs. Brown," on which its valorization of disorder and fragmentation as truer to consciousness appears to draw.

12. For Richardson's use of this term, see *Selected Letters of Samuel Richardson,* ed. John Carroll (Oxford: Clarendon Press, 1964), 78 (26 Jan. 1747); for Fielding's, see *Joseph Andrews and Shamela,* ed. Douglas Brooks-Davies, rev. and intr. Thomas Keymer (Oxford: Oxford University Press, 1999) (hereafter *JA*), 8 (preface).

13. Ian Watt, *The Rise of the Novel: Studies in Defoe, Richardson, and Fielding* (London: Chatto & Windus, 1957), 291, 294.

14. John Richetti, *The English Novel in History, 1700–1780* (London: Routledge, 1999), 271.

15. Watt, *Rise of the Novel,* 291.

16. See Jonathan Lamb, "Sterne's System of Imitation," *Modern Language Review,* 76 (1981), 794–810.

17. Melvyn New, "Swift as Ogre, Richardson as Dolt: Rescuing Sterne from the Eighteenth Century," *Shandean,* 3 (1991), 49–60 (at 50,55); Melvyn New, *Tristram Shandy: A Book for Free Spirits* (New York: Twayne, 1994), 103 (and see also pp. 17–18).

18. Parnell, "Swift, Sterne," 239.

19. New, "Swift as Ogre," 50.

20. Jack Lynch puts it nicely in his account of the book as "made up of the 'shreds and clippings' of other discourses," such that "the eminently Erasmian *Tristram Shandy* is Bakhtinian heteroglossia writ large" ("The Relicks of Learning: Sterne among the Renaissance Encyclopedists," *Eighteenth-Century Fiction,* 13 [2000], 1–17 [at 16]).

21. Miguel de Cervantes, trans. Tobias Smollett, *The History and Adventures of the Renowned Don Quixote,* 2 vols. (1755), 1:x.

22. *CH,* 126. James G. Basker attributes this second review to Smollett himself (*Tobias Smollett: Critic and Journalist* (Newark: University of Delaware Press, 1988), 260), a supposition lent weight by Smollett's fondness for the proverbial "Jack Pudding" allusion (as in Tobias Smollett, *Peregrine Pickle,* ed. James L. Clifford, rev. Paul-Gabriel Boucé [Oxford: Oxford University Press, 1983], 387: "the grimaces of a jack-pudding"). Foppington is also proverbial, from Cibber's celebrated creation of the role in Vanbrugh's *The Relapse* (1696) and his own *The Careless Husband* (1704).

23. *Oxford Dictionary of English Proverbs,* 3rd ed. (Oxford: Clarendon Press, 1970), 865. Another of Herbert's imports from France is a version of Maria's "*God tempers the wind . . .* to the shorn lamb" (*Oxford Dictionary of Proverbs,* 312–13; see *SJ,* 369).

24. Milton, *Paradise Lost,* ed. Alastair Fowler (London: Longman, 1971), bk, i, lines 134–36.

25. John Cleland, *Memoirs of a Woman of Pleasure,* ed. Peter Sabor (Oxford: Oxford University Press, 1985), 15.

26. *Notes,* 153, citing William V. Holtz, *Image and Immortality: A Study of Tristram Shandy* (Providence, R.I.: Brown University Press, 1970), 43.

27. See Martin C. Battestin with Ruthe R. Battestin, *Henry Fielding: A Life* (London: Routledge, 1989), 366 and plate 35.

28. William Toldervy, *The History of Two Orphans,* 4 vols. (1756), 1:25.

29. Ibid., 1:80.

30. Smollett, *Peregrine Pickle,* 39, 239, 665.

31. *CH,* 270 (letter to George Gregory, 5 Dec. 1787). Seward takes a similar view of Sterne's debt to, and transcendence of, Smollett's characterization: "You observe that Toby Shandy is the Commodore Trunnion of Smollett. It is long since I read *Peregrine Pickle,* and it made so little impression, that I have no remembrance of the Commodore. It is impossible that I should ever, even after the slightest perusal, have forgotten . . . Toby Shandy."

32. "A Short Discourse on Novel Writing," in *Constantia: or, A True Picture*

of Human Life, 2 vols. (1751), 1:x; William Warburton, preface to *Clarissa* (1747–48), 3:iii.

33. Ronald Paulson, *Don Quixote in England: The Aesthetics of Laughter* (Baltimore: Johns Hopkins University Press, 1998), ix; on Sterne, see 150–58.

34. Francis Coventry (?), *An Essay on the New Species of Writing Founded by Mr. Fielding,* ed. Alan D. McKillop, Augustan Reprint Society Publication no. 95 (Los Angeles: Clark Library, 1962), 46 (see also 33).

35. Edward Kimber, *The Juvenile Adventures of David Ranger, Esq.,* 2 vols. (1756), 1:1.

36. Tobias Smollett, *Ferdinand Count Fathom,* ed. Damian Grant (Oxford: Oxford University Press, 1971), 8; see also Shaun Regan, "Translating Rabelais: Sterne, Motteux, and the Culture of Politeness," *Translation and Literature,* 10 (2001), 174–99.

37. Henry Fielding, *Tom Jones,* ed. Martin C. Battestin and Fredson Bowers (Oxford: Clarendon Press, 1975) 13.1. 686; Smollett, *Ferdinand Count Fathom,* 7–8; *Critical Review,* 2 (Nov. 1756), 357.

38. On Montaigne's currency in the period, see Claude Rawson, *God, Gulliver, and Genocide: Barbarism and the European Imagination, 1492–1945* (Oxford: Oxford University Press, 2001), 69–70; also Fred Parker, *Scepticism and Literature: An Essay on Pope, Hume, Sterne, and Johnson* (Oxford: Oxford University Press, 2003).

39. Henry Fielding, "An Essay on Conversation," in *Miscellanies I,* ed. Henry Knight Miller (Oxford: Clarendon Press, 1972), 124, 142, 146. See also Sterne's *Sermons,* 5.194: "Conversation is a traffick."

40. Notably, in the first category, Wolfgang Iser, *Laurence Sterne: Tristram Shandy* (Cambridge: Cambridge University Press, 1988), 60–71; in the second, Elizabeth W. Harries, *The Unfinished Manner: Essays on the Fragment in the Later Eighteenth Century* (Charlottesville: University Press of Virginia, 1994), 41–55; Helen Ostovich, "Reader as Hobby-horse in *Tristram Shandy,*" *Philological Quarterly,* 68 (1989), 325–42.

PART II

Public Performance and Print Culture

Laurence Sterne and Literary
Celebrity in 1760

PETER M. BRIGGS

◆　◆　◆

"Formerly *Poets* made *Players,* but nowadays 'tis
generally the *Player* that makes the *Poet."*
—ABEL BOYER, *The English Theophrastus, Or,*
The Manners of the Age (London, 1702)

ON THE EVENING OF 31 December 1759, David Garrick presented at Drury Lane a new afterpiece of his own composition
called *Harlequin's Invasion,* complete with music by William Boyce.
Advertised as a "Christmas Gambol, after the manner of Italian
comedy," the piece imagines an invasion from France by Harlequin
and the forces of Pantomime, aiming to scale the heights of British
Parnassus. Harlequin himself is a protean comic villain, dangerously able to improvise new behaviors and to assume what disguises
he will. As one of his inept British adversaries warns,

> Nobody can comprehend [i.e., apprehend] him, he's too nim-
> ble for 'em. . . . They hunted him last week all about town,
> and he turn [*sic*] himself into ten thousand shapes. First he
> shrunk himself into a dwarf, then he stretched himself into
> a giant. Then he was a beau, then a monkey, then a peacock,
> then a wheel barrow. And then he made himself an ostelige,
> and he walked about so stately and looked so grand, and
> when I went up to him he clapped his wing so (*mimics the*
> *ostrich*) that my very heart leaped within me.

Fortunately Mercury, representing Jove, takes the part of the British against the French, urging them to live up to the memory of

Shakespeare and their own theatrical heritage. Harlequin and the powers of Pantomime, ineffectually resisted by comical Londoners at Charing Cross, are eventually turned back by Mercury who summons a storm to destroy their fleet. The piece ends with Shakespeare rising through one stage trap as Harlequin descends through another, followed by spirited dance and song, praising Britain, Nature, and Shakespeare forever:

> Now let immortal Shakespeare rise,
>   Ye sons of Taste adore him.
> As from the sun each vapor flies,
>   Let folly sink before him.[1]

Meanwhile at York, 175 miles to the north, a second harlequin's invasion was preparing—one that would eventually reflect a similar appreciation of the powers of comic eccentricity and public theatricality. It was during the same week that volumes 1 and 2 of *Tristram Shandy* were first produced at the printshop of Ann Ward. The Reverend Laurence Sterne, their author and himself a protean figure who had already been affectionately caricatured as a harlequin by his friend Thomas Bridges,[2] also aspired to scale the heights of Parnassus. Many particular details surrounding the publication of *Tristram Shandy* have been lost, but the general outlines of the story are clear. Sterne sent an early, more satirical draft of the novel to Robert Dodsley, the London publisher, in May 1759. In June Dodsley returned the manuscript, declining it as too risky. During the summer and early fall Sterne rewrote the manuscript and then contracted with Ann Ward to print a first edition at his own expense, part to be sold by John Hinxman at York, the rest shipped to London where James Dodsley, Robert's brother, would handle sales. As might be expected when a local clergyman turns novelist, *Tristram Shandy* sold well at York, well enough for Sterne's daughter Lydia to be teased about it at school. But as Sterne knew, if Parnassus was to be scaled, conquering the London market was crucial.

Sterne's novel arrived in London sometime early in January 1760. Helped by Catherine Fourmantel, the singer with whom he was carrying on a flirtation, Sterne managed to have *Tristram Shandy* recommended to David Garrick and possibly to other tastemakers. By the beginning of February Sterne, still at York, received reports that his novel was indeed being talked up by Garrick, that early journalistic reviews were favorable, and that the success of the novel had generated considerable speculation as to the character of its unknown and still unnamed author. Was there a real Tristram Shandy? Or was the author perhaps Yorick? ("It is by some supposed to be the Character of the Author, as he himself Chuses it should be exhibited," commented the *London Chronicle* for 5 February, possibly with Sterne's prompting.[3]) Then in early March— and seemingly by the accident of being offered a free ride—Sterne himself went to London where he was immediately greeted as *the* literary event of the season. For the next eleven weeks he was passed from hand to hand through the upper echelons of London society. Befriended by Garrick, painted by Joshua Reynolds, patronized by William Warburton and Lord Bathurst (once supporters of Alexander Pope), interviewed by James Boswell, put in communication with William Hogarth the artist and with William Pitt the prime minister, presented at court by the marquis of Rockingham and the duke of York, now under a generous contract with James Dodsley as publisher—Sterne cut a wide swath among the people who mattered and at the same time established a broad public visibility.[4] When he finally left London for York, shortly after the publication of the first two volumes of *The Sermons of Mr. Yorick* on 22 May 1760—with 661 subscribers, including all the best names—Sterne no longer needed a free ride. He rode in a carriage bought with his own money, and the summit of Parnassus seemed well within Harlequin's reach.

My reason for going over these well-known facts is not just to commemorate Sterne's sudden success but rather to provide a context within which to examine some of the guises of authorial fame in 1760. More specifically, my aim is to raise questions about literary celebrity in an age and society not yet overloaded and jaded with celebrities. Clearly Sterne wished to succeed as an author, but success and public celebrity are not necessarily the same things nor translatable, one to the other. And even if Sterne did wish to become a notable, celebrity involves public performance and polished performance requires know-how—which leads to the interesting question, how did he know *how* to be one? Similar questions arise when one views the same events in a broader social perspective. Literary talent may be a personal possession, but literary acclaim is a social phenomenon, a concerted will that prompts and promotes certain persons into prominence. How is public celebrity achieved and sustained? Furthermore, as we are all well aware that famous persons appearing in public do not actually behave like real people but rather specifically like celebrities, who, if anyone, legislates the codes of behavior and the underlying values that seem to accompany celebrity? And who, if anyone, is able to raise the substantive question of what is worth celebrating? Finally, what does literary celebrity really signify to those who possess it, to those who create it, and to those of us who arrive after the fact to study it?

Of course, "celebrity history" as such does not exist, nor should it perhaps, given the facts that most celebrities are insubstantial and ephemeral creatures passing in parade and that celebrity itself is such an elusive thing, so protean, so easily manipulated, so often confused with real fame. And when a great writer happens to become (or indeed, *works* to become) a celebrity, we are mistrustful and therefore tend to set that fact somewhat apart from his or her real merit. A broad public, seeing the outward manifestations of supposed greatness, is unlikely to sense or savor those things that give an author distinctive worth and lasting value. Fair enough— and yet. . . . Celebrities *are* parts of the cultural history of their times, creatures and reflections of prevailing moods, issues, and fashions. And while true fame may be the gift of the distinguishing few, the acclaim of the popular many was not a negligible force in the crowded, increasingly commercialized cultural marketplace where Sterne like so many others sought a place for himself. Publicity had much to do with commercial success, and who dared to suppose it had *nothing* to do with lasting fame? Moreover, celebrity was part of the real daily experience of a Laurence Sterne, an Alexander Pope, a Samuel Johnson. It shaped and constrained how they lived, how and what they wrote, how they perceived and valued themselves—even while they in their turns shaped the ways in which their audiences were to focus and understand the temper and potentialities of the times. Celebrity was and is too important to be left to the publicists, too important to be ignored.

Let me begin by taking for granted three things which will help to clear our way: first, that *Tristram Shandy* is indeed a great book which truly deserved the fame that it eventually earned; second, that cultivated society in 1760 and at most other times is generally anxious to embrace and celebrate "genius," particularly if genius is smart enough to show up in a well-bred and entertaining form (as Sterne was). Third and more complexly, we must recognize at the outset that celebrity is finally a collaborative social form and process, a sort of dance, a coming together of attitudes, aspirations, and behaviors on the part of the celebrity with patterns of expectation and response on the part of an audience. In other words, the phenomena which constitute celebrity depend heavily upon the mental habits of all concerned, and public gestures associated with celebrity which, taken in isolation and out of social context, might appear bizarre or simply unaccountable are in fact parts of a shared social idiom. To put the matter in its simplest form, *one* celebrity is a contradiction in terms; celebrities must exist in the plural in order to be socially recognizable, for they acquire whatever meanings they have by implicit reference to one another, to their chosen audiences, and to codes of social behavior which they, taken as a group, make visible. For better or for worse, then, the celebrated tend to resemble one another and to reflect the mind— often the divided mind—of the society that creates, debates, and eventually consumes them. ("Popular favourites are too much like the innocent victims of superstition, led out, garlanded with flowers, to slaughter and to sacrifice," as William Hazlitt would later remark.[5]) By the same token, the creation of celebrities, an activity with broad cultural implications, can also be deeply self-regarding, as individuals use the celebrated as visible test cases of the social codes and boundaries within which everyone must eventually find their way and live their lives. But we are getting ahead of ourselves.

As far as they can be documented, Sterne's own reactions to the events of that dizzying spring of 1760 represent an interesting mixture of naive wonder and well-calculated self-promotion. At least with Catherine Fourmantel, he had begun good-humoredly to play the role of Yorick, the eccentric, unworldly and amiable country parson who "loved a jest in his heart," before he ever left York.[6] After he arrived in London, he continued this Yorick pose and complicated it by adding a Tristram pose; he wrote shandaical letters to London friends, full of witticisms and broken sentences and dramatic posturing—and apparently he, like Harlequin, acted out multiple and shifting roles in companies with whom he could establish a facetious relationship. Posing is in itself an effective and self-protective way of relating to large numbers of relative strangers, as Tristram himself would be the first to assure us:

> —Here—pray, Sir, take hold of my cap,—nay, take the bell along with it, and my pantoufles too.—
>
> Now, Sir, they are all at your service; and I freely make you a present of 'em, on condition, you give me all your attention to this chapter. (*TS,* 3.18.222)[7]

The thrill of sudden fame and fortune was certainly real for Sterne, as his letters to Catherine Fourmantel, still at York, repeatedly attest; with breathless abandon he reported the many invitations, the compliments, and the unexpected favors showered upon him. And years later John Croft would remember Sterne, just returned from his new publisher, "skipping into the room" and announcing himself "the richest man in Europe" (*Letters,* p. 98n).

Sterne's seemingly naive pleasure in his success occurred simultaneously with continual self-promotion. No one needed to tell a poor, middle-aged country parson to play up to the well-born and well-endowed who might do him some good, but Sterne's campaign went well beyond being anxious to please, entertaining, and grateful. For one thing, he was consciously building a network of social contacts: "Pray have you no interest, lateral or collateral, to get me introduced to his Lordship?" he asked Garrick (*Letters,* p. 93). For another, he was collecting endorsements and famous names—Garrick, Warburton, Hogarth, Pitt—to adorn the second edition and subsequent volumes of *Tristram Shandy.* For a third, it seems probable that Sterne was deliberately courting attacks in the public press, realizing that controversy would help to sell his books: "—There is a shilling pamphlet wrote against Tristram.—I wish they would write a hundred such."[8] Within two months of his arrival in London Sterne's campaign was going well enough so that he could strike the Popean attitude of the famous author hemmed in by his own celebrity: "—Every Minute of this Day & to morrow is pre-engaged, that I am as much a Prisoner as if I was in Jayl" (*Letters,* p. 109). Finally it seems clear that Sterne was marketing not just the first two volumes of *Tristram Shandy* and not just himself but also preparing the way for future productions—later volumes of *Shandy,* perhaps a play, certainly *The Sermons* (originally announced as *The Dramatic Sermons*) of *Mr. Yorick.* (Someone, Sterne or his friends, had to *gather* all those 661 subscriptions and the broad-based endorsement of the author's piety and social respectability which they implicitly represented.)

In his own eyes, at least, Sterne was simply making the most of his opportunities, making one opportunity lead to the next. When Joshua Reynolds was able to complete the famous "Lansdowne" portrait of Sterne after eight sittings on 21 April 1760, Sterne evidently got the portrait into the hands of Simon Ravenet, the engraver, the very next day: "There is a fine print going to be done of me—so I shall make the most of myself, & sell [my head] both inside & out." Exactly a month later, on 22 May, the first two volumes of *The Sermons* appeared with Ravenet's engraving of Sterne as their frontispiece (*Letters,* pp. 105–106). From one point of view, what all these details add up to is a very concentrated version of contemporary literary success: London was enjoying its latest "sensation" and Sterne was doing his best to sustain the effect, keeping himself, his work, even his image in public view and under public discussion—in fact, doing on a grand scale most of the things that young James Boswell, "sensation"-in-waiting, would try (with much less success) two and one half years later and faithfully record in his *London Journal.*

But there is at least one significant difference. Sterne conspicuously did not hurry to present himself to the contemporary literary community, nor did the members of that community rush to embrace him—no presentation to Dr. Johnson, no tea with Samuel Richardson, no interview with Tobias Smollett—and most of literary London was left simply to gossip about Sterne from afar.

There is also something extremely ironical and incongruous about Sterne's choosing to present himself in London as a candidate for fame in the character of Parson Yorick. Everyone knew Hamlet's Yorick, of course, but what everyone (including Sterne) remembered of him was, first, that he was only a jester, and second, that he was an epitome of the vanity of all human hopes for lasting fame—"Where be your gibes now, your gambols, your songs, your flashes of merriment, that were wont to set the table on a roar?" (*Hamlet* V.i.183–85).

We must remind ourselves that we tend to read the story of Sterne's appearance in London backward, secure in our own knowledge of his eventual success. Of necessity, Sterne himself had a different perspective. As a first-time novelist and a highly unconventional one at that, Sterne was very much at risk in venturing to the great world; he knew it, and therefore he carefully positioned himself to fail *or* succeed: "Yorick" could be ironically detached from the hope for fame, whereas Laurence Sterne could not. Samuel Johnson, Horace Walpole, and other well-qualified observers suggested that *Tristram Shandy* could not last, that its apparent success was due merely to its novelty—and there is every reason to suppose that Sterne himself feared exactly what they hoped. A newspaper biography of Sterne published in May 1760 suggested that sudden fame had not turned the author's head, but what that article interprets as modesty could equally be a reflection of authorial vulnerability and fear: "He says he is now just like a fashionable mistress, whom every body solicits, because 'tis the fashion, but who may walk the street a fortnight [hence], and in vain solicit corporal Stare for a dinner."[9]

Yet Sterne did want fame terribly much. "I wrote not to be *fed,* but to be *famous,*" he remarked to an unknown correspondent, reversing in a self-congratulatory way a phrase borrowed from Colley Cibber, the actor, dramatist, theatrical manager, and autobiographer.[10] Moreover, Sterne sensed, as Johnson and Boswell also did, that the lineaments of literary fame and celebrity were changing rapidly in the mid-eighteenth century, that audiences were increasingly interested in authors as "personalities" rather than simply as artistic makers; idiosyncrasies that had gone unreported in an earlier generation were now seized upon as symptoms of personal character, pieces in a mosaic of personality which the reading public wished earnestly to complete.[11] So Sterne deliberately became a "personality," or rather several, for public consumption—and idiosyncrasies lent themselves to publicity besides. Yet this new emphasis upon human particularities had to be balanced against an older attachment to the ceremonials which served to distance, generalize, and dignify human worth. Rituals of celebrity shadow forth values—or sometimes conflicts of values—which both the object of admiration and his celebrants feel to be culturally central, and all particular celebrities stand, knowingly or unknowingly, as semi-allegorical creatures, personifications of general concerns and urgencies which they momentarily and in the eyes of their public embody. In other terms, the rituals of fame tend to reflect and to reconstitute, or occasionally even to challenge, existing patterns of cultural authority.[12]

A particular instance might help to clarify the point. In March 1742 young Joshua Reynolds, then only nineteen, was allowed by his master, Thomas Hudson, to attend an auction of the late Lord Oxford's pictures in Covent Garden. There he had the good fortune to see Alexander Pope. Nearly fifty years later, in December 1791, Reynolds recalled the scene vividly for James Boswell who recorded it:

> The room was much crowded. Pope came in. Immediately it was mentioned he was there, a lane was made for him to walk through. Everyone in the front rows by a kind of enthusiastic impulse shook hands with him. Reynolds did like the rest and was very happy in having that opportunity. Pope was seldom seen in public, so it was a great sight to see him. . . . Sir Joshua said he had an extraordinary face, not an everyday countenance—a pallid, studious look; not merely a sharp, keen countenance, but something grand, like Cicero's.[13]

This scene is highly theatrical and almost luminous—and not just because Boswell, dramatist manqué though he was, recorded it. The gentlemen in the auction room were responding unanimously to a shared sense of occasion, enacting a spontaneous ceremonial in which they all knew their parts and Pope, by then a much-practiced performer, knew his. What they were acting out without prompting or collusion was the acknowledgment and celebration of majesty—in this case, literary majesty, though the case would not have been very different for a temporal or spiritual eminence. By acknowledging the poet's special power, the gentlemen in attendance in fact ritually reconstitute and share it.

To witness majesty in the flesh was a rarity—"a great sight" and memorable in detail, even after half a century: Pope and this audience between them create a moment that stands above ordinary time. Moreover, this moment of spontaneous ritual which serves to incorporate the poet into the group also serves to dramatize his essential separateness: he is a liminal figure, set apart by special abilities, accomplishments, and responsibilities but also by age and crippled ill health, seeming to step down for a moment out of a world of larger significances into ordinary reality. The absolute silence of this ritual scene is also striking; William Cooke, the second recorder of the scene, characterizes it as "a dead calm," sudden silence after the ordinary bustle of a crowded auction room. Even though Pope's power as a poet is specifically a verbal one, his importance in this ritual scene is his presence, not anything he has to say but what he *is.*

Finally Reynolds draws attention to Pope's face. It is not surprising that Reynolds as an aspiring portrait painter should pay particular attention to the countenance of a famous poet, but the mode of his attention is noteworthy. As Leo Braudy acutely remarks, "Images of greatness gather their power from traditions of seeing"[15]—and Reynolds's way of seeing Pope, assisted no doubt by fifty years to reflect upon the event, tends to legitimate and amplify the poet's special status and significance. Pope's was "an extraordinary face," pallid, studious, keen, with "something grand, like Cicero's." Reynolds, of course, had never seen Cicero; instead he had seen busts and paintings of Cicero, enshrined as a hero of public virtue. What Reynolds's imagination was doing in response to Pope's face, then, was to translate the living poet into a sort of icon, something fixed and austere and legible; what might in other circumstances have been a description of the animated qualities of Pope's face as he meets a roomful of admirers becomes instead a still portrait, even a statue, a timeless monument to civic virtue, artistic integrity, social hierarchy, and moral assurance.

The obvious lesson to draw from this instance is that the further significances of fame and of celebrity as well reside largely in the eyes and felt needs of the beholders—after all, Pope was just going to see some pictures at an auction. A less obvious but equally important implication is that famous people, insofar as they are public players, often find themselves responsible for fulfilling expectations and needs which they may not have created nor anticipated—or at least, for not dashing such expectations. In a way, living up to one's own celebrity can become a strange sort of public trust, one that honors and constrains its object simultaneously. As Hazlitt would later suggest, "No man is truly himself, but in the idea which others entertain of him."[16] And even Samuel Johnson felt compelled to purchase new and uncharacteristic clothes—"a scarlet waistcoat, with rich gold lace, and a gold-laced hat"—in order to appear in public as the author of *Irene*.[17]

In any event, Pope's drawing room celebrity and enduring fame certainly did represent goals worth aspiring to. But was this the sort of acclaim that Sterne hoped for, as he planned his harlequin's assault on London? The answer, I think, is both yes and no. Yes, insofar as Sterne was unlikely to turn aside adulation in any form or refuse to be hailed by some as the avatar of a distinctly new literary moment (as he was). But mostly no. Sterne's talent did not lie in the direction of high seriousness, as Pope's often did, particularly as he grew older. Moreover, literary recognition is a historical construction, variable with the times, and it was not at all clear that the strategies for achieving celebrity or claiming an enduring fame which had worked in Pope's life and times (remembering that Pope was *already* famous even before Sterne was born in 1713) would still work in 1760. Then, too, the adulation of Pope witnessed by Reynolds in 1742 was not sudden fame, but the hard-won reward for a long career of artistic achievement. The same might be said of most earlier writers to whom Sterne could have looked for models—Dryden, Congreve, Addison, Swift, Fielding.

All had had some early successes, but general acclaim came much later if at all. Perhaps it was already too late for Sterne, sickly and middle-aged, to build incrementally toward a solidly based fame. "Slow rises worth, by poverty depressed," Samuel Johnson had soberly observed in *London* (line 177), and for Sterne there was no worse poverty than provincial obscurity. Surely there must be a shorter road to public acclaim than that traveled by Pope, Johnson, and the others.

What other roads were available? The avenues to fame vary not only with the times but also by profession, and it is instructive to notice not just that Sterne avoided professional literary circles, but also what he seems to have embraced in their place. From a certain point of view his behavior seems surprisingly consistent. In the spring of 1760 Laurence Sterne came down from York (1) paraphrasing the autobiography of one theatrical character, Colley Cibber; (2) while playing the role of another theatrical character, poor Yorick; and (3) immediately presented himself before the leading actor and theatrical manager of the age, David Garrick. He tried to get Garrick to take a particular interest in him by holding out the possibility of writing for the stage.[18] And although Sterne mostly ignored literary society, he had, within a day or so of his arrival in London, been granted free access, not only to high society but also to the Drury Lane theater, Garrick's theater, for the remainder of its season. There seems ample reason for supposing, then, that Sterne differentiated between *kinds* of celebrity and the available paths to fame and that he deliberately chose to present himself upon the great stage of London society not as a literary candidate for slow fame but as a theatrical candidate for sudden fame. As everyone in 1760 surely knew, dramatic fame *could* be both sudden and sustained, as Garrick's overnight success nineteen years earlier and his subsequent career had amply demonstrated.

Colley Cibber was repeating a lament traditional among actors when he remarked that dramatic success, which can be so overwhelming, should also be so ephemeral:

Pity it is, that the momentary Beauties flowing from an harmonious Elocution, cannot like those of Poetry, be their own

Record! That the animated Graces of the Player can live no longer than the instant Breath and Motion that presents them; or at best can but faintly glimmer through the Memory, or imperfect Attestation of a few surviving Spectators.[19]

The split that Cibber supposed between an actor's instantaneous dramatic presence and an artifact's (poetry's) quieter staying power is exactly the one that Sterne was trying to overcome through his appearance in London. Part of the genius and triumph of *Tristram Shandy* as a novel is the way in which it sustains an illusion of dramatic presence—not just authorial presence, Tristram at our elbow, directing our attention, discussing his story with us even as he tells it, but also the presence of his characters—Trim's gestures or Yorick's, the variable tones of Walter Shandy's theorizing or Uncle Toby's whistling.[20] When Sterne showed up in London acting the parts of Yorick and Tristram and perhaps others, he was basically offering confirmation of an illusion of presence already established by his novel; now Tristram *was* at one's elbow, just as he had seemed to be before. The tonal variety of the novel, its delicate balance of facetiousness and seriousness, sentiment and posturing, was now compounded by the variousness of an actor, Sterne's own ability to play off his audience and its responses, to adjust tone and gesture and implication, even in mid-sentence, as mood and occasion dictated.[21]

Young James Boswell was quite right, then, when he described Sterne not as a person but rather as a series of public performances, a protean figure in an improvised and forever unfinished scenario, just like the harlequin. In a poetic epistle unpublished at the time but addressed to "Doctor Sterne, Parson Yorick, and Tristram Shandy," Boswell celebrated Sterne as a happily compounded figure, an improbable mixture of fact and fiction:

By Fashion's hands compleatly drest
He's everywhere a wellcome guest:
He runs about from place to place,
Now with my Lord, then with his Grace,
And, mixing with the brilliant throng,
He straight commences *Beau Garcon.*

In Ranelagh's delightfull round
Squire Tristram oft is flaunting found;
A buzzing whisper flys about;
Where'er he comes they point him out . . .
"That there is he, do, Thomas! look,
Who's wrote such a damn'd clever book."[22]

Sterne *had* written a damn'd clever book, of course, but many who witnessed his public performance had probably not read it nor did they need to in order to enjoy the show. And insofar as Sterne was palpably playing his improvised roles, he presumably had an actor's advantage over his audience: audiences understand that the self-exposure which goes with acting makes it a risky business and they share vicariously in the riskiness (*we* gasp when the tightrope walker falters and *we* are embarrassed if Hamlet forgets his lines). In short, audiences generally *want* performances to succeed and experienced actors heighten their performance accordingly. That is why Boswell witnessed Sterne not just performing but "flaunting" the fact of his performance.

The notion that authorial self-presentation might best be understood as a kind of "theater" was certainly not a new one in 1760; after all, those older authorial appearances at court and in the houses of the great were nothing if not theatrical. Still, the rules of the game for both literal and figurative "theater" were changing over the course of the eighteenth century, as the audience for cultural things became larger and more popular, and Sterne had much to learn from the very different careers and styles of such worthies as Colley Cibber and David Garrick. Melvyn New has argued persuasively that the breathless, informal, and self-projecting style of *Tristram Shandy* has significant affinities with the cheeky style of Cibber's autobiographical *Apology:*

> —Reader, take heed! for I find a strong impulse to talk impertinently; if therefore you are not as fond of seeing, as I am of shewing myself in all my Lights, you may turn over two Leaves together, and leave what follows to those who have more Curiosity, and less to do with their Time, than you have.[23]

But Sterne had even more to learn from the general shape and tone of Cibber's long public career. In the 1690s Cibber had had difficulty earning the star billing which he felt he deserved. He finally solved this problem by writing a major comic part, that of Sir Novelty Fashion in *Love's Last Shift* (1696), which only *he* was suited to play. His comedy and the part of Sir Novelty succeeded wonderfully. In Vanbrugh's *The Relapse* (1696) Sir Novelty Fashion was elevated to Lord Foppington, a part specifically designed for and played by Cibber, again with great public success—and Cibber then proceeded to spend much of the rest of his long life (he died in 1757 at age 85) acting out the Lord Foppington role, the epitome of confident vanity, both on and off the stage.[24] In short, Sterne was not the first to invent a comic character and then to adopt it as his persona to carry him through that long series of theatrical engagements which make up the public life of a celebrity.

But there are subtler affinities between Cibber and Sterne as well. Both tended to alternate between pretensions of brassy self-confidence and repeated confessions of weakness or uncertainty designed to win sympathy from their audience. And both became masters of a public pretense to a certain kind of candor—not true candor, of course, but a teasing or ironically qualified kind of candor, one that makes public assertions or gestures and yet at the same time avoids complete commitment to them. Either Tristram or Sterne himself could easily have subscribed to the cheerful admission of his follies and limitations offered by Cibber:

I will not go out of my Character, by straining to be wiser than I *can* be, or by being more affectedly pensive than I *need* be; whatever I am, Men of Sense will know me to be, put on what Disguise I will; I can no more put off my Follies, than my Skin; I have often try'd, but they stick too close to me; nor am I sure my Friends are displeas'd with them; for, besides that in this Light I afford them frequent matter of Mirth, they may possibly be less uneasy at their *own* Follies, when they have so old a Precedent to keep them in countenance: Nay, there are some frank enough to confess, they envy what they laugh at.[25]

It is a wise fool indeed who can arrive at such carefully contrived "candor" and who further realizes that the licensed follies of a celebrity finally exist to palliate or even legitimate the more timid follies of his admirers. Both Cibber and Sterne in their roles as public players learned to practice a continual flirtation between seriousness and game, creating fragile yet surprisingly durable dramatic parts which allowed them brash self-assertion and shameless self-promotion and simultaneously a self-protective retreat into irony, evasion, or special pleading. What a perceptive critic said of Cibber could equally be said of the public Sterne: "His very Nakedness is a Disguise."[26]

Sterne had a different set of lessons and a different kind of equipoise to learn from David Garrick. The reasons for courting Garrick were obvious ones in 1760. Generally celebrated as the greatest actor of the day, Garrick was pioneer of a "natural" style of acting that, it might be supposed, Tristram in his apparent spontaneousness and in his calculated hesitancy was endeavoring to imitate. Garrick was himself a generous patron of the arts and someone who had easy access to other patrons, to publishers, to aristocrats and politicians, to the press, and to the cultivated public at large. He could open many doors for Sterne and in fact did so. Moreover, Garrick and his lovely and accomplished wife, the former Eva Maria Veigel, a Viennese opera dancer, were among the "beautiful people" of their time, celebrated as the epitome of virtues toward which many people in that highly theatrical London society aspired—grace, taste, control, "presence"—virtues which had value both onstage and off. The painter Gainsborough once advised an aspiring young actor: "Stick to Garrick as close as you can, for your life, you should follow his heels like his shadow in sunshine . . . Garrick is the greatest creature living, in every respect; he is worth studying in every action. Every view and every idea of him, is worthy of being stored up for imitation."[27]

Apart from Garrick's social connections and his general exemplariness, there were more particular things that Sterne might have hoped somehow to assimilate by associating with him. For one thing, the knowledge necessary for *being* successful as opposed to merely becoming so: Garrick had succeeded spectacularly where so many famous performers fail, by managing to turn overnight celebrity in 1741 into lasting fame and fortune ever since—and he had done so without being trapped by an adoring public into a few choice roles, endlessly repeated, or by dwindling into a mere caricature of himself, the diminished version created by the simplifying pressures of public expectation. Garrick was the most versatile actor of the age and he could continually renew and extend his fame by taking on new roles—a course that Cibber and, as it turned out, Sterne were for the most part unable to follow. But there was an even subtler art to be glimpsed and perhaps learned in Garrick. More than anyone else of the time, Garrick had shown an ability to "manage" himself as a theatrical celebrity—keeping up his craft, of course, but also avoiding unnecessary controversies, supporting popular causes, being seen with the right people, keeping up good taste and good manners in his public dealings, bending a bit to get along with others. Sustaining celebrity demanded self-control and ensemble performance, both onstage and off, together with *not* letting the dissonances and loose ends of real experience show too prominently; in the eyes of their public celebrities must be dependably and confidently "themselves."[28]

But Garrick's control of how he would be seen extended yet further. It was no accident, I think, that the two theatrical figures whom Sterne seems to have had most in mind as he traveled to London, Cibber and Garrick, were not just successful actors but actors who were *also* scriptwriters and successful theatrical managers. (Furthermore, to appear in London as "poor Yorick" was to allude to *Hamlet,* and Prince Hamlet is in his theatrical manipulations directed against Claudius also an actor-writer-manager.[29]) These exemplars had shown the power of a theatrical triple role— they supplied the dramatic texts, acted the central roles in the plays they supplied, and directed and managed their own performances, on stage and off—and it was exactly this triple combination that Sterne was laboring to enact in 1760 and throughout his subsequent career. Of course, no public performer ever controls all the variables that shape and sustain his or her acclaim, and all celebrities, knowing the fickleness of audiences, must dread bad publicity, uncontrollable public occasions, and what Johnson and

Garrick jointly called "the wild vicissitudes of taste," the endless chase after "the new-blown bubbles of the day":

> Ah! let not censure term our fate our choice,
> The stage but echoes back the publick voice.
> The drama's laws the drama's patrons give,
> For we that live to please, must please to live.
> ("Drury-Lane Prologue," 1747, lines 48, 50–54)

Still, a writer-actor-manager can control many *more* variables of performance and of public perception than a simple writer can, and it was this realization that put Laurence Sterne on the trail of David Garrick and, more distantly, on that of Colley Cibber.[30]

In some respects, at least, things must have been easier back in that older dispensation when Milton's version of Phoebus Apollo, god of poetic inspiration and transcendence, could assure the doubting poet that true fame—the only acclaim that finally meant anything—was located elsewhere:

> Fame is no plant that grows on mortal soil,
> Not in the glistering foil
> Set off to th' world, nor in broad rumor lies,
> But lives and spreads aloft by those pure eyes,
> And perfect witness of all-judging Jove;
> As he pronounces lastly on each deed,
> Of so much fame in Heaven expect thy meed.
>   ("Lycidas," 1637, lines 78–84)

Certainly this was a happy faith for those who could sustain it— Milton's otherworldly attitudes were in fact proudly, stubbornly anachronistic even when he penned these lines—but by 1760 it seemed clear to most observers that fame, and particularly authorial fame, definitely grew on mortal soil, that it would gladly make use of whatever glistering foil was available, and that broad rumor was just the right thing to assure success. Fame had become, was continuing to become, more worldly, more journalistic, more popular and often vulgar, more oriented toward the printing press, the commercial marketplace, the teeming city. To have a "name" was to have a toehold on survival in a very competitive environment. In his *Life of Richard Nash* (1762) Oliver Goldsmith described clearly the nexus between publicity, fashion, and fortune in the ever more crowded cultural marketplace of London:

> In the populous city where [Nash] resided, to be known was almost synonimous with being in the road to fortune. How many little Things do we see, without merit, or without friends, push themselves forward into public notice, and by self-advertizing, attract the attention of the day. The wise despise them, but the public are not all wise. Thus they succeed, rise upon the wing of folly, or of fashion, and by their success give a new sanction to effrontery.[31]

The new muses of publicity were for the most part an undiscriminating lot, more interested in "sensations" than in substance, and it was hard for literary quality to come to the fore in such a marketplace. Moreover, as Goldsmith pointed out in another essay, publicity created more publicity and the *expectation* of publicity on the part of beholders; one celebrity might have seemed an oddity or a monster, but many celebrities in cacophonous concert created a system of public awareness and of supposed "merit." In fact, the public often seemed positively to enjoy being imposed upon by what were finally self-chosen delusions: "Like children we dress up the puppets in finery, and then stand in astonishment at the plastic wonder."[32]

For obvious reasons the qualities that made this new cultural marketplace so vital and open could also make it seem terrifying. As Samuel Johnson pointed out in the *Rambler,* to throw oneself upon the public and bid for approval was to put one's wholeness and happiness into the hands of others who were often busy or distracted or indifferent—and, as Johnson laconically put the matter, "praise may always be omitted without inconvenience." The general public had little memory or gratitude, a short attention span, and an insatiable desire for ever more novelties. The other sad fact, Johnson went on to suggest, was that even in a growing marketplace there simply wasn't enough applause to go around to all claimants. And to court celebrity, even if one succeeded, was only to find one's place in a market where all gains and losses finally balance:

> Whoever claims renown from any kind of excellence, expects to fill the place which is now possessed by another, for there are already names of every class sufficient to employ all that will desire to remember them; and surely he that is pushing his predecessors into the gulph of obscurity, cannot but sometimes suspect, that he must himself sink in like manner, and as he stands upon the same precipice, be swept away with the same violence.[33]

Given such realities, Sterne did remarkably well, "shandying" his way about London (his verb), and the manner of his doing well is instructive. For one thing, his strategy for creating a cultural "place" for himself should be recognized as a carefully hedged one. He wanted to be a "sensation" in the popular marketplace, but he was unwilling to entrust himself wholly to it, so he also followed more traditional authorial patterns—seeking proper introductions, courting aristocratic patrons, collecting subscriptions, being presented at court, and so on. Sterne could see that the popular and aristocratic markets were not necessarily opposed to one another, that they might be brought together by the common social denominator of play-acting. He further had the wit to invent characters, Tristram, Yorick, and others, humorous yet serious, eccentric enough not to be particularly identified with either popular or aristocratic tastes, yet winning enough to engage both—and he was then able to enact such sensibilities rather than just commending them in fiction. In his ostentatious play-acting Sterne was also conforming to one of the fundamental realities of the city itself: in a place where so many came from someplace else and so few could see the full shape of other people's lives, all were judging from outward appearances and all were performing for one another. ("I have discovered that we may be in some degree whatever character we choose," Boswell announced cheerfully from London in 1762.[34]) Sterne's self-dramatizing practices only made more explicit and therefore emphatic some social rules by which others lived. What Tristram says of Uncle Toby's bowling-green wars might equally be said of Sterne's public playing. If anyone *else* had done it, it might have been taken for satire.

Paradoxically enough, what was most effective about Sterne's public performances was his final elusiveness as a character; had the public known what to make of him, they would soon have paid less attention. Boswell reported of Samuel Johnson that he was in the habit of dropping broad hints about his undisclosed activities and personal associations, so as to have the pleasure of being an object of curious speculation—"He loved thus to keep things floating in conjecture: *Omne ignotum pro magnifico est*" ["The unknown passes for something grand"].[35] Whether by instinct or by design, Sterne was able to achieve something of the same effect by flaunting the fact of his performances, by switching roles, by continually improvising, by hedging everything he said or did in public with self-conscious irony.[36] He could never quite become the "perfect" celebrity, a figure embodying great, urgent, and probably conflicting cultural energies, an inexhaustible object of public curiosity and yearning, forever revealing qualities or aspects forever new. He was not a versatile enough player, and a mere novelist, an entertainer, a harlequin could not wield such cultural power. Still, Sterne could through the combination of his writings and his public playing raise important questions by making them socially visible. What *was* the cultural pertinence nowadays of a country clergyman, an author, a wit, a jester? And what *was* a proper balance between seriousness and play, head and heart, in relation to such culturally charged topics as romantic love or old war wounds or the birthing and naming and raising of a child? And how could one draw a clear line between social decorum and indecorum for such an ambivalent creature as man? And what were the essential qualities of language, of theatrical gestures, of disguise, all three so powerful to capture and organize realities, yet all three equally apt to misrepresent them or to wander away from them?

As a writer and public performer Sterne never ceased to appear an exemplary figure, a catalyst for potential meanings—and that, of course, is what all the most intriguing celebrities, then or now, finally are. But exactly *what* he was exemplifying on any given day seemed forever up for grabs: he was naive and knowing, reverent and devil-may-care, brash and whimsical, sentimental and skeptical and comical by turns. The variables of his public performance, his impersonations, were all described (often ambivalently) somewhere in his published writings, but it seems clear that the shape of his personal script he discovered from moment to moment, even in the act of performing before others. The significance of his performance was further hedged by the various vantage-points of his audience. To some observers he seemed a hero of social sympathy, personal sensibility, and good humor, while to others he was a scandal, running into the ground his various professions as minister, author, husband, and gentleman. To still others, the eventual majority, he appeared an essentially "literary" figure, a self-conscious invention designed to confirm favorite English mythologies concerning eccentricity and good-heartedness, a character to be placed in the tradition of Don Quixote, Roger de Coverley, Parson Adams, the Vicar of Wakefield, and their literary kin. (As John Berger shrewdly observes, modern cultures use the arts of mythology and publicity in tandem to propagate through carefully chosen images each culture's belief in itself.[37])

Probably to the greatest number of his contemporaries, Sterne was simply a "sensation," a highly charged and controversial figure capable of lending amusement or drama to long gray afternoons; increasingly through the eighteenth century, cultivated life, guided by its newspapers, seemed to require and therefore to create a steady diet of "sensations" to be savored and consumed.[38] Sterne understood the still-emerging rules of the new, more entrepreneurial cultural marketplace and he was willing to live by them. But he understood something further. Part of the essential modernity of Sterne lies in his knowledge that *every* space, a blank page, an empty room, an ambiguous word, an undefined character or a new social relationship, was potential dramatic space, imaginative space to be invested with energy and color and personality— and understanding this, he further knew how to take advantage of, to find instruction and amusement and consolation in, a world of variable meanings.

Notes

Epigraph: Quoted in Leo Braudy, *The Frenzy of Renown: Fame and Its History* (New York: Oxford University Press, 1986), p. 401. Although I am more interested in the public performances associated with fame rather than in fame itself, my general indebtedness throughout this article to Braudy's groundbreaking study should be evident.

1. David Garrick, *Plays,* ed. Harry William Pedicord and Fredrick Louis Bergmann (Carbondale: Southern Illinois University Press, 1980), I, 215, 203–204, 224. For a fuller account of this production see George Winchester Stone Jr. and George M. Kahrl, *David Garrick: A Critical Biography* (Carbondale: Southern Illinois University Press, 1979), pp. 220–23.

2. See Arthur H. Cash, *Laurence Sterne* (London: Methuen, 1975–86), I, 299–300 and plate I. In general, I have relied heavily upon Cash's excellent account of Sterne's life, but for one particularly interested in the "performance" side of Sterne's career, there is also material of value in Willard Connely's *Laurence Sterne as Yorick* (London: Bodley Head, 1958), *passim.*

3. Quoted in Cash, *Laurence Sterne,* I, 296.

4. For a fuller account of this wonderful spring, see Cash, *Laurence Sterne,* II, 1–53.

5. "The Theatres and Passion-Week," published in *The Examiner* for 6 April 1828, *Complete Works,* ed. P. P. Howe (London: J. M. Dent, 1930), 18, 386.

6. See *Letters,* pp. 81–82, where Sterne signed a 1759 letter as "Yorick."

7. Compare also Richard Steele's famous statement closing out the first series of the *Spectator* papers, when he explains the difference between writing in the voice of the fictional Spectator and in his own: "It is much more difficult to converse with the World in a real than a personated Character. That might pass for Humour, in the *Spectator,* which would look like Arrogance in a Writer who sets his Name to his Work. The Fictitious Person might contemn those who disapproved him, and extoll his own Performances, without giving Offence. He might assume a mock-Authority, without being looked upon as vain and conceited. The Praises or Censures of himself fall only upon the Creature of his Imagination, and if any one finds fault with him, the Author may reply with the Philosopher of old, *Thou dost but beat the Case of Anaxarchus.* When I speak in my own private Sentiments, I cannot but address my self to my Readers in a more submissive manner, and with a just Gratitude" (*Spectator* no. 555). For other anticipations of Shandean social behavior see *Spectator* no.

14 and *Rambler* no. 208, in which Addison and Samuel Johnson respectively argue the liberating effects of wearing masks and disguises in social gatherings; see also Sandra Billington's interesting *A Social History of the Fool* (Sussex: Harvester Press, 1984), chap. 6, in which she argues the rising social acceptance of fool figures in polite society over the course of the eighteenth century. And for a provocative modern discussion of the psychodynamics of the masquerade tradition, see Terry Castle, *Masquerade and Civilization: The Carnivalesque in Eighteenth-Century English Culture and Fiction* (Stanford: Stanford University Press, 1986), particularly chaps. 1 and 2.

8. *Letters,* p. 107. For an interesting general discussion of the relationship between contemporary journalism and the writing of *Tristram Shandy,* see Morris Golden, "Periodical Context in the Imagined World of *Tristram Shandy,*" *Age of Johnson,* 1 (1987), 237–60.

9. Quoted in Cash, *Laurence Sterne,* II, 20.

10. *Letters,* p. 90. In *An Apology for the Life of Colley Cibber,* ed. B. R. S. Fone (1740; rpt. Ann Arbor: University of Michigan Press, 1968), Cibber admitted that he complied with the popular tastes of his times because he "had not virtue enough to starve, by opposing a Multitude, that would have been too hard for me" (p. 280). In *A Letter from Mr. Cibber to Mr. Pope* (London, 1742; rpt., 1973, Augustan Reprint Society, no. 158) Cibber amplified the thought: "All I shall say then . . . is, that I wrote more to be Fed, than to be Famous, and since my Writings still give me a Dinner, do you rhyme me out of my Stomach if you can" (p. 9). In his *Life of Johnson* James Boswell traced the reversible fed/famous phrase to a more remote Latin ancestor—*fami non famae scribere,* "to write for hunger, not fame"—a comment written by French historian Thuanus (Jacques-Auguste de Thou [1553–1617]) about the famous but impoverished classical scholar Wilhelm Xylander (1532–1576). The G. B. Hill–L. F. Powell edition of Boswell's *Life* (Oxford: Clarendon Press, 1936–64), I, 208n., lists the original source as Thuanus's *Historia,* lib. lxii, cap. v.

11. It is exactly this shift of interest, of course, which becomes the enabling principle for *Tristram Shandy.* As Tristram himself observes, "I know there are readers in the world, as well as many other good people in it, who are no readers at all,—who find themselves ill at ease, unless they are let into the whole secret from first to last, of every thing which concerns you" (*TS,* 1.4.4–5). Compare also Joseph Addison's *Spectator* no. 1, particularly the opening paragraph.

12. My views on the rituals attending social celebrity have been shaped by readings in cultural anthropology, notably Arnold van Gennep, *The*

Rites of Passage, trans. Monika B. Vizedom and Gabrielle L. Caffee (Chicago: University of Chicago Press, 1960), *passim*; Victor Turner, "Social Dramas and Ritual Metaphors" in *Dramas, Fields, and Metaphors: Symbolic Action in Human Society* (Ithaca: Cornell University Press, 1974), pp. 23–59; Clifford Geertz, "Centers, Kings, and Charisma: Reflections on the Symbolics of Power" in *Local Knowledge: Further Essays in Interpretive Anthropology* (New York: Basic Books, 1983), pp. 121–46; and Marshall Sahlins, "Other Times, Other Customs: The Anthropology of History," *American Anthropologist* 85 (1983), 517–44.

13. *Portraits by Sir Joshua Reynolds,* ed. Frederick W. Hilles (New York: McGraw-Hill, 1952), p. 24. Interestingly enough, the same scene was recorded a second time by William Cooke, the biographer of Samuel Foote the comedian, also relying on Reynolds's memories. Cooke's account is similar, yet significantly less vivid than Boswell's, a reason for praising Boswell—or for mistrusting him. Cooke's version: "When Reynolds was a young man, he was present at a sale of very scarce pictures, which attracted a great crowd of *connoisseurs* and others: when, in the moment of a very interesting piece being put up, Mr. Pope entered the room. All was in an instant, from a scene of confusion and bustle, a dead calm. The auctioneer, as if by instinct, suspended his hammer. The audience to an individual, as if by the same impulse, rose up to receive the poet; and did not resume their seats till he had reached the upper end of the room" (*Memoirs of Samuel Foote* [London, 1806], II, 156).

14. Compare *Tatler* no. 122 by Addison: "It is said of *Virgil,* when he enter'd a *Roman* Theatre, where there were many Thousands of Spectators present, That the whole Assembly rose up to do him Honour; a Respect which was never before paid to any but the Emperor." Later in the same number Addison recalled an analogous story of Socrates: "This venerable Person often frequented the Theatre, which brought a great many thither, out of a Desire to see him. On which Occasions it is recorded of him, That he sometimes stood to make himself the more conspicuous, and to satisfie the Curiosity of the beholders." Samuel Johnson reported of Pope that he received a general ovation from the audience when he entered the theatre to attend the opening of Thomson's *Agamemnon* in 1738; see "James Thomson," *Lives of the English Poets* (London: J. M. Dent, 1925, 1958), II, 288. Compare more generally the importance of kingship metaphors in Oliver Goldsmith's "Life of Richard Nash" and in Boswell's *Life of Johnson.* The general point, of course, is that the symbolism of power and authority is a flexible and transferable resource in a well-integrated

culture, a phenomenon richly illustrated and thoughtfully explored throughout Braudy's *Frenzy of Renown.*

15. *Frenzy of Renown,* p. 205. For a much more jaundiced, but still pertinent view of the same traditions, especially as they are exploited by modern celebrities and their attendant media, see Daniel J. Boorstin, *The Image: A Guide to Pseudo-Events in America* (New York: Atheneum, 1961, 1975), particularly pp. 45–76.

16. The *Plain Speaker* no. 12 (1826), *Complete Works,* XII, 117. Compare Samuel Johnson's discussion of the peculiar burdens of being a public notable, a known author, in *Rambler* No. 16; speaking through a persona, Johnson writes wryly, "such is now the importance of my opinion, that I am afraid to offer it, lest, by being established too hastily into a maxim, it should be the occasion of error to half the nation; and such is the expectation with which I am attended, when I am going to speak, that I frequently pause to reflect whether what I am about to utter is worthy of myself." Compare also Hazlitt's famous argument in his essay, "Whether Actors Ought to Sit in the Boxes?" (1821–22): "Actors belong to the public: their persons are not their own property. . . . [An actor] is the centre of an illusion that he is bound to support, both . . . by a certain self-respect which should repel idle curiosity, and by a certain deference to the public, in whom he has inspired certain prejudices which he is covenanted not to break" (*Complete Works,* VIII, 272–73).

17. Boswell, *Life of Johnson,* I, 200. Recall also Johnson's remark to Boswell recorded in the *Journal of a Tour to the Hebrides:* "A man who is not publickly known may live in London as he pleases, without any notice being taken of him; but it is wonderful how a person of any consequence is watched" (ed. R. W. Chapman [London, 1965], pp. 325–26).

18. Letters, p. 87. But compare Joseph Cradock, *Literary and Miscellaneous Memoirs* (1828; rpt., Westmead: Gregg International, 1972), I, 207–208, where Sterne is recalled conceding in conversation that he lacked the talent for writing stage comedy.

19. *Apology,* p. 60.

20. Many modern commentators on *Shandy* have noticed the importance of theatrical conventions and concerns in its development. For a good overview of the pertinent affinities, see Ronald Hafter, "Garrick and *Tristram Shandy,*" *SEL,* 7 (1967), 475–89; for a more modernistic post-Humean, mind-playing-theatrically-with-its-own-objects approach, see Peter Steele, "Sterne's Script: The Performing of *Tristram Shandy,*" in *Augustan Studies: Essays in Honor of Irvin Ehrenpreis,* ed. Douglas L. Patey and Timothy

Keegan (Newark: University of Delaware Press, 1985), pp. 195–204. In "Laurence Sterne and the Eighteenth-Century Stage," *PLL,* 4 (1968), 144–57, Lodwick Hartley warns against *over*stressing the connections between Sterne's novel and contemporary stagecraft.

21. Compare Oliver Goldsmith's famous attack on Sterne's bawdry and "pertness" in *Letters of a Citizen of the World,* no. 53—which attack should be understood, I think, as being directed not against an author so much as against a public performer, a harlequin.

It was exactly this "performance" quality that Thackeray also felt in reading Sterne and resisted as cheaply exploitative; significantly, he too used the image of the theatrical jester: "[Sterne] fatigues me with his perpetual disquiet and his uneasy appeals to my risible or sentimental faculties. He is always looking in my face, watching his effect, uncertain whether I think him an impostor or not; posture-making, coaxing, and imploring me. . . . This man is a great jester, not a great humourist. He goes to work systematically and of cold blood; paints his face, puts on his ruff and motley clothes, and lays down his carpet and tumbles on it" (From *The English Humourists of the Eighteenth Century* [1853] in *Works of William Makepeace Thackeray* [London: Macmillan, 1911], VII, 168–69).

22. *CH,* 83 ("A Poetical Epistle to Doctor Sterne, Parson Yorick and Tristram Shandy").

23. *Apology,* p. 17. New, "The Dunce Revisited: Colley Cibber and Tristram Shandy," *South Atlantic Quarterly,* 72 (1973), 547–59.

24. See *Apology,* pp. 118–20, and Helene Koon, *Colley Cibber: A Biography* (Lexington: University Press of Kentucky, 1986), pp. 26–32, 83–84. Compare also Joseph Spence's comment on Cibber, quoted by Koon, p. 218: "Old Colley is himself a Comedy." For a vigorous defense of Cibber's posing, see Lois Potter, "Colley Cibber: The Fop as Hero," in *Augustan Worlds,* ed. J. C. Hinson, M. M. B. Jones, and J. R. Watson (New York: Barnes and Noble, 1978), pp. 153–64.

25. *Apology,* p. 15.

26. *The Laureat* (1740), possibly by Aaron Hill, quoted in Lois Potter, "The Fop as Hero," p. 163.

27. Quoted in Stone and Kahrl, *David Garrick,* p. 468.

28. It is testimony to the growing power of newspapers and pamphlets as cultural arbiters that well-established figures feared negative publicity so much. According to Thomas Davies who knew him well, Garrick was a perpetual hostage to bad press and his feelings of vulnerability grew in proportion to his celebrity: "He, indeed, carried this quick sense or feeling

of the mind too far: a false report would alarm him; a paragraph or a letter in a newspaper, or a pamphlet, would, for a time, greatly affect him. . . . He had justly acquired a very great reputation, and he feared lest the base, unfounded aspersions of men who had no character of their own to lose, should make more impression on the world than it was possible they could. . . . His fears increased with his fame" (*Memoirs of the Life of David Garrick* [1780; rpt., New York: Benjamin Blom, 1969], II, 411–13). Compare also Samuel Johnson's comment to Boswell that he would have liked to visit the charming but notorious Margaret Caroline Rudd, adventuress, blackmailer, and acquitted forger—"were it not that they have now a trick of putting every thing into the newspapers" (*Life of Johnson*, III, 79). Boswell, being Boswell, of course went to visit her and, some years later, became for a time her lover; for full details and an interesting commentary, see Gordon Turnbull, "Criminal Biographer: Boswell and Margaret Caroline Rudd," *SEL*, 26 (1986), 511–35.

There are many histories available of the rise of newspapers and of print culture generally in eighteenth-century Britain. Two of the most thoughtful are Alvin Kernan's study of changing notions of authorship in *Printing Technology, Letters, and Samuel Johnson* (Princeton: Princeton University Press, 1987), *passim*, and Lance Bertelsen's study of a group of writer-publicists who lived by, for, and through newspaper publicity, *The Nonsense Club: Literature and Popular Culture, 1749–1764* (Oxford: Clarendon, 1986), particularly pp. 136–60.

29. For an interesting and pertinent reexamination of "player" themes in *Hamlet*, see Jonathan Baldo, "Theatricality, Generality, Drama: Variations on the Theme of Context in *Hamlet*," *Criticism* 27 (1985), 111–131. I am grateful to Professor Richard Wertime for bringing this resource to my attention.

30. Cibber particularly prided himself as a professional man of the theater for having taken measures to exclude theatrical patrons from seating upon the stage where they had too often interfered with the actors and from the backstage area where they had no proper business: "while they were admitted behind our Scenes, we but too often shew'd them the wrong Side of our Tapestry; and . . . many a tollerable Actor was the less valued, when it was known, what ordinary Stuff he was made of" (*Apology*, pp. 316–18).

31. *Collected Works*, ed. Arthur Friedman (Oxford: Clarendon Press, 1966), III, 295.

32. *Citizen of the World*, letter xciii; *Collected Works*, II, 375–76.

33. *Rambler* no. 46; Johnson takes up the same melancholy themes again in no. 203.

34. *London Journal, 1762–1763,* ed. Frederick A. Pottle (New York: McGraw-Hill, 1950), p. 45. One could reasonably argue that what was *truly* exceptional about Sterne's appearance in London in the spring of 1760 was his ability to tear himself away to meet other obligations after only eleven weeks; most authors, though they received considerably less encouragement than Sterne did, chose nevertheless to remain in London.

35. *Life of Johnson,* III, 324; the Latin tag is from Tacitus, *Agricola,* xxx.

36. For a reading of *Tristram Shandy* emphasizing these same provisional qualities, see my earlier article "Locke's *Essay* and the Tentativeness of *Tristram Shandy,*" *SP,* 82 (1985), 493–520.

37. *Ways of Seeing* (Harmondsworth: Penguin, 1972, 1977), pp. 139–40.

38. For a broad and interesting array of illustrative instances see Richard D. Altick, *The Shows of London* (Cambridge: Belknap Press, 1978), particularly chaps. 3 and 7; Roy Porter, *English Society in the Eighteenth Century* (Harmondsworth: Penguin, 1982), ch. 6; and Neil McKendrick, John Brewer, and J. H. Plumb, *The Birth of a Consumer Society: The Commercialization of Eighteenth-Century England* (Bloomington: Indiana University Press, 1982), *passim.*

Tristram Shandy as Aesthetic Object

PETER J. DE VOOGD

◆　◆　◆

L AURENCE STERNE PUBLISHED his masterpiece *The Life and Opinions of Tristram Shandy, Gentleman* in nine slender volumes in the final decade of his life, between 1759 and 1767. The first two volumes appeared in York, Dublin, and London by January 1760. On 25 March the advertisement for the second (London) edition proudly announced a frontispiece designed by William Hogarth. Volumes 3 and 4 (again with a frontispiece by Hogarth) appeared a year later, in January 1761, and in December of that same year volumes 5 and 6 came out, with the unusual announcement that "Every book is signed by the author." And indeed, to protect his book from being pirated, Sterne signed all copies of the first and second (revised) editions of volume 5, and of the first editions of volumes 7 and 9 on the first text page: 12,750 signatures in a neat (and still perfectly legible) hand. Volumes 7 and 8 appeared in January 1765, the last volume in 1767, shortly before Sterne's death (he died of consumption). Contrary to Samuel Johnson's famous dictum that "Tristram Shandy did not last," the novel was a success. Some thirty different editions appeared in his lifetime, and many, many more have appeared since then.

From the very beginning Sterne devoted almost excessive attention to matters of typographical detail. His letters to his publishers attest to his demands regarding format, quality of paper, type, and layout. The first advertisements for his book stressed that it was "Printed on a super-fine Writing Paper" and with a "new Letter," and that it was "neatly bound." He saw each new volume through the press himself, which is the more remarkable since he had to travel all the way from Coxwold in Yorkshire to London in the worst possible season (all volumes came out in winter). He wrote to his London publisher, Dodsley, about the first York imprint, that he had corrected every proof himself, and the extant manuscripts of his other masterpiece *A Sentimental Journey through France and Italy* are evidence that Sterne corrected his proofs with very great care, revising his text in minor detail, specifying typographic accidentals such as italics, upper- and lowercase with professional precision, and devoting much care to layout and paragraphing. He had always been finicky, even in 1759, when Caesar Ward in York had printed his satirical pamphlet *A Political Romance.* Sterne wrote Ward: "do not presume to alter or transpose one Word, nor rectify one false Spelling, nor so much as add or diminish one Comma or Tittle" (*Letters,* 68).

The text of *Tristram Shandy* is characterized by the highly unusual nature of its many nonverbal features. Many of these appear, if they appear at all, in modern editions of the novel in a form which differs from the one originally insisted upon by the author. No one who knows *Tristram Shandy* only in the Penguin, the Random House, or the Everyman edition can know the extent of Sterne's experiments with the visual effect of the printed word.[1] In this paper I will regard his novel as a "coexistential" verbo-visual whole. I will discuss the function and effects of the nonverbal aspects of the text of the first editions of *Tristram Shandy* in the light of the aesthetic effect of the printing and layout of its 1,594 duodecimo pages.

Let me explain that term *coexistential.* The verbal and visual elements of a text can be said to be either mutually "referential" (as when a newspaper article is illustrated by a photograph), or "co-referential" (as when a graph elucidates a text). But the closest relationship between a word and an image is a coexistential one, when the text's verbal and visual elements are so intimately interwoven that they form an aesthetic whole. Text and picture cannot be divorced from one another without serious loss. The picture *is* the text, the text the picture. A striking example in *Tristram Shandy* (amply commented upon) is the marbled page in volume 3, which is part of the text of the novel, as its pagination and margins show. Indeed, what first made me turn to the first editions of the individual volumes of *Tristram Shandy* was the very unicity of those baffling marbled pages, each page hand-marbled, each side different and unique, each side hand-stamped, each leaf stuck in, the sheer scope of the undertaking a tell-tale indication of the extent to which Sterne was prepared to go in turning his book into an aesthetic object: the marbled pages in volume 3 required 8,000 times folding of the leaf, marbling, and stamping.[2] In between the extremes of, on the one hand, a unique text (in all its original typographical aspects) and, on the other, a cheap featureless reprint, I propose a sliding scale by which we may measure the degree of coexistentiality of any text's verbo-visual elements and features. To give one example, many of W. M. Thackeray's illustrations are merely referential and can be (and often, unfortunately, are) left out in modern reprints without loss of understanding of the text. But Thackeray occasionally throws in a clearly coexistential drawing, as in *The Rose and the Ring* (1854), where on page 87 he uses an almost Sternian dash to indicate the delicate pause in which he decides to draw the picture rather than describe the scene: "The landlady came up, looking—looking like this—" and there she is (Fig. 1), rising from the page.

Another example, in which indeed the coexistentiality of the aesthetic whole makes it almost impossible to say whether we are dealing with a text or with a picture, can be found in Tom Phillips's *A Humument: A Treated Victorian Novel.* Tom Phillips started "treating" William H. Mallock's 1892 *A Human Document* in 1966, using the typographical "rivers" in the type of the original, scoring out unwanted words, coloring in type areas, making each page new, and inviting the reader/spectator to share in his Barthesian textual *jouissance*.

Sterne's novel contains all the verbo-visual features outlined above. This is not surprising, since in volume 5, chapter 7, Sterne himself voiced the idea "that of all the senses, the eye . . . has the quickest commerce with the soul,—gives a smarter stroke, and leaves something more inexpressible on the fancy, than words can either convey—or sometimes get rid of." This paper's scope does not allow more than passing treatment of the purely "referential" dimension. Given the variety of Sterne illustrations this is a pity. From Hogarth onward illustrators have risen to the challenge (Henry William Bunbury is one of the more intriguing artists in a long line), and obviously one of the more interesting subjects here is which "pregnant" moments (in Shaftesbury's sense of that term) have been chosen by illustrators. Uncle Toby's hobby-horse was quite popular. Another favourite, of course, was Mad Maria, with her goat. That rather disturbing animal was later, when Sentimentalism had won, replaced by a little lamb, and, in the 19th century, by a poodle.

Tristram Shandy contains at least one open invitation to the reader to supply his own "referential" picture on the blank page in volume 6, chapter 38, where the reader may draw his own portrait of the Widow Wadman (and the author exclaims: "Thrice happy book! thou wilt have one page, at least, within thy covers, which MALICE will not blacken, and which IGNORANCE cannot misrepresent"). The page has remained disappointingly blank in all the copies I have seen, although elsewhere inventive publishers have unwittingly supplied fine "referential" illustrations: the 1779 Dublin edition of *Tristram Shandy* has placed the phrase "Alas, poor Yorick!" *in* the black page, thus turning it into a perfect tombstone, and in many editions Uncle Toby's favorite song *Lillabullero* is printed, lyrics and score, unasked for by Sterne's text. As to the coreferential and coexistential dimensions of Sterne's text, most one-volume editions of *Tristram Shandy* merely offer the reader the verbal contents of the text. Some copy in one form or another some of the nonverbal effects characteristic of the novel, but none, alas, do full justice to the startling originality of the novel as it was published by Sterne. Obviously, the marbled pages must be seen in color, but other examples come to mind. The graphs in volume 6 charting the plot lines (and originally signed "Inv. T.S. & Scul. T.S.") are mostly copied, but they strike one differently in the original text, as does Trim's flourish in volume 9. The difference is easily explained: the flourish (Fig. 2) is much larger a gesture than the one we find in modern editions. This one fills more than half the page (the absence of a catchword adding to the effect). The Penguin page contains two and a half times as much text as Sterne's original pages do. This simple fact diminishes the effect Trim's flourish can have in Penguin considerably, and likewise makes the graphs in volume 6 far more secondary in Penguin than they are in the original.

A quick check of the following most outstanding typographical "oddities" will show how appallingly bad most modern editions are. There must be two black pages in volume 1, chapter 12; and two marbled ones (each side different, and in color) in volume 3, at the end of chapter 36; there must be a gap in the pagination of volume 4, since chapter 24 is missing; a blank page is asked for in chapter 38 and a series of graphs in the last chapter of volume 6; in volume 7, chapter 25, the broken syllables chanted by the Abbess of Andouillets and Margarita must get smaller and smaller; the fine woodcut depicting Corporal Trim's flourish must be in chapter 4 of volume 9, of which chapters 18 and 19 must be blank, though later they *are* printed, with different chapter headings. And there are countless smaller indications that words and characters are visual objects in the pages of *Tristram Shandy,* as when "sentiment" sails down the Ganges and round the world in volume 5, chapter 12, or when the city of Nevers is never reached in chapter 2. And in chapter 13, Mrs Shandy almost would have listened at the door "till the end of the chapter." Thus it is fitting that in volume 3 the actual moment of Tristram's birth is not described; at that point in the work there is instead "The Author's PREFACE." After all, Tristram Shandy, Gentleman is both a character, an implied author, and a title.

Here are two more examples of verbo-visual surprise. In Fig. 3

the left (Latin) and right (English) pages suggest a literal translation, and indeed nearly all modern editions number the chapter
on both pages identically, thus deviating from the original where,
as one sees, the Latin text gives chapter 25 of Ernulphus, the English
text chapter 11 of Tristram. An interesting variant is first found in
the edition of 1782, where the English chapter numerically suc-
ceeds the Latin one. But even thus regularized the surprise effect
is gone. And a closer look at the pagination of the missing chapter
in volume 4 (the text jumps from page 146 to 156) brings to light
the awkward (and I am sure deliberate) misnumbering of the right-
hand page (p. 156). As compositors and binders know only too well
(their work hinges on the very principle) right-hand pages are
always odd-numbered. To have them even-numbered from here
to the end of the volume on page 220 (indeed *recto*) creates total
and recurrent typographical alienation. This is a printer's nightmare not unlike the glorious grammatical impossibility of that
triumphant nonsentence in volume 3, chapter 38: "a cow broke in
(to-morrow morning)." Naturally, all modern editions number the
pages of *Tristram Shandy* "correctly" (that is to say, they ruin one of
Sterne's better jokes).

Many of these are obviously based on the serial appearance of
the volumes. A good example is the fate of Sterne's suggestion to
his fictional reader (himself a character *in* the volume) in the beginning of volume 6 that "as we have got thro' these five volumes"
he "sit down upon a set" (of those volumes: their very small size
adds to the joke). But the point was obviously missed when the
format of the novel was changed: In later editions "set" is often
silently "emended" to "seat." I often advise my students to cut up
their Penguin edition into nine separate parts—it helps. Although
of course nothing can ever turn Penguin's Linotype Georgian pages
(38 lines, 60 characters wide) into Sterne's hand-set Caslon Pica
ones, 22 lines long, each page 40 characters wide.

And this brings me to my main point. *Tristram Shandy* was designed by Laurence Sterne to be set in Caslon Pica; indeed, he had
insisted upon this in his first letter to Dodsley, in October 1759.
Sterne, who had just seen the first two volumes of *Tristram Shandy*
through Caesar Ward's press in York, wrote Dodsley in London,

not quite truthfully (since the volumes had been printed already): "I propose . . . to print a lean edition, in two small volumes, of the size of Rasselas, and on the same paper and type, at my own expense" (*Letters,* 80). Johnson's *Rasselas* had just been published in two slender duodecimo volumes. Sterne did not copy Johnson's entire title page. He obviously disliked the customary division between title and imprint, and got rid of the double rule separating them. But he did almost exactly copy the rest of the format of *Rasselas*: the type Caslon Pica, the type area 21 text lines, the paper smooth writing paper. And he used with abandon the many characteristic features of the type he chose, a type which he would also have known from his favorite reference work, the second (1738) edition of Ephraim Chambers's *Cyclopaedia: or, an Universal Dictionary of Arts and Sciences,* which has s.v. "Letter" a copy of Caslon's first type specimen of 1734. Caslon's is a highly irregular letter, more suitable for poetry than for prose, and a difficult letter for compositors and printers to work with, especially on smooth "superfine" writing paper. The "T" is asymmetric, the "g" too slanting, the verticals of the "W" are not parallel, the "N" slants and is too wide, the "A" looks topped off, the italics are highly irregular, almost too italic, and the ampersand is quite exuberant (and cheerfully used for full effect by Sterne, for instance in volume 4 where whole strings of &c. &c. &c.'s disrupt the order of the page). The letter Sterne chose is one reason why the pages of *Tristram Shandy* have their nervous look, especially since the relatively small type area and the generous margins give Caslon's Pica full rein.

But Sterne went further. He developed an intricate system, rhetorical rather than grammatical, of hyphens and dashes and asterisks, adding an occasional cross (when someone crosses himself), or index hand (to score a point), and once (in volume 5, chapter 10) he had two small dots printed to indicate that Corporal Trim snaps his fingers. He also considerably varied letterpress, asking for black letter, Greek type, French and Latin, undercase, uppercase (sometimes both in one line, and often, as in the phrase "insensible MORE or LESS," he insisted upon a double shift to uppercase for single words)—compositors must have considered him exceedingly demanding, and this might explain why Dodsley did not renew his contract. It is also quite typical of Sterne that a very complex joke necessitates bad French, in volume 1, where it is hoped that the baptismal strategies invented by the doctors of the Sorbonne will do no harm "a le père." This was silently and incorrectly "corrected" to "au père" by nearly all compositors after the first edition. Interestingly, the relevant (and correct) page in the first (York) edition is a cancel, which seems to indicate that Sterne had demanded restoration of his joke.

But the most immediately striking visual feature of Sterne's text is his remarkable use of the asterisk and the dash. The contemporary use of the asterisk (to indicate footnotes and hiatus or ellipsis) is expanded considerably. In *Tristram Shandy* it often stands for distinct words or whole sentences (thus "**** *** ** *** ******" in volume 5 is, in context, perfectly legible, what with there being no ******* ***); sometimes it stands for unspecified sentences or narrative passages in general, filling whole blocks of text. Such asterisked text lines (asterisks occur in 163 lines, sometimes for half a page) often have their own punctuation: the starry paragraphs are indented, or rounded off with a period, or they are interrupted by a dash; indeed, a row of asterisks is used twice for a catchword. Even more spectacular (and mysterious) is the Shandeian dash, which varies in length from 3 mm to 3 cm, and, like the asterisk, is often treated as though it were a word in a sentence. The fine Florida Edition of *Tristram Shandy* (1978) points out (in an important note on pp. 835–37) that Sterne lengthened the dash in the second edition of volumes 5 and 6, which he carefully supervised, by one em in 90 percent of cases: "perhaps he did ask the printer to open up the text in this way . . . for Sterne the dash was primarily important not as a grammatical or oratorical sign, but as a visual one—it affects the appearance of the page." The extent to which the dash is used is truly staggering (9,560 times in 1,594 pages of text, or rather in 27,899 text lines, that is to say there is on average one dash in every three lines). The dash's visibility is great in the small type area of the original text. Gardner D. Stout suggests on p. 53 of his edition of *A Sentimental Journey* that the dash is usually preceded by other punctuation in volumes 1 to 4, and that in the remaining volumes, as in *A Sentimental Journey,* there is "almost exclusive use" of the single dash, the shift "commencing in vols. III and IV." This is not entirely true. There is considerable flux and variation throughout the nine volumes, although in general the longer dash in stead of a comma or period occurs more often from volume 7 onward. The subject is too complex to treat here, but my computer data indicate that in all volumes different combinations with dashes occur, the patterns being totally unpredictable and certainly not as linear as Stout would wish.

Finally there is Sterne's intriguing use of a contemporary printer's convention, the use of a catchword on the signature line of the page to indicate the first word on the next. There are indications that Sterne did not really like that convention (one remembers that there is no catchword to spoil Trim's flourish).[3] But as they had to be there, Sterne used them, on one occasion so subtly interweaving text and footnote that no modern edition seems to have noticed what does happen. In Figure 4 one can clearly see how the two texts on page 133—main text and footnote text—continue to the next page via their respective catchwords "but" and "If." There the footnote text stops, any catchword being strikingly absent, although the text would suggest that the next page will "follow," as it does, but from the other catchword, the main text's "ME—." In other words, typographically main text and footnote are merged in new main text, a confluence that has gone unnoticed so far. Catchword order (to coin a phrase) is restored on the next pages.

As my last examples will show, to read the original text of Sterne's book one must to a very great extent submit to a lexical and visual guessing game. Needless to say, one's guesses are not infrequently wrong, and expectations are often frustrated. Sterne's use of catchwords can be compared with one important feature of rhyme. The skilled reader tries to anticipate what follows while the poet tries to surprise. And in the case of *Tristram Shandy* one not only seldom knows how the sentence (or for that matter the story) will continue, one does not know either what the next page is going to look like. *Tristram Shandy* is one of those novels where blanks are as meaningful as text. Each page is a living unit, each new page a visual surprise. Any modern edition in comparison is drably uniform, its type area too large and its type too small to be as flexibly versatile as Sterne's twenty-odd Pica lines per page. Figures 5 to 7 demonstrate the full effect of a sequence of pages. Some indication of context is required: throughout the volume the Widow Wadman and her servant Bridget want to know precisely (anatomically) where in or near the groin Uncle Toby, a retired infantry captain, was wounded during the siege of Namur (which might be a pun on "ne amour" or on "no more"), but their persistent inquiries always lead to Uncle Toby's explaining, geographically, with the help of a map of the fortifications of Namur, where he stood when he got wounded. His faithful batman, Corporal Trim, here explains in his own way that the Widow has nothing (or everything) to fear. The striking position of the two textlines on p. 118 is the more striking when one realizes that this is the only time that the word *map* (which occurs 20 times in the novel) is capitalized, and that this is the only one of the 312 chapters placed thus on an otherwise blank page: here hangs a map indeed. In the next pages dashes lead the eye while the right-hand catchwords raise expectations that are not fulfilled. "We" are not Toby and Trim, but Widow and Bridget. What "It" will be can never be guessed, and few will guess that it is Trim who "knows" on p. 124. Notice on pages 120 and 121 how the long dashes and the blank lines between paragraphs slow down the narrative, and remark that Bridget's gesture is said to be a "sentence"; notice also how the lines of asterisks on page 122 end in a period; above all, notice how these pages vibrate with life, their ever-surprising layout furthered by the fact that the text is hand-set in a letter which refuses to yield straight and uniform lines.

This is why only the original text will do. No matter how faithfully the more obvious idiosyncrasies of Sterne's text are copied, the modern linotype page cannot but be a gray and uniform typographical block, whereas Sterne's pages are wide open. Just as the text of the novel is typically and nervously conversational (the text must be read aloud to make full sense), its typography is never still but in constant flux. Yet the conversational flow is all the time interrupted by the typography, and a great deal of the full effect of this unique novel stems from that very contrast between textual point and visual counterpoint. In a word, in *Tristram Shandy* we witness the writing in time in a book in space. But we can participate fully only when we accept the coexistence of word and image in this novel that can only be read as it was originally composed.

Notes

1. This problem was particularly acute when the present essay was first published in 1988. Since then, new and much improved editions have appeared: Penguin brought out a paperback version of the Florida text, edited by Melvyn New, in 1997 and 2003; Everyman's Library published a new edition by Tim Parnell in 1999; and Robert Folkenflik's edition came out in the Modern Library in 2004. But even though these new editions are much more aware of the typographical intricacies of Sterne's text than the precursors I mention in the following paragraphs, none of them follows the original edition in all its aspects, if only because the marbled leaf is reproduced in black and white in all three of them.

2. See my "Laurence Sterne, the Marbled Page, and the Use Of Accidents," *Word & Image*, 1 (1985), 279–87. Also Alain Bony, "La Couture et le gond: La page marbrée dans *Tristram Shandy*," *Études Anglaises*, 37 (1984), 14–27; Susan Otis Thompson, "*Tristram Shandy*: The Marbled Leaf," *Library*, 28 (1973), 160–61; W. G. Day, "*Tristram Shandy*: The Marbled Leaf," *Library*, 27 (1972), 143–45; Horst Meyer, "Das Geheimnis der marmorierten Seite oder Tristram Shandys typographische Extravaganzen," *Börsenblatt für den Deutschen Buchhandel*, 21 (1986), 130–34. See also Roger Moss's interesting "Sterne's Punctuation," *Eighteenth-Centuries Studies*, 15 (1981–82), 179–200; and Max Nänny, "Similarity and Contiguity in *Tristram Shandy*," *English Studies*, 60 (1977), 422–35. An equally curious case could be the work of Julius Caesar Ibbetson (1759–1817), a painter, whose *An Accidence, or Gamut, of Painting in Oil and Watercolours*, "Printed for the author, by Darton and Harvey" in 1803 (a second edition appeared in 1828) has a highly unusual frontispiece: a circular fully finished original oil painting of a mountain landscape with villa, trees, and river, 4.25 inch in diameter, set in an aquatint frame.

3. As Kenneth Monkman puts it (in the 1978 Florida edition of *Tristram Shandy*, p. 929) in his commentary on the fact that in the second edition of volume 5 the catchword "CHAP." is omitted in ten out of eleven cases:

The landlady came up, looking—looking like this—

" What are you a hollering and a bellaring for here, young man? "
says she.

FIGURE 1

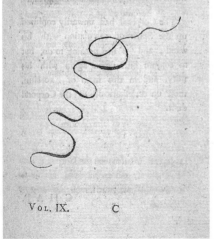

[17]

Nothing, Trim——said my uncle
Toby, mufing——

Whilft a man is free—cried the Corporal, giving a flourifh with his ftick
thus——

Vol. IX.   C

FIGURE 2

36

Textus de Ecclefiâ Roffenfi, per Ernul-
fum Epifcopum.

C A P. XXV.

EXCOMMUNICATIO.

EX auctoritate Dei omnipotentis, Pa-
tris, et Filij, et Spiritus Sancti, et
fanctorum canonum, fanctæque et inte-
meratæ Virginis Dei genetricis Mariæ,

As the genuinenefs of the confultation of the *Sorbonne* upon the queftion of baptifm, was doubted
by fome, and denied by others,——'twas thought
proper to print the original of this excommunication; for the copy of which Mr. *Shandy* returns
thanks to the chapter clerk of the dean and chapter
of *Rochefter*.

Atque

FIGURE 3

37

C H A P. XI.

" **B** Y the authority of God Almighty,
" the Father, Son, and Holy Ghoft,
" and of the holy canons, and of the un-
" defiled Virgin *Mary*, mother and patro-
" nefs of our Saviour." I think there is
no neceffity, quoth Dr. *Slop*, dropping the
paper down to his knee, and addreffing
himfelf to my father,——'as you have read
it over, Sir, fo lately, to read it aloud;—
and as Captain *Shandy* feems to have no
great inclination to hear it,——I may as
well read it to myfelf. That's contrary to
treaty, replied my father,——befides, there
is fomething fo whimfical, efpecially in
the latter part of it, I fhould grieve to
lofe the pleafure of a fecond reading. Dr.
Slop did not altogether like it, — but my
uncle *Toby* offering at that inftant to give

C 3   over

FIGURE 3

It is a terrible misfortune for this fame
book of mine, but more fo to the Re-
publick of Letters ; — fo that my own
is quite fwallowed up in the confidera-
tion of it,—that this felf-fame vile pruriency for frefh adventures in all things, has
has got fo ftrongly into our habit and
humours,—and fo wholly intent are we
upon fatisfying the impatience of our
concupifcence that way,—that nothing
but

powers of the midwives, by determining, That
tho' no part of the child's body fhould appear,——
that baptifm fhall, neverthelefs, be adminiftered to
it by injection,—*par le moyen d' une petite Canille.*—
Anglicè *a fquirt.*—'Tis very ftrange that St. *Thomas Aquinas,* who had fo good a mechanical head,
both for tying and untying the knots of fchool divinity,—fhould, after fo much pains beftowed upon
this,—give up the point at laft, as a fecond *La chofe
impoffible,*—" Infantes in maternis uteris exiftentes
(quoth St. *Thomas*) baptizari poffunt *nullo modo.*"—
O *Thomas ! Thomas !*

5   If

'but the grofs and more carnal parts of a
compofition will go down:—The fubtle
hints and fly communications of fcience
fly off, like fpirits, upwards ;——the
heavy moral efcapes downwards ; and
both the one and the other are as much
loft to the world, as if they were ftill left
in the bottom of the ink-horn.

I wifh the male-reader has not pafs'd
by many a one, as quaint and curious as
this one, in which the female-reader has
been detected. I wifh it may have its
effects;—and that all good people, both
male and female, from her example, may
be taught to think as well as read.

I 3   M e-

If the reader has the curiofity to fee the queftion
upon baptifm, *by injection,* as prefented to the Doctors of the *Sorbonne,*—with their confultation there-
upon, it is as follows.

FIGURE 4

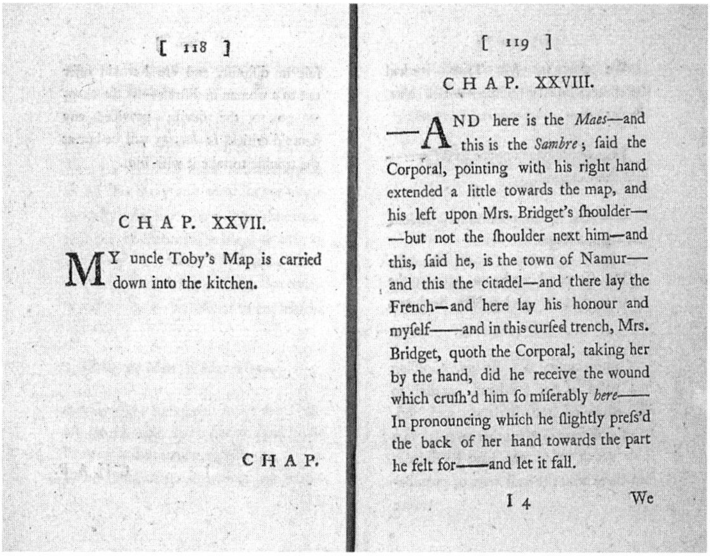

CHAP. XXVII.

M Y uncle Toby's Map is carried down into the kitchen.

CHAP.

CHAP. XXVIII.

A ND here is the *Maes*—and this is the *Sambre*; said the Corporal, pointing with his right hand extended a little towards the map, and his left upon Mrs. Bridget's shoulder——but not the shoulder next him—and this, said he, is the town of Namur—and this the citadel—and there lay the French—and here lay his honour and myself——and in this cursed trench, Mrs. Bridget, quoth the Corporal, taking her by the hand, did he receive the wound which crush'd him so miserably *here*——In pronouncing which he slightly press'd the back of her hand towards the part he felt for——and let it fall.

I 4

We

FIGURE 5

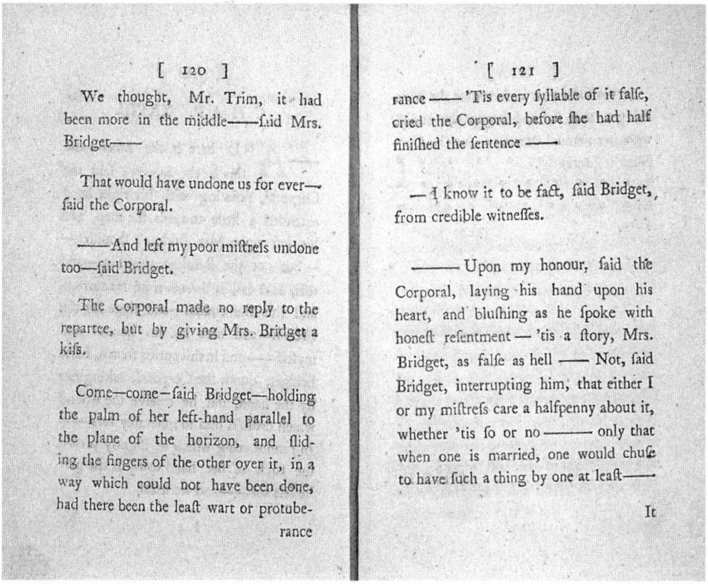

We thought, Mr. Trim, it had been more in the middle——said Mrs. Bridget——

That would have undone us for ever——said the Corporal.

——And left my poor mistress undone too—said Bridget.

The Corporal made no reply to the repartee, but by giving Mrs. Bridget a kiss.

Come—come—said Bridget—holding the palm of her left-hand parallel to the plane of the horizon, and sliding the fingers of the other over it, in a way which could not have been done, had there been the least wart or protuberance

rance ——'Tis every syllable of it false, cried the Corporal, before she had half finished the sentence ——

—— I know it to be fact, said Bridget, from credible witnesses.

—— Upon my honour, said the Corporal, laying his hand upon his heart, and blushing as he spoke with honest resentment — 'tis a story, Mrs. Bridget, as false as hell —— Not, said Bridget, interrupting him; that either I or my mistress care a halfpenny about it, whether 'tis so or no—— only that when one is married, one would chuse to have such a thing by one at least——

It

FIGURE 6

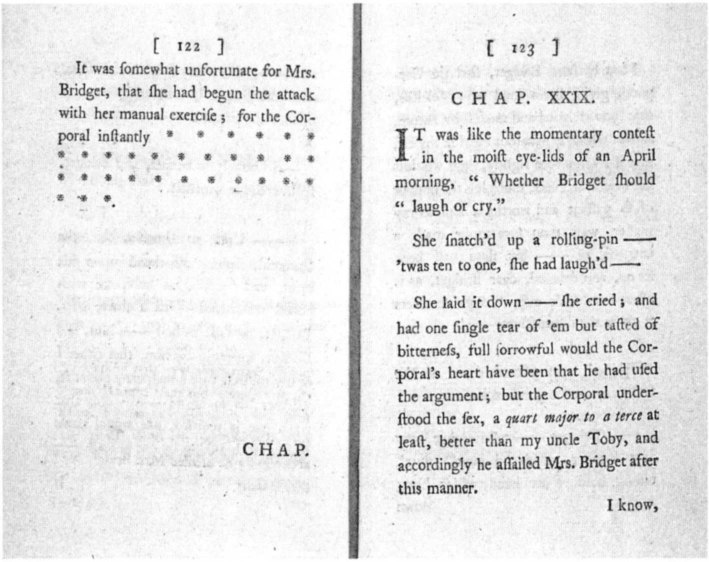

It was somewhat unfortunate for Mrs.
Bridget, that she had begun the attack
with her manual exercise; for the Corporal instantly * * * * * *
* * * * * * * * *
* * * * * * * * *
* * *.

CHAP.

CHAP. XXIX.

IT was like the momentary contest
in the moist eye-lids of an April
morning, " Whether Bridget should
" laugh or cry."

She snatch'd up a rolling-pin ——
'twas ten to one, she had laugh'd ——

She laid it down —— she cried; and
had one single tear of 'em but tasted of
bitterness, full sorrowful would the Corporal's heart have been that he had used
the argument; but the Corporal understood the sex, a *quart major to a terce* at
least, better than my uncle Toby, and
accordingly he assailed Mrs. Bridget after
this manner.

I know,

FIGURE 7

The decision to remove them certainly improves the look of the printed page, but was contrary to contemporary practice, and "CHAP." reasserts itself in volumes 7 and 8, and consistently throughout volume 9, in which, probably to spin out Sterne's text, each chapter begins on a new page and so calls for a

catchword

PART III

Language of the Body

Tristram Shandy and
the Wound of Language

ROSS KING

◆　◆　◆

D URING THE EIGHTEENTH CENTURY, philosophy combines
with physiology in such a way that, for some philosophers,
all human faculties are traced back to their origins in sensation.
As a result, mental experience is often contextualized by writers—
by novelists as well as philosophers—within the sensory networks
of the physical body.[1] If the cult of sensibility and corollaries like
sentimental fiction mark this turn,[2] so also do aesthetic theory and
the "aestheticization" of politics and ethics after 1688.[3] However,
perhaps the exemplary literary genre in the first decades of the
century, satire, maintains a more historically sustained preoccupation with the body: From Rabelais and Cervantes to Swift and
Sterne, somatic space, often filthy or deformed, represents a prof-
itable site of a satirical humor.[4] The nature of the preoccupations
with the gross materiality of the flesh differs within the genre, of
course, with Swift generally singled out as the writer whose "hatred
and horror of physiological degradation," as Henri Fluchère puts
it, "have never been surpassed."[5] Swift's hatred and horror of the
body—notably the female body—has been identified as part of a

more specific satire in the "scatological poems" on the degenerate woman who becomes an admonitory emblem of a putatively feminized and capitalized culture.[6] The body in this case becomes the locus of a "broader concern with the fate of writing in an effeminate, modern culture where, as Swift conceives it, not even satire can redeem."[7]

By contrast with Swift's bitterly misogynistic repulsion, Sterne seems positively indulgent about the body. According to Fluchère, physiological themes in *Tristram Shandy* are "in an entirely different spirit" from those in Swift: "Man's subjection to his organic functions excites in him neither anger nor disgust. On the contrary, to evoke them helps his comic intention, as if the only way of overthrowing their tyranny was to assign them a comic function."[8] In this light it seems significant that for Sterne, unlike for Swift, male bodies become the principle focus of interest; yet if they are not so degenerated as Swift's female monsters, these male bodies are nonetheless typically disfigured or diseased. Indeed the scarred or diseased body is so ubiquitous in *Tristram Shandy* that, despite the novel's humor, readers may be forgiven for dwelling more on infirm and suffering figures than on Sterne's buffers of mirth. The body certainly appears much less salubrious here than in *A Sentimental Journey,* where it becomes the site of blushes, touches, dilating vessels, pulsating arteries, vibrating nerves, and floods of tears. Bodies in *Tristram Shandy,* on the other hand, are invariably partial or deficient, and images of diseased flesh recur throughout the text: from the consumptive Tristram with his "vile cough," to Walter's metaphor of the distempered body of the state, to the catalog of "colds, coughs, claps, tooth-aches, fevers, stranguries, sciaticas, swellings, and sore-eyes" which begins volume 8, to the dying Le Fever whose very name itself inscribes illness.[9] Such debilitations through disease, often associated with sexual wounds and later recounted in *Journal to Eliza* through the prolific symptoms of the morbid body, correspond across the disintegrating flesh with even more pronounced physical injuries—wounds and disfigurements sustained, for example, in battles or accidents.

In the dedication to William Pitt in the second edition of the first two volumes of the text, Sterne raises the specter of his own diseased body and reverts to an image that will be deployed throughout the text at large, that of the infirm or disabled body which seeks palliation through the powers of language. The novel was written, he claims, as part of a "constant endeavour to fence against the infirmities of ill health"; and he hopes its apotropaic power will now similarly beguile Pitt "of one moment's pain" (*TS*, 1.Dedication.iii). Suffering from tuberculosis, and perhaps also from syphilis,[10] he appears to regard language and the act of writing as in part the obviation of mortality and physical misfortune. Linguistic procedures of compensation form a general plot in the text as a whole, which exhibits a continual and repetitive movement from loss, interruption, or accident (often associated with the mutilation or disfigurement of the body, frequently of a sexual nature) to a restoration pursued through linguistic media.

This procedure of textual compensation for bodily loss testifies to a specific view of the powers and uses of language. Because of Walter's conviction that *nomen est omen,* proper names like "Dinah" or "Trismegistus" are not in his view simply inert markers or static descriptions of extralinguistic reality. Rather, the denominative act determines or constitutes reality, acting performatively on "characters and conduct" (*TS*, 1.19.58). And, critically for Walter, in so doing the act of naming possesses the power to compensate physical loss and supplement deficiencies—in particular those which, as in the case of Susannah's negligence with Tristram at the window, are associated with the loss of masculine proficiency and often reveal the correspondence Jonathan Lamb points to between "women and wounds" in the text.[11] Yet Walter's denominative acts and other verbalizations in the face of physical calamity and loss are not so much evasions of a ruinous life, as Lamb suggests,[12] rather attempts at a textual recuperation of the body, a reconstitution of masculine virility through the therapeutic power of the word.

In what follows I shall examine some of the text's performative linguistic events in order to argue that in the context of this recuperative movement the body in Sterne is not merely a site of comic opportunity but rather a privileged, though vulnerable, location of patriarchal power. As this site of power degenerates through wounds and disease, compensation offers itself in the form of a series of textual prostheses. Through the performance of the speaking or writing body, as in the case of the *Tristrapaedia* or Tristram's intended name, the body is transformed into text as language attempts to supplement or repair physical infirmities and deficiencies. Yet in *Tristram Shandy* such techniques of compensation inevitably fail, for bodily impuissance is not repaired by language but reduplicated in it, as becomes apparent from the many cases of linguistic invirility—those moments in the text when language, like the impaired body, fails to perform. This failure of the performative I shall try to set in a linguistic context which will succeed from local issues of influence—whether, that is, Sterne's concept of the sign is Lockeian or Hartleian[13]—to encompass some broader questions broached by the text regarding the nature and employment of representation. In conclusion I will suggest how these questions can be made contiguous with a reading of the text as a unique mode of political satire.

Why the wounded body should seek compensation through performative language has been suggested by Shoshana Felman, who argues that the speech act by its very nature—as *both* speech *and* act—interweaves language and body, pointing to the indissoluble relations between the linguistic and the physical.[14] Such overlap is emphasized in several of Corporal Trim's rhetorical performances, speeches intended to affect or raise passions in their listeners: his delivery of Yorick's sermon on conscience, for example, where proper articulation through the body, including a specific posture and disposition of the limbs, is intended to effect "the true persuasive angle of incidence" (*TS,* 2.17.140). Or when he learns of Bobby Shandy's death he again produces a mixed discourse of words and actions:

> "Are we not here now;"—continued the corporal, "and are we not"—(dropping his hat plumb upon the ground—and pausing, before he pronounced the word)—"gone! in a moment?" The descent of the hat was as if a heavy lump of clay had been kneaded into the crown of it.—Nothing could have

expressed the sentiment of mortality, of which it was the type and fore-runner, like it. (5.7.432)

Like Walter's following speech—the abstract of Socrates' oration—Trim's forms part of the text's rhetoric of consolation, other examples of which include Yorick's epitaph and his funeral sermon for Le Fever: rhetorical performances designed to comfort or palliate the body's ultimate loss in death. More typically the performance of the speaker is intended to supplement slightly less drastic losses, normally the deficiencies or infirmities of the body. A common feature of many of the text's performative utterances is their relationship to the diseased or, more often, the injured body, typically masculine. Such, for example, is the case with Ernulfus's curse, a sort of verbal charm made available to Dr. Slop after he wounds himself with a pen knife (*TS*, 3.10.199–200). The execution of the curse in fact serves a double function in relation to the body. Like other linguistic processes of compensation, it alleviates pain or anxiety, giving vent, as Walter explains, to the sufferer's stirring humors; but it also in turn inflicts physical suffering on both the enunciated subject and sensitive listeners like the Shandy brothers: " 'May he be cursed in his reins,' " reads Slop, " 'and in his groin,' (God in heaven forbid, quoth my Uncle Toby)—'in his thighs, in his genitals,' (my father shook his head) 'and in his hips, and in his knees, his legs, and feet, and toe-nails' " (*TS*, 3.11.209). Language possesses the power to wound as well as to heal; but most important, in either case it appears to hold the power to *act,* to perform material effects on the body under certain prescribed conditions (Walter insists, for instance, that the curse must be read aloud).

A much more important source of linguistic compensation, for Walter at least, is Tristram's intended name, Trismegistus. After his son's nose has been crushed flat at birth by Dr. Slop's "vile instruments" (*TS*, 3.27.253), Walter foresees a restitution of the family fortunes through another instrument, namely language, or more specifically through a name whose "magic bias" will act as a countervailing power to the obstetrical forceps (*TS*, 4.8.334). Had the child "arrived safe in the world, unmartyr'd in that precious part of him," Walter would not be so adamant in his theory regarding the formative influence of Christian names: "But alas! . . . as the greatest evil has befallen him—I must counteract and undo it with the greatest good" (*TS*, 4.8.334). The wound to Tristram's body, and by extension the blow to the House of Shandy, may therefore be mitigated, Walter believes, by the imposition of a single word.

This rhetoric of compensation bears similarities with ancient convictions regarding the therapeutic word over the ailing physical body, a faith whose history stretched from pre-Hippocratic medicine's techniques of the charm or conjuration (*epôdê*) and other curative words to the "talking cure" of Freudian psychotherapy.[15] As Roy Porter has observed in a study of the rhetoric of quackery in the eighteenth century, it is no accident that Apollo is the god of eloquence and poetry as well as medicine, since "language has ever been crucial to the profession and practice of medicine."[16] For Toby as much as for Walter, the word holds this promise of an extenuation of physical misfortune. From the loss sustained at the siege of Namur—the wound in his groin—Toby moves toward linguistic compensation, for his recovery depends upon his being able "to talk upon" his injury (*TS*, 2.3.101), to explicate his story for curious visitors. Restoration of the body in this case requires the offices of language. This story will become a kind of logotherapy, a verbal or textual prosthesis for the wounded body whose corrupt or damaged matter is transformed into words.

Yet palliation through language becomes problematic and uncertain as linguistic impotence frequently accompanies or matches physical impotence. Writing of attempts by Swift and Defoe to transcend corporeality through language, Carol Houlihan Flynn argues that if in order to escape matter "the writer turns the struggle with the material itself into text, that text becomes matter that can turn corrupt, and even turn against its maker."[17] In *Tristram Shandy* the problem of corporeality similarly becomes one of textuality. Far from being an elixir for injury or disfigurement, language often obstructs the cure, renders it problematic, or else remains altogether incapable of performing the task. Failure and ill consequences, for instance, attend Yorick's epitaph. In the case of the parson's death, caused by a logomachy, bodily loss is not reflected or compassed by the consoling inscription, rather by the *absence* of words: the "Alas, poor YORICK!" engraved on marble and repeated by passersby collapses into the black and silent abyss of the blank page. Yorick's profusions of language—the "multitude of small book-debts" (*TS*, 1.12.30)—contract into three words on the marble slab, and these in turn finally revert to the linguistic void of death which words both caused and are meant to alleviate.

It is Walter Shandy, however, who most conspicuously employs language to shape reality and redress physical loss—and it is Walter, too, who is most conspicuously disappointed. Language fails his purposes in the case of the textually fragmentary *Tristrapaedia* which casts back, mirror-like, the shards of the fragmented and incomplete masculinity it was intended to repair (*TS*, 5.26.458). Or again, prior to this particular failure of textual equiponderance, his confidence in the abilities of denominative language to restore loss has already been undermined by the disappointing conclusion of his hobbyhorsical obsession with names. Like most other performative events in the play, the christening of Trismegistus Shandy goes awry, in this case for want of Walter's breeches: a symbolic unmanning of the father whose place is assumed by Susannah, the female maid, a "leaky vessel" who fragments or "scatters" the letters of the chosen name (*TS*, 4.14.344). In the botched ceremony Tristram accidentally receives the unheroic name for which Walter entertains his unconquerable aversion. Like his nose, and later his penis, Tristram's name is drastically abbreviated and becomes yet another signifier of retrenched masculinity. In such cases the word proves as fragile and as susceptible to loss as the body it seeks to reconstitute, and the failure and debility of the performative duplicate the failure and debility of the body.

The performance of language is at issue in the text as pervasively and intriguingly as the performance of the body. Perhaps more than any other fictional work of the eighteenth century, *Tristram Shandy* explores the conditions for the successful performance of conventional acts or procedures, specifically acts or utterance and their contextual surroundings. This should not be surprising, perhaps, given Philippe Lejeune's assertion that the identity of autobiography is contractual, grounded in speech acts like the promise.[18] Thus when Fluchère observes that physiological acts like procreation, pregnancy, heredity, and birth occupy so large a part of Sterne's text,[19] we must note that these acts are at once also linguistic insofar as they are accompanied by conventions and procedures enacted through language. In Sterne's mock-autobiographical text, exemplary models of the performative like baptisms or christenings are set into play and extensively analyzed, first in a long footnote drawing on deliberations at the Sorbonne in 1733; and then, after Tristram's unsuccessful christening, at the visitation dinner presided over by Didius, the Canon lawyer who will advise whether or not Tristram may be legally rebaptized. At this latter venue Didius and Kysarcius debate the subtle conditions under which a priest's speech act over the font is either valid or invalid, depending, for instance, on his intentions and his proficiency in Latin (*TS*, 4.29.388ff). Or to cite another conspicuous example of the text's ironic play with speech acts, at the beginning of volume 5 Tristram makes his famous vow not to plagiarize:

> By the great God of day, said I, looking towards the sun, and thrusting my arm out of the forewindow of the chaise, as I made by now, "I will lock up my study door the moment I get home, and throw the key of it ninety feet below the surface of the earth, into the draw-well at the back of my house." (*TS*, 5.1.407)

As critics have long noted, the form of his vow is plagiarized (like the preceding dedication of the volume to Lord Spencer) from the preface to Robert Burton's much-pillaged *Anatomy of Melancholy* (1621), a treatise which, like Tristram's, catalogs the morbidities of body and mind. By incorporating a fragment from Burton into his text, Tristram violates his vow in the very act of making it, and the covenant made with the reader is thereby invalidated. The vow's compromised status is then emphasized several paragraphs later when with self-conscious irony he incorporates into his text snippets from a copious selection of previous authors—Zoroaster, St. John Chrysostom, Moses, Plato, Aristotle, and Horace.

As these examples should indicate, the speech act is prone to error, accident, and abuse. The first thing to remember about performances, J. L. Austin states at the beginning of his discussion of the subject, "is that, since in uttering our performatives we are undoubtedly in a sound enough sense 'performing actions,' then, as actions, these will be subject to certain whole dimensions of unsatisfactoriness."[20] Among many other things, *Tristram Shandy* concerns those performative events which miscarry or fail. Almost all of the speech acts in the text—vows, christenings, curses, contracts—are subject to some sort of "unsatisfactoriness" which reveals the ineffectuality of the speaker, of the performative word, or perhaps more broadly, of the empowering institutions themselves. If the speech act often represents the root of tragedy, as for instance in *Hamlet* or *Oedipus Rex*,[21] its failure, like the failure of the body, becomes among other things a source of Sterne's humor and satire.

The performance and nonperformance of both body and language bear, like most acts in *Tristram Shandy,* conspicuously sexual resonances. According to Felman, the link between body and text in the performative is inevitably sexual inasmuch as the performance is "modelled on the metaphorics of the 'performance' of the sexual act."[22] Indeed performance, whether physical or linguistic, is, according to Freud, always related to its prototype in *sexual* performance. According to Lacan, Freud's theory of sexuality

> consists in noting that everything having to do with sex is always a failure. It is the basis and the principle of the very idea of fiasco. Failure (misfire) itself can be defined as what is sexual in every human act. That is why there are so many *actes manqués.* Freud indicated perfectly clearly that an *acte manqué* always has to do with sex. The *acte manqué par excellence* is precisely the sexual act.[23]

In *Tristram Shandy* the *acte manqué,* linguistic or sexual, specifically involves the deflation or abridgment of the masculine power which language is to repair. Linguistic acts are closely bound up with patriarchy: As should be clear by now, many of the textual acts function as compensation for the loss or impairment of peculiarly sexual abilities linked with the masculine prerogative. To cite one of the most obvious examples, after his inadvertent circumcision inflicted by the descent of the sash-window and then the inept ministrations of Dr. Slop, Tristram supplements his father's *Tristra-paedia*—itself intended by Walter to extenuate the loss of the masculine trinity of Tristram's "geniture, nose, and name" (*TS,* 5.16.455)—with an admonitory "chapter upon sash-windows" (*TS,* 5.26.458), as if this textual interpolation will redress his own genital dismemberment. The performative's attempt to shore up the masculine order also appears in the marriage settlement, a contract by whose provisions Walter will "grant, covenant, condescend, consent, conclude, bargain, and fully agree" to Elizabeth's journey to London for her lying in (*TS,* 1.15.43). The plethora of performatives in this instance attempts to bolster a threatened order which, for Walter, refracts political furrows into the familiar Court-Country and female-male oppositions embraced by Augustan Tories.[24] Language vouchsafes the rights of the pregnant body—an affiliation of law and the gestating body already playfully mocked in the earlier avowal that the homunculus is "a BEING guarded and circumscribed with rights" (*TS,* 1.2.3)—but, more important for Walter, it also guards and circumscribes patriarchal rights and hence safeguards the "body national" (*TS,* 1.18.52). The two bodies are, of course, genetically bound to one another, and care of the latter entails control, through legal language, of the former.[25] As a follower of Sir Robert Filmer, Walter regards authority in the body politic as the product of a paternal power originally exercised in the family, that is, by the procreative male body. This argument he develops in the preface to his own patriarchalist document, the *Tristrapaedia,* which assigns the "original of society" to "a man,—a woman—and a bull" (*TS,* 5.31.466)—a trinity whose cogency diminishes somewhat by the end of the novel when suspicions are raised regarding the potency of the Shandy bull.

The connections between the body, performative language, and patriarchal power—or more properly their failed connections—display themselves most clearly in Walter's theory of Christian names. If the hopes Walter invests in a patriarchal symbol like a long nose have been cruelly disappointed at Tristram's nativity, his other hobbyhorse, that appellations govern subjectivity, may be satisfied by the choice of a proper name; hence the resolution to christen his new son Trismegistus. Why this particular name should serve his purposes so well Walter explains to Toby: "This *Trismegistus . . .* was the greatest (*Toby*) of all earthly beings—he was the greatest king—the greatest law-giver—the greatest philosopher—and the greatest priest" (*TS*, 4.11.339). Thus by virtue of his onomastic power, the intended Trismegistus Shandy will encompass those patriarchal roles—ruler, philosopher, priest—the possibilities for which Slop's malfeasant forceps have placed in jeopardy.

But this exemplary model of patriarchal power also comprises more roles than those to which Walter testifies at this point. A putative ancient Egyptian divinity, teacher of mysteries, and scribe of the gods, Hermes Trismegistus is the inventor who gave the world arithmetic, astronomy, geometry, games like draughts and dices, and, to cap it all, letters. The Egyptian equivalent of Prometheus and the supposed source of the *Hermetica,* Trismegistus is cognate with Thoth (or Theuth), memorably described by Socrates in the *Phaedrus* as the inventor of writing who presents his gift to the skeptical phonocentric, King Thamus. As Keir Elam has noted in a different context, he is "a copiously linguistic or semiotic deity," a "deity of texts and their interpretation" ("hermeneutics" derives from his name), one whose powers are specifically graphic rather than oral.[26] Trismegistus's patriarchal status as priest, philosopher, and lawgiver therefore appears to coincide with, perhaps is enabled by, his mythological function as the god of writing—a highly appropriate deity, it would appear, for the scriptomaniac Tristram.

As compensation for physical/sexual loss, Walter's child will therefore receive not just any name but that of the originary bringer of letters; the deity of writing, and by extension the powers of writing and of language, will palliate physical misfortune manifesting itself in impaired masculinity. But with the failure of his christening Tristram becomes a sort of anti-Trismegistus, if we understand Trismegistus not only as the bearer of patriarchal status and authority (as Walter sees him) but also as the advocate of a system of signification based on presence and plenitude (as he is in the *Phaedrus*), a system in which no difference exists between the written word of the text and the living speech of the body. For

Socrates' Thoth, the written word carries decipherable meaning, faithfully inscribing knowledge that will "make the Egyptians wiser and improve their memory."[27] However, Sterne's text continually broaches the relations between Trismegistus's gift of letters and his other productions, more specifically the vexed association (frequently observed in empirical philosophy) of writing with knowledge. In such moments Tristram resembles King Thamus, the mythological antagonist of his would-be namesake. The nature of Thamus's pessimistic attitude toward Thoth's gift is pointed out in *The Divine Legation of Moses Demonstrated* (1737–41), the gargantuan treatise of Sterne's uneasy patron (and Tristram's proposed tutor), the polemical divine William Warburton (1698–1779).[28] In a discussion of the primal scene of writing recounted in the *Phaedrus,* Warburton observes that Thamus recognizes how, if adopted, letters will call attention "away from THINGS" and direct it instead to "exterior and arbitrary SIGNS, which would prove the greatest hindrance to the progress of knowledge."[29] Warburton's Thamus claims that, with the advent of writing, things are decanted into the unreliable vessel of language. Both Tristram and Thamus are therefore aware of the double nature of the inscription, the fact that, as an arbitrary sign, as a displacement of the originary thing, it does not merely give, as Thoth argues, but also takes away— and so the means of language to palliate loss are always vexed by its privative qualities.[30]

Something of the nature of these privative qualities becomes clear in Toby's linguistic predicament. As Toby discovers in the course of his talking cure, not just any language will do. The words he pronounces in the sickroom are not sufficient to effect a cure, and in the end they even aggravate his wound. The story of his wounding in the siege is confused and impeded, and palliation frustrated, because of a linguistic plight often identified by philosophical nominalism as a root of epistemological error. According to Tristram, his uncle's "perplexities . . . arose out of the almost insurmountable difficulties he found in telling his story intelligibly, and giving such clear ideas of the differences and distinctions between the scarp and counterscarp,—the glacis and covered way,—

the half-moon and ravelin,—as to make his company fully comprehend where and what he was about" (*TS*, 2.1.94).

Toby's autobiographical impulse comes up against a classic problem in epistemology: the contentless sign, the word of "indeterminate . . . sense" or "little meaning" (*TS*, 2.2.100). For Toby's auditors, specialist terms of military fortification like *counterscarp* and *half-moon* remain empty signifiers, devoid of conjunction with any things or "clear ideas" of things. Toby himself is puzzled by these signifiers and often "would get so sadly bewilder'd and set fast amongst them, that frequently he could neither get backwards or forwards to save his life" (*TS*, 2.1.94–95). In such instances language acts not as an agent of cure or "fence against . . . infirmities," but on the contrary as a bearer of bodily "pains and sorrows," duplicating the physical damage inflicted by the stone falling from the parapet in the siege of Namur. Far from finding solace, because he is hemmed in by language and cannot "keep [his] discourse free from obscurity," Toby suffers "sharp paroxisms and exacerbations of his wound," and his life is "put in jeopardy by words" (*TS*, 2.1.94–95; *TS*, 2.2.101). If the physical and linguistic are indissolubly joined, then the nonperformance of language merely reproduces or reflects the nonperformance of the body. Toby's autobiographical lenitive falters and stalls in its textual articulation, the wound in the flesh becoming the wound of language.

As Toby's problems indicate, the difficulty of the misfiring performative in *Tristram Shandy* constitutes part of a more encompassing problem with language during the eighteenth century: a problem with its representational as well as its performative function. Porter argues that the latter function requires the cogency of the former, the curative properties of the word in the medical armamentarium being predicated on a potent "marriage between words and things, names and power."[31] This affiliation of names and power clearly informs Walter's faith in the "magic bias" of words, the extralinguistic performance of the kinetic charm or *epôdê*. The magic bias suggests an organization of the sign according to what Foucault calls "resemblance," the semiotic element by which from the Stoics through the Renaissance the sign, including that elucidated in magic, became transparent, "almost the same thing" as that which is designated, through similitudes like analogy and emulation.[32] But Foucault argues that the fate of the sign in the post-Renaissance period is one of ever decreasing transparency as the "profound kinship" of words and things is dissolved when they are no longer held together by divinely ordained bonds of resemblance or affinity.[33] Thus Porter finds that the traditional association between language and physical cure bears a strain by the eighteenth century, after the Scientific Revolution's "radical distrust of language" insists on the separation of words and things.[34] This gap between words and things or ideas, and hence the untrustworthiness of language, is constantly underscored by philosophers like Hobbes, Locke, and Berkeley, for whom words-without-ideas mark the original sin of empirical inquiry. In an image which strikingly anticipates Toby's situation of being set fast among words, unable to move either forward or backward, Hobbes warns in *Leviathan* (1651) that since

> *truth* consisteth in the right ordering of names in our affirmations, a man that seeketh precise *truth,* had need to remember what every name he uses stands for; and to place it accordingly; or else he will find himselfe entangled in words, as a bird in lime-twiggs; the more he struggles, the more belimed.[35]

Earl Wasserman long ago read Sterne in the context of this sort of Foucauldian epistemic break, finding in his texts the collapse of analogical ordering systems which gave shape and meaning to Renaissance and Augustan literature.[36] In the signifying logic of the Shandy world, meaning is produced not by resemblance or analogy but through systems of difference; it is not immediately present in a word, rather only a function of a relation to another word. The exemplary exposition of this Shandean *différance* is Toby's account of ravelins and half-moons, two of the terms whose distinctions are so difficult to appreciate in Toby's sad explanation: "For when a ravelin, brother, stands before the curtin," he explains to Walter, it is a ravelin; and when a ravelin stands before a bastion, then the ravelin is not a ravelin;—it is a half-moon;—and a half-moon likewise is a half-moon, and no more, so long as it stands before its bastion;—but was it to change place, and get before the curtin—'twould be no longer a half-moon; a half-moon, in that case, is not a half-moon;—'tis no more than a ravelin. (*TS*, 2.12.129)

In this system one word may, depending on its context, present a vast manifold of ideas. Even apparently more commonplace words like *whiskers, nose,* and *fiddlesticks* spill forth cataracts of meaning: The latter, for instance, supposedly pullulates with no less than fourteen thousand senses (*TS*, 9.19.789). For a single word to possess such a superabundance of meaning is really to possess no straightforwardly or universally intelligible meaning at all, and hence the many communicative failures in the Shandy household—those, for example, in the conferences between Toby and Walter or the Widow Wadman, where wild divarications of interpretation turn on the pivot of a single word. In such moments Sterne playfully exhibits the philosophical nightmare of polysemia described by Aristotle, whose *Metaphysics* insists on a linguistic univocity by which the name "has one meaning," a condition necessary for both social intercourse and self-identity. If the meanings of words "were not limited," writes Aristotle, "but one were to say that the word has an infinite number of meanings, obviously reasoning would be impossible; for not to have one meaning is to have no meaning, and if words have no meaning, our reasoning with one another, and indeed with ourselves, has been annihilated."[37]

Because of the loosening of word and thing, Toby's suffering will be relieved only when he escapes the prison house of language, or better yet, its fortress or citadel. Such is the recommendation of Hobbes, who, Thamus-like, criticizes "those men that take their instruction from the authority of books, and not from their own meditation."[38] Using another avian metaphor, he castigates those who "spend time fluttering over their bookes; as birds that entring by the chimney, and finding themselves inclosed in a chamber, flutter at the false light of a glasse window."[39] True knowledge requires the circumvention of misleading words and a concentration on ideas, a point made by Socrates in the *Phaedrus* and also, with startling confidence, by Berkeley in his introduction to *A Treatise Concerning the Principles of Human Knowledge* (1710), which attempts "to get clear of all controversies purely verbal"[40] and concentrate instead on ideas and things.

For Sterne, however, the curtain of words cannot be folded back so easily; on the whole he remains much less sanguine than the philosophers about the capacity of language to fix the identity of ideas or of the ability of language users to extricate themselves from the tangle of words. In true empirical fashion, Toby's solution to his linguistic perplexities is first of all to avoid them altogether through recourse to things themselves, in this case through a putatively more reliable language of physical gesture. The intricacy, ambiguity, and emptiness of a verbal language of ravelins and counterscarps will be supplemented by a single act whereby he inserts a pin into the map of Namur and environs. Concentrating on things instead of words, this nostrum of physical gesture apparently achieves what Toby's spoken words fail to deliver and in so doing frees him from a linguistic "world of sad explanations" (*TS*, 2.1.96). The novel provides many cases of this sort of gestural communication, acts which debar the apparent incongruity between body and text by purporting to transpire outside the impregnable walls of the textual fortress: the digital manipulations Corporal Trim employs to discreetly narrate Tristram's mishap with the sash-window (*TS*, 5.20.453), or the flourish Toby makes with his walking stick in order to explicate the benefits of celibacy (*TS*, 9.4.743). Such acts comprise part of what in his study of *Tristram Shandy* Wolfgang Iser calls a "body semiotics" which proceeds beyond failed verbal communication. "What characterizes all the physical gestures," Iser asserts, "is the fact that they bring about immediate understanding. . . . Body language becomes the medium for successful communication."[41]

The semiotics of the gesturing body is examined several decades before Sterne by Bishop Warburton. In *The Divine Legation of Moses Demonstrated* Warburton describes how, because of the poverty of

language in antiquity, "in the first ages of the world, mutual converse was upheld by a mixed discourse of words and ACTIONS,"
or what he calls "the mode of *speaking by action*."[42] The Scripture
contains many examples of these speaking actions, such as when
the prophet Jeremiah breaks a potter's vessel in the sight of the
people. By such actions, Warburton claims, "the prophets in-
structed the people in the will of God, and conversed with them
in signs."[43] However, as Ian Balfour has pointed out, Warburton
"fails to recognize the way that prophetic words speak louder than
actions, since the nature of the analogy between action and its
allegorical referent must be spelled out by God's words to the
prophet."[44] Thus when Jeremiah breaks the potter's vessel before
his people, this physical act is not sufficient in itself, for the Lord
also commands the prophet to say on his behalf: "Even so will I
break this people and this city, as *one* breaks a potter's vessel, that
cannot be made whole again."[45]

Sterne recognizes how a bodily semiotics of pure action raises
difficulties which both Warburton and Iser fail to acknowledge. In
Toby's amendment of his talking cure, the motions of the body
perhaps appear, at first, to compensate for the deficiencies of language. These motions comprise the "combined looks of simple
subtlety" which in *A Sentimental Journey* Yorick compares favorably
with "all the languages of Babel" (*SJ,* 74). Yet Sterne seems less
optimistic about body semiotics than the account by Iser implies,
for all attempts to avoid the equivocations of language, to divest
oneself of words and resort to mute physical gestures, inevitably
lead to the reinscription of language. In *A Sentimental Journey* Yorick
discovers that in order to find points of social, emotional, or sexual
contact he must translate "the several turns of looks and limbs,
with all their inflections and delineations, into plain words" (p. 77).
The body does not speak for itself but requires translation and
interpretation, for gesture can work itself out only through writing
and orality. If understanding is to ensue, the language of gesture
and the physiology of the nervous system which activates it must
be recontextualized in "plain words." Further, the semiotics of the
body are as prone to confusion and equivocation as linguistic communication—as Yorick discovers, for instance, when he mistakes

the crimson tint of sunlight on the face of the fille de chambre for an amorous blush (p. 121).

Initially troubled by the equivocations of language, Toby's attempts to "comprehend where and what he was about," to capture and express the presence and identity lost at Namur, are finally conducted not through physical gestures but rather specifically linguistic codes or media. The wordless inscription of presence on the map proves inadequate or incomplete because, however satisfactory at first, ultimately it redoubles his desire for knowledge, a desire which, "like the thirst of riches, increases ever with the acquisition" of its object (*TS*, 2.3.102). This self-consuming supplement to knowledge must itself be supplemented with other maps, plans, and, significantly, with the volumes of military writers like Gobesius, Ramelli, and Cataneo. Predictably, these texts with which he attempts to satisfy his desire form a *regressus ad infinitum:* they lead him into bafflingly elusive terrain, down a "thorny and bewilder'd track" and into an "intricate . . . labyrinth" (*TS*, 2.3.103) where truth forever recedes before its representations. Finally articulated three-dimensionally as battlefield simulacra, they rehearse but never explain his loss, constituting, like all words and signs, only a privative means of understanding. Toby's hobbyhorse in fact becomes a paradigm of all signification and narrative, a kind of Lacanian topology of castration: his experience of lack, the wound in his groin, leads him into a potentially infinite procession whereby books, maps, and scale models form a prosthetic chain of signifiers along which he proceeds in a dialectic of desire and lack, seeking to fill the inexpressible gap in his identity breached at Namur.

But if language, itself a series of gaps, cannot redress gaps in the physical, neither can the body be separated from language through recourse to a mode of "speaking by action," the language of countenance, movement, or gesture posited by Warburton. As Austin observes of the dream of such mute motions, the "vague and comforting idea" exists that "doing an action must come down to the making of physical movements with parts of the body; but this is about as true as saying that something must, in the last analysis, come down to making movements of the tongue."[46] Or as Felman succinctly puts it: "There is no act without linguistic inscription."[47] The movements of the limbs or expressions of the face are therefore inseparable from the movements of the tongue or pen; and, as Sterne shows, the product of each is as susceptible to damage and loss as the other.

In certain respects Sterne's satires on both language and the body are coterminous with a more general satire on eighteenth-century political society. By comparison with the bitter party invectives of the Augustans, however, the political satire in *Tristram Shandy* may seem very mild, and indeed it is rarely if ever overestimated. Sterne's own abbreviated political career and departure from the *York Gazeteer,* in which he satirized Tory opponents in 1741–42, makes appealing evidence in the case for the reining in of his satirical powers, as does the withdrawal from circulation of a later satire, *A Political Romance* (1759), and his claim to his daughter in 1767 that he withdrew from satire and journalism because he was not a "party-man . . . and detested such dirty work: thinking it beneath me" (Letters, 4). On the balance of such evidence Carol Kay states that in *Tristram Shandy* he "contrived an alternative, nonsatiric, political aesthetic, a politics of play that made differences of opinion fun."[48] She argues, for example, that the textual fragments interpolated throughout the novel, many of which I have discussed as performative events, underscore Sterne's retreat from the vitriol of party politics after 1742 insofar as they are not components of satire but rather form a depoliticized discourse: Sterne, the former hired pen and Whig polemicist, now makes his writing "innocent" by "invoking forms of writing that usually function as authoritative social acts and converting them into play."[49] A fragment such as Yorick's sermon, for instance, "intended to be delivered by a member of the state church entrusted with the education of the nation, is here delivered by a servant in a parlor."[50]

Yet to convert authoritative patriarchal discourse into play, and thereby to deprive it of all perlocutionary force, in itself represents a drastically political act and says much about the state of the authoritative body whose appendage that discourse is. If words require for their perlocutionary force an observance or circumscription of conventions and procedures, their failure adumbrates a breakdown in those institutions which give it existence, and which, as Kay notes, are notably political, associated with both Church and State. The performative bears an explicit political identity in eighteenth-century discourse, for after 1688–89 it becomes a form of social practice paradigmatic of new economic and political relationships. By the end of the seventeenth century, commerce is based increasingly on credit and contract, constituting more than anything else, as Joyce Oldham Appleby points out, "a system of promises."[51] Further, and more important for the world of *Tristram Shandy,* Carole Pateman has argued that, with the end of the Stuart monarchy, performatives like the promise and the contract underwrite Whig-liberal theories of political subjectivity, and that in practice this subjectivity is constructed through oaths of obedience and abjuration, putatively acts of obligation freely assumed and unambiguously asserted.[52] Post-1688 political society is therefore held together in part by a series of performative events, the prototype for which is the "Original Contract between king and people" asserted by the Convention Parliament.[53] In his portrayal of a language bereft of all perlocutionary force, however, Sterne parodies the tenets and assumptions of this Whig contractarianism inaugurated theoretically in Locke's *Two Treatises of Government* (1690) and practically by the Convention Parliament. In *Tristram Shandy* the inability to force words into action thus bears political as well as linguistic and sexual implications.

Notes

1. The links between physiology and epistemology during the Enlightenment have generated much scholarship. See, for example, G. S. Rousseau, "Nerves, Spirits, and Fibres: Towards Defining the Origins of Sensibility," in *Studies in the Eighteenth Century* (Toronto: University of Toronto Press, 1966), 137–57; Karl Figlio, "Theories of Perception and the Physiology of Mind in the Late Eighteenth Century," *History of Science* 12 (1975): 177–212; and Christopher Lawrence, "The Nervous System and Society in the Scottish Enlightenment," in *Natural Order: Historical Studies of Scientific Culture,*

ed. Barry Barnes and Steven Shapin (Beverley Hills and London: Sage Publications, 1979), 19–40.

2. See John A. Dussinger, "The Sensorium of the World in 'A Sentimental Journey,' " *Ariel* 13 (1982): 3–16; John Mullan, "Hypochondria and Hysteria: Sensibility and the Physicians," *ECS* 35 (1984): 141–74; and Ann Jessie Van Sant, *Eighteenth-Century Sensibility and the Novel: The Senses in Social Context* (Cambridge: Cambridge University Press, 1993).

3. See Howard Caygill, *Art of Judgement* (Oxford: Basil Blackwell, 1989), 38–102; and Terry Eagleton, *The Ideology of the Aesthetic* (Oxford: Basil Blackwell, 1990), 13–69.

4. For a discussion of the role of the body in the satirical tradition, see John R. Clark, *The Modern Satiric Grotesque and Its Traditions* (Lexington: University Press of Kentucky, 1991), 116–30.

5. *Laurence Sterne: From Tristram to Yorick,* trans. Barbara Bray (London: Oxford University Press, 1965), 207. For readings of Swift's satires on the physicality of the body, see Donald Greene, "On Swift's 'Scatological Poems,' " *Sewanee Review* 74 (1967): 672–89; and Thomas B. Gilmore, "The Comedy of Swift's Scatological Poems," *PMLA* 91 (1976): 33–43.

6. See Susan Gubar, "The Female Monster in Augustan Satire," *Signs* 3 (1977): 380–94; Terry J. Castle, "Why the Houyhnhnms Don't Write: Swift, Satire and the Fear of the Text," *Essays in Literature* 7 (1980): 31–44; Ellen Pollak, *The Poetics of Sexual Myth: Gender and Ideology in the Verse of Swift and Pope* (Chicago: University of Chicago Press, 1990), 88–109.

7. Pollak, 169.

8. Fluchère, 207.

9. *TS,* 7.1.575; 1.18.52–53; 8.3.658; 6.6.499ff.

10. Sterne's most recent biographer, Arthur H. Cash, conjectures that the diagnosis of syphilis described in *Journal to Eliza* may have been, as Sterne himself believed, incorrect. See *Laurence Sterne: The Later Years* (London: Methuen, 1986), 289–91. Cash suggests that the entire constellation of symptoms described in *Journal to Eliza* may be unified under a diagnosis of tuberculosis (p. 290).

11. *Sterne's Fiction and the Double Principle* (Cambridge: Cambridge University Press, 1989), 79.

12. Observing that he "quotes Spenser at Tristram's damaged penis, and paraphrases Locke during the destruction of his nose," Lamb argues that Walter's faith is "relentless in the power of books to recall or invent alternatives to the havoc he would otherwise have to acknowledge" (141–42).

13. For discussions of these questions, see John Traugott, *Tristram Shandy's World: Sterne's Philosophical Rhetoric* (Berkeley: University of California Press, 1954); Helene Moglen, *The Philosophical Irony of Laurence Sterne* (Gainesville: University Presses of Florida, 1975); Howard Anderson, "Associationism and Wit in *Tristram Shandy*," *PQ* 48 (1969): 27–41; and Jonathan Lamb, "Language and Hartleian Associationism in *A Sentimental Journey*," *ECS* 13 (1980): 285–312.

14. See *The Literary Speech Act: Don Juan with J. L. Austin, or Seduction in Two Languages,* trans. Catherine Porter (Ithaca: Cornell University Press, 1983), 92–94.

15. See Pedro Lain Entralgo, *The Therapy of the Word in Classical Antiquity,* trans. L. J. Rather and John M. Sharp (New Haven: Yale University Press, 1970).

16. "The Language of Quackery in England, 1660–1800," in *The Social History of Language,* ed. Peter Burke and Roy Porter (Cambridge: Cambridge University Press, 1987), 73.

17. Flynn, *The Body in Swift and Defoe* (Cambridge: Cambridge University Press, 1990), 219.

18. *Le pacte autobiographique* (Paris: Editions Seiul, 1975).

19. See Fluchère, 208.

20. *How to Do Things with Words,* 2nd ed., J. O. Urmson and Marina Sbisà, eds. (Cambridge, Mass.: Harvard University Press, 1975), 21.

21. See Felman, 95–96; and Myra Gann, "The Performative Status of Verba Offenses in *A Secreto agravio, secreta venganza,*" in *Things Done with Words: Speech Acts in Hispanic Drama,* ed. Elias Rivers (Newark, N.J.: Juan de la Costa, 1986), 39–49.

22. Felman, 108.

23. "Le Symptôme," *Scilicet* 6/7 (1976): 19; quoted in Felman, 110.

24. On these oppositions in eighteenth-century politics, see H. T. Dickinson, *Liberty and Property: Political Ideology in Eighteenth-Century Britain* (London: Weidenfeld and Nicolson, 1977); and Isaac Kramnick, *Bolingbroke and His Circle: The Politics of Nostalgia in the Age of Walpole* (Cambridge, Mass.: Harvard University Press, 1968).

25. For the inequalities of the sexual contract during this period, see two works by Carole Pateman: *The Problem of Political Obligation: A Critique of Liberal Theory* (Oxford: Basil Blackwell, 1985); and *The Sexual Contract* (Cambridge: Polity Press, 1988), 3–4, 55–59.

26. *Shakespeare's Universe of Discourse: Language-Games in the Comedies* (Cambridge: Cambridge University Press, 1984), 151.

27. *Phaedrus,* trans. C. J. Rowe (Warminster, Wilts.: Aris and Phillips, 1986), 123.

28. For Sterne's relations with Warburton, see Cash, 5–8, 52, and 115; and Melvyn New, "Sterne, Warburton, and the Burden of Exuberant Wit," *ECS* 15 (1982): 245–74.

29. *The Divine Legation of Moses Demonstrated on the Principles of a Religious Deist,* 2 vols. (London: 1737–41), 2:154–55.

30. See Paul de Man's observation, regarding a similar problem of textual recuperation in Wordsworth, that since "language is a figure . . . it is indeed not the thing itself but the representation, the picture of the thing. . . . Language, as trope, is always privative." "Autobiography as De-Facement," in *The Rhetoric of Romanticism* (New York: Columbia University Press, 1984), 80.

31. Porter, 73.

32. Michel Foucault, *The Order of Things: An Archaeology of the Human Sciences,* trans. Alan Sheridan (New York: Vintage, 1973), 64. For Foucault's discussion of the sign in Renaissance magic, see p. 33.

33. Foucault, 43.

34. Porter, 73.

35. *Leviathan,* ed. C. B. Macpherson (London: Penguin, 1968), 105.

36. *The Subtler Language: Critical Readings of Neoclassic and Romantic Poems* (Baltimore: Johns Hopkins University Press, 1959), 169–71.

37. *The Works of Aristotle,* ed. W. D. Ross, vol. 8, 2nd. ed. (Oxford: Clarendon Press, 1928), 1006b5–10.

38. Hobbes, 106.

39. Hobbes, 105.

40. *A Treatise Concerning the Principles of Human Knowledge,* ed. G. J. Warnock (LaSalle, Ill.: Open Court, 1986), 61.

41. *Laurence Sterne: Tristram Shandy,* trans. David Henry Wilson (Cambridge: Cambridge University Press, 1988), 45–48. For a similar observation, see Lamb, *Sterne's Fiction and the Double Principle,* 69.

42. Warburton, 2:133, 136.

43. Warburton, 2:134.

44. "The Rhetoric of Romantic Prophecy," Ph.D. dissertation, Yale University, 1985, 127.

45. Jeremiah 19:11.

46. *Philosophical Papers,* 3rd. ed., J. O. Urmson and G. L. Warnock, eds. (Oxford: Oxford University Press, 1979), 178.

47. Felman, 93.

48. *Political Constructions: Defoe, Richardson, and Sterne in Relation to Hobbes, Hume, and Burke* (Ithaca: Cornell University Press, 1988), 203. For Sterne's rather unhappy political involvements, see Arthur H. Cash, *Laurence Sterne: The Early and Middle Years* (London: Methuen, 1975; rpt. London: Routledge, 1992), 87–115.

49. Kay, 210.

50. Ibid.

51. *Economic Thought and Ideology in Seventeenth-Century England* (Princeton: Princeton University Press, 1978), 188.

52. See Pateman, *The Problem of Political Obligation*, 1–36.

53. Quoted in J. P. Kenyon, *Revolution Principles: The Politics of Party, 1689–1720* (Cambridge: Cambridge University Press, 1977), 10.

Consuming Time: Narrative and
Disease in *Tristram Shandy*

CLARK LAWLOR

◆　◆　◆

> TB is a disease of time; it speeds up life, highlights it,
> spiritualizes it. In both English and French,
> consumption "gallops."
> —SUSAN SONTAG, *Illness as Metaphor*

> Time wastes too fast: every letter I trace tells me with
> what rapidity Life follows my pen.
> —LAURENCE STERNE, *Tristram Shandy*
> (9.8.754)

ONE WOULD THINK THAT the subject of time and Sterne,
especially in *Tristram Shandy*, had been entirely exhausted, like
Yorick's broken-winded horse. The second quotation in my epigraph is only too well known to anyone having the least acquaintance with Sterne's writing, dramatizing what has traditionally
been conceived as the futile effort of the Modern to write to the
moment, and enacting the ultimate victory of time over the writer
and therefore over the narrative.[1] Sterne criticism has identified
various types of time at play in *Tristram Shandy*, the most notable
being the psychological Lockean time of the individual who associates randomly within his own mind and, relatedly, the temporal
structure of the entire narrative as it emanates from Tristram's
erratic consciousness.[2] Some attention has even been paid to
Sterne's own physical-personal time and its relation to the periodic
publication of the novel in two-volume installments. Such analyses
have tended to place the novel even further in its own era by

emphasizing the historicity and unfinished nature of the novel, countering Wayne C. Booth's famous formalist argument about its intentionally finished nature.[3] There has even been a certain amount of work on a perspective that has been largely ignored in the plethora of writing on the philosophical and psychological aspects of time in *Tristram Shandy:* Sterne's, Tristram's, Walter's, Yorick's, and even Yorick's horse's disease, consumption.[4]

These bring us to the crucial word *wastes* in the second quotation above, and Sontag's identification of consumption (or tuberculosis as it came to be known) as *the* disease of time in the first. Sontag is really talking about consumption as a Romantic disease, however: Very little research has been done on the "external" cultural status of consumption in the eighteenth century, although "internal" medical histories abound. As I will show, consumption looms large in Sterne's world. The very nature of the disease is a crucial factor in structuring the narrative of *Tristram Shandy.* It is also a determining element in much of his other writing, especially *A Sentimental Journey* and the "Journal to Eliza," although I will not be examining those texts here. Tristram's flight away from Death (by consumption) to the Mediterranean in volume 7 and beyond is a central instance of disease actually triggering the narrative and dictating its time accordingly. I will be contrasting idealized notions of the way the time of both narrative and disease are supposed to behave with their actual manifestations in the life of Sterne and *Tristram Shandy.* Rather than arriving at a picture of continuity and control, we are left with a form of narrative improvisation that responds to the irregular, accidental, and traumatic "times" of consumption.

The kind of analysis that has been done already in this direction has tended to be along the lines of W. B. C. Watkins's *Perilous Balance: The Tragic Genius of Swift, Johnson and Sterne,* which portrays Sterne as its romantic title suggests: a tragic genius whose soaring mind struggles to free itself from the shackles of its earthly frame. The imminently dangerous nature of disease focuses the author on the high value of his remaining time in the world. As Sterne wrote to John Wodehouse in 1765: "Few are the minutes of life, and I do not think that I have any to throw away on any one being."[5] Time wastes too fast for Sterne: His visibly "wasting" and consumptive frame literally embodies this notion. This romantic image of the heroic writer struggling against the odds to sustain his narrative is not one I wish to follow here, however appropriate or otherwise it might be to any particular writer suffering from any specific disease. In this essay I will attempt to construct a more culturally embedded and historicized version of Sterne, his narrative, and his consumption. It is necessary to understand the way in which Sterne and his eighteenth-century contemporaries perceived consumption and the way in which he incorporates the idiosyncratic rhythms of his disease into the narrative of *Tristram Shandy,* whether it be done consciously or unconsciously.

In order to do this I will examine the already unstable and even conflicting views of some contemporary doctors, both populist and "serious," that Sterne is likely to have read. It is known that Sterne was well versed in medical literature, contemporary, and antiquarian, if only, as I have argued elsewhere, for the simple reason that he had suffered a lung hemorrhage while still at university in Cambridge ("It happened in the night and I bled the bed full") and so felt the need as a sufferer to understand his condition.[6] Also, as Dorothy and Roy Porter have shown, patients had a considerable amount of leverage against doctors in the eighteenth century and often took an approach to treatment that suited their own medical mythology and predilections. Hence an educated person could attempt to take charge of his own condition by reading all the medical theories and practices concerning it.[7] I have largely confined myself to the contents of Sterne's library sale catalog (which also includes some items from other collections), although he certainly had access to other medical books in the library of York Minster, for example.[8] My argument is not that he had definitely read all these texts, although he certainly digested many, but that the general medical culture of consumption embraced Sterne and that the various "times" and rhythms of the disease outlined by such a culture manifest themselves in Sterne's narratives. Of course Sterne absorbed popular and religious definitions of phthisis; these will also be examined in relation to the times of *Tristram Shandy.*

Defining Consumption: Traumatic Narratives

The term *tuberculosis* only came into use with advances in medicine in the early nineteenth century; before then consumption (also "phthisis" or "tabes") was not a single disease entity but an umbrella term for a number of wasting conditions that tended to intermingle and have various possible stages or outcomes which could vary according to the management of a variety of factors, particularly the six "non-naturals."[9] Consumption of the lungs, the commonest type, was initially thought to result from an imbalance in the humors and later blockage of the blood flowing through the lungs. Such congestion led to ulcers or abscesses and then the disintegration of the lungs, made evident by the patient's productive cough. This process could be slow or quick and be retarded or accelerated by various factors usually related to the non-naturals: failure to follow a regimen of emotional self-control; intemperance in food and drink, especially alcohol; irregular hours of sleep at reasonable times; exposure to bad environmental and weather conditions, and so on.[10] Although not a paradox in medical terms, the potentially dual rhythm of consumption's "narrative," acute ("galloping") or chronic ("slow"), could seem contradictory to the sufferer, and is central to Sterne's traumatic experience of the disease as we shall see in greater detail later.[11] Sterne himself suffered from the chronic form of consumption, although with occasional acute and potentially deadly episodes in the form of lung hemorrhages. The intermittent timing of such attacks fundamentally alters the form and content of Sterne's narrative, most obviously at the start of the seventh book, when Tristram parallels Sterne's flight down to the warm sun of the south in a desperate search for a cure.

Before specifying the rhythms of consumption further, however, the issue of a precursor condition must be clarified. The newcomer to eighteenth-century medical history might wonder why Tristram often complains of his "asthma," as in the ominous early mention of living in "one of the vilest worlds ever made" and his difficulty in breathing due to "an asthma I got in scating

against the wind in *Flanders*."[12] Again, much later in volume 8 after
his flight from death, he displays an acute awareness of the threat-
ening time of consumption:

> To this hour art thou not tormented with the vile asthma
> that thou gattest in skating against the wind in Flanders? and
> is it but two months ago, that in a fit of laughter, on seeing
> a cardinal make water like a quirister (with both hands) thou
> brakest a vessel in thy lungs, whereby, in two hours, thou
> lost as many quarts of blood; and hadst thou lost as much
> more, did not the faculty tell thee—it would have amounted
> to a gallon? (*TS*, 8.6.663)

Although couched in comic terms, the narrative enacts the repetition of a trauma that we saw introduced early in the first volume;
the compulsive repetition of "vile[est]" in relation to asthma and
the primal scene of the disease's apparent symptomatic origin at-
tests to the psychological impact of such an occurrence, as does
the precise chronological and quantitative measurement of his case
history. The problem exists in a form of continuous present ("to
this hour"), but the potentially disastrous loss of blood from the
lungs recurs within this structure as a similarly continuous possibility. Any small incident or accident like laughter that physically
disrupts the motion of the lungs can bring on a hemorrhage.
Even the much-vaunted Sterneian/Burtonian laughter against the
spleen is not enough to guard against a deterioration in his condition. Ironically, the bodily effects of laughter even exacerbate the
problem by further damaging the lungs. At this point in the narrative an intensified awareness of consumptive time is specified to
the most recent trauma ("two months") and the duration of this
rapid and alarming happening, losing "in two hours [. . .] as many
quarts of blood," with the possibility of bleeding in even more
disastrous quantities.

The mention of the medical "faculty" reminds one that the
problem is severe enough to require constant dealings with doctors
and their own narratives, and it is to these stories of the body that
I turn to make sense of Sterne's use of the word *asthma* and its
significance for his narrative. In his treatise on asthma Sir John

Floyer stated that few people will die of an asthma fit. "But the Frequency of that often occasions Consumptions in lean habits."[13] Later in the book he makes this point in starker terms, language that someone who was constitutionally thin and suffering from "asthma" would find impossible to ignore: "The Asthma usually ends in a Consumption in lean Bodies" (p. 175). Richard Morton had said the same in his famous *Phthisiologia,* as had the more contemporary John Stephens.[14] Floyer goes on to mention the commonly held belief that the cold east wind often causes asthma fits (p. 56). Cold winds ("sharp" air) were also thought to cause consumption by damaging the lungs as opposed to the balmy and healing warm air of the Mediterranean where consumptives were sent to recover.[15] Hence received medical doctrine predicted that, given Tristram's (and Sterne's) constitution, the initial problem of asthma, caught skating against the wind, would usually develop into the more serious state of consumption. The time of disease here allows a modulation of the condition itself. The repeated asthma fits lead to a deterioration in the lungs and the onset of pulmonary consumption.

The irregularity of this disease time traumatizes the narrative of *Tristram Shandy:* but there is also a teleology to the time of consumption itself that increases the danger to the narrative and its author, who will write as long as he lives.[16] This teleology is stated commonly throughout the medical literature of the eighteenth century and before: Gerard Van Swieten's commentaries on Boerhaave's aphorisms contain one section with the chilling heading "Phthisis—Why It Is Always Mortal."[17] Metaphors of time usually accompany descriptions of consumption, as another sentence on the same page emphasizes: "In diseases arising from some putrid matter lying in the body, all the humours are dissolved, nutrition fails, and the patient dies of a slow consumption." Chambers's *Cyclopaedia* is rather more cautious, but still provides the kind of diagnosis that led Keats in the next century to pronounce his own blood-spitting as his "death warrant": "A true phthisis, even in its beginning, is a dangerous disease, and admits but of a very dubious prognostic; but when in an advanced state, it is always fatal."[18] Another term for "advanced state" was "confirmed": that stage in the disease narrative at which the plot, as it were, is made definite. As William Oliver put it: "A confirm'd Phthisis or Consumption, is beyond the Power of our Bath-Waters."[19] In a Shandyesque statement, Chambers makes the prospects for a frisky personality like Tristram/Sterne even more gloomy: "People of a dry habit are much sooner carried off by it than those of a moist one; as are also those of a brisk disposition, than those of a more languid temper."[20] Much though Sterne might resist such prognoses through a "True Shandeism" that should "open the heart and lungs," it is not difficult to see how his perception of narrative might be filtered through the ever-present threat of a consumptive terminus.[21]

When Sterne is truly threatened by death, the effect of this trauma is a change of tempo, albeit a panicked one. It has often been noticed that the rhythm of Sterne's narrative moves from a trot to a gallop at the beginning of the seventh volume of *Tristram Shandy*, and that this shift is caused by the continuing hemorrhages that inspired Sterne himself to escape the cold north with its dangerous fogs, (east) winds, and miasmas for the balmy air of the warm south.[22] The volume famously begins with Tristram/Sterne's explicit connection between the motion of his writing and that of his consumption:

> No—I think, I said, I would write two volumes every year, provided the vile cough which then tormented me, and which to this hour I dread worse than the devil, would but give me leave—and in another place—(but where, I can't recollect now) speaking of my book as a *machine,* and laying my pen and ruler down crosswise upon the table, in order to gain the greater credit to it—I swore it should be kept a going at that rate these forty years if it pleased but the fountain of life to bless me so long with health and good spirits. (*TS,* 7.1. 575–77)

That word *vile* reappears, signaling the recurrence of Tristram's traumatic lung hemorrhage and its hellish implications as it "torments" him and which he dreads "worse than the devil" because it imperils both life and narrative. Neither writer nor narrative can be in control of time because the condition of the body will not allow it.

Sterne's awareness of the fragility of the body and narrative, and the uncertainty inherent in the times of both, is partly derived from the medical sphere as well as the religious, although the two naturally overlap. The theme and threat of the cessation of time through physical mishap is a common one in eighteenth-century medical writing, but nowhere more strikingly so than in the work of the physician-poet Edward Baynard, who had written the second part of *Psukhrolousia: The History of Cold Bathing,* with Sir John Floyer producing the first part.[23] Although Sterne seems to have read Floyer's more studious history thoroughly, it was Baynard's lively mixture of commonsense observations and poetic expressions of medical knowledge and morality that engaged his imagination. Baynard had also written *Health, A Poem: Shewing How to Procure, Preserve, and Restore It,* published in London in 1719, which had gone through ten editions by 1764, several extracts of which appear in *The History of Cold Bathing.* Baynard's talent for translating medical knowledge into a popular idiom evidently influenced Sterne stylistically, as I have begun to argue elsewhere.[24] The opening of volume 7 of *Tristram Shandy* echoes Baynard's poetic strictures on the evils of intemperance:

> When (low drawn) Time's upon the Tilt,
> Few Sands and Minutes left to run;
> And all our (past gone) years are spilt,
> And the great Work is left undone:
>
> When restless Conscience knocks within,
> And in Despair begins to baul,
> Death like a Drawer then steps in,
> And asketh, Gentlemen! d'ye call?
> (*History of Cold Bathing,* p. 419)

The centrality of time to medical narratives, which in their turn map out the lifetime, or the unfolding of a life in time, with all the discontinuities and variant stages prompted by the (mal)functioning of the body, is stressed clearly in this very Shandean passage, albeit written decades earlier than Sterne's novel. These stanzas would naturally fit the themes generated by Sterne/ Tristram's panicked position in volume 7 very well: the brevity of life being all too obvious to a man afflicted with an apparently acute consumption and, at a narrative level, facing the prospect of leaving "the great Work" of *Tristram Shandy* "undone" by death. Of course by the logic outlined in several of Tristram's statements, including the one cited above, *Tristram Shandy* could only ever have remained unfinished. The traditional image of the hourglass here gels perfectly with our opening quotation from volume 9 that "Time wastes too fast," in which Tristram alludes both to the sands of time and his own wasting flesh (*TS,* 9.8.754).

There is also a more precise reference to the third stanza in Sterne's novel. The personification of Death appears early in volume 7:

> when DEATH himself knocked at my door—ye bad him come again; and in so gay a tone of careless indifference, did ye do it, that he doubted of his commission—
>
> "—There must certainly be some mistake in this matter", quoth he. [. . .]
>
> "—Did ever so grave a personage get into so vile a scrape?" quoth Death. (*TS,* 7.1.576)

Thomas Patch's well-known "Caricature of Laurence Sterne and Death" is taken from this scene. In the illustration the emaciated Sterne bows politely to Death's skeletal person stepping across the threshold of the door, carrying both a scythe and a bat-winged, almost fully drained hourglass.[25] Death is often personified, but Baynard's cheerful vision of Death as an inn "drawer" or waiter parallels Sterne's defensive reduction of "so grave a personage", who, like a servant mistakenly thinking he has heard his master's call, is peremptorily sent away. The reversal of power relations between the human and superhuman is structured by the presence of a religiomedical view of time which is embodied in the gothic image of Death bearing an hourglass, itself a traditional *memento mori.* Sterne has recourse to this image partly because medicine had as yet developed little beyond its medieval past. Stuart Sherman's investigation into the significance of the new chronometry of the eighteenth century, embodied in more accurate clocks and watches that could measure not just the hours but the minutes and seconds, shows how this technology was concomitant with a new cultural conception of time which gradually became dominant as the century wore on, a form which was also woven into the narratives of the age.[26]

Here Baynard and, as implied by Patch, Sterne use an obsolete chronometric device because the helplessness of medicine in the face of consumption and indeed disease in general forces the author to seek meaning in a different discourse: the religious rather than the medical. Sherman has argued that time before the mid-seventeenth century had been structured by religious notions of significant events rather than the mere secular progression of quantified and evenly spaced series of discrete units of time, opposing the tolling of the church tower bell to the "tick tick tick" of the modern clock. The treatment (as opposed to diagnosis) of consumption had not palpably evolved since the ancients. Controlling one's lifestyle, environment, exercise in the form of riding and so on, travel and change of air—all these had remained unchanged more or less for hundreds of years with the same erratic potential for cure. If anything, the incidence of consumption rose throughout the eighteenth century to reach new heights in the nineteenth.[27] One indication of a patient's perspective on the advance of medical skill is given in Edward Baynard's admittedly entertaining account of a consumptive case:

> The virtuous Mrs. Celia Panton, the famous Western Beauty, Daughter of Dr. Panton, who from a florid and good habit of Body seemingly, fell into a Hectic suddenly, thence into a galloping Phthisis in a very few Months; she was advised to Riding, and Ass's milk; in which Course she persever'd strictly, but it sunk her; her Hectic and Cough were incessant: And a little before she dy'd, said, *That she wonder'd that Physicians should depend so much upon Ass's Milk, for she had found by Experience, that Ass's milk was an Ass's Remedy.* (*History of Cold Bathing*, p. 471)

Ass's milk had been a (useless) remedy for consumption since the classical physicians. The optimism generated by chronometric refinement that culminated in the ability to calculate longitude, the Holy Grail of seafarers, could not exist in the medical sphere. The medieval figure of Death in all its gloomy fatality remained central to Baynard, Sterne, and Patch because there was nothing to replace it, no new secular deity of medical technology like the watch in chronometry.

Death's visit to Tristram is inspired by the traumatic memory of Sterne's lung hemorrhage in Paris, 1762, and no doubt the ones before that stretching back to the first in Cambridge.[28] It has often been noted that Sterne jests anxiously here; naturally he uses humor as a psychological defense mechanism. As we have seen in the medical narratives of the time, the threat of consumption as a fatal but chronic disease was all too real. Part of the black humor of the scene is that the consumptive person in the later stages of the disease was thought to be "the very picture of death; and in fact, his whole body looks like a moving skeleton, or a wandering spirit," as Dr Stephens put it (p. 118). Tristram refers to "these two spider legs of mine" just after his meeting with Death, and later is taken for a man on the verge of decease by a priest, who offers the last rites on seeing Tristram's "face as pale as ashes."[29] The symptomatic use of the trigger word *vile,* put into the mouth of Death rather than Tristram this time, alerts one to the seriousness of the danger in this situation, both physical and psychological. In the light of tales like that of Mrs. Panton, Sterne's transformation of disease into a "galloping" narrative is productive of the blackest of traumatic humor.

Accidental Narratives

Sterne's presentation of Death as a mistaken caller draws attention to a constant theme in *Tristram Shandy:* that of the accidental (mal)formation of life, death, and narrative. Although he draws upon a religious image of death, the kind of death Sterne imagines for himself and Tristram is all too secular. The lung hemorrhage that could finally be the death of him may come suddenly and be without apparent meaning. Chambers's *Cyclopaedia* lists one of the causes of consumption as the "accidental": that is, something that is not hereditary or "natural."[30] This consumptive time is irregular, disorderly, without narrative structure. Again the writing of Edward Baynard reinforces this notion from a medical perspective, although the often conflicting nature of eighteenth-century medical explanations of most diseases, especially consumption, would also be bound to instill a fundamental feeling of uncertainty in the reader searching for a rational meaning or narrative for his disease.[31]

In *The History of Cold Bathing* Baynard inserts a section of poetry taken from his poem on *Health* that warns the reader to control what he can with regard to his body because life is full of unexpected physical dangers that no doctor can prevent or cure:

> All finite things tend to their own undoing,
> But Man alone's industrious to his Ruin;
> For what with Riot, Delicates and Wine,
> Turns Pioneer himself to undermine.
> Besides the hidden Snares laid in our Way,
> The sudden Deaths we hear of every Day,
> The Smoothest Paths have unseen Ambuscades,
> And Insecurity Security invades;
> For no Man knows what's the next Hour's Event,
> Man lives, as he does die, by Accident.
>
> (*History of Cold Bathing,* p. 403)

The Tobyesque mention of "unseen Ambuscades" for the body creates a sense of time as an always potentially interruptable narrative, "for no man knows what's the next Hour's Event." Traditional narrative form depends precisely on the author's knowing what the next event will be, whereas the Sterneian narrative is less certain of its destination and even purpose because Sterne (and Tristram) cannot depend on their health. There are continual allusions throughout *Tristram Shandy* to the role of the accidental, particularly in the development of the body. Tristram's disastrously managed birth is a core example of this inconstant constant in the

Shandy world: "My mother, madam, had been delivered sooner than the green bag infallibly—at least by twenty *knots.*——Sport of small accidents, *Tristram Shandy!* that thou art, and ever will be!"[32] One wonders whether Sterne had in mind, both in these passages and throughout the novel, the physician Sir Thomas Browne's comment in his letter concerning the death of a consumptive: "The whole course of Time runs out at the Nativity and Death of things."[33]

Sterne's figure of "Death surpris'd," as it were, is an apparent reworking not merely of Death as a Drawer, but also of a later occurrence of this personification in Baynard's poem:

> Diseases, like true Blood-Hounds, Seize their dam,
> And prey upon the Carcass where they sprang.
> Be always on thy Guard, watchful and wise,
> Lest Death should take thee napping by Surprize.
>
> (*History of Cold Bathing,* p. 404)

Sterne reverses the roles so that Death is surprised by Tristram's breezy indifference. Again, Baynard's use of Death emanates from the religious edict that one should always be in a state of spiritual preparation for the end of life, a condition that consumption was traditionally supposed to enable the sufferer to attain. Although classic humoral theory stated that pulmonary consumption derived from a flux of corrosive humors from the head which then corrupted the lungs, a Christian tradition arose in which consumption was seen as the disease suitable for a good death. In 1656, Thomas Fuller wrote: "What is thy disease—a consumption? Indeed a certain messenger of death; but know, that of all the bailiffs sent to arrest us to the debt of nature, none useth his prisoners with more civility and courtesie."[34] Sir Thomas Browne's description of the "soft death" of a consumptive in his "Letter to a Friend" was similarly influential from its publication in 1690 right into the nineteenth century.[35] Consumption was regarded as a disease that, unless "galloping," allowed time for the good man to prepare himself for death. In this context its progress was supposedly slow and predictable, nor did it cloud the mind, thus enabling one to confront death in good moral order, ask God's forgiveness, and repent.

Hence consumption acted as a physical *memento mori*, encouraging one to meditate upon one's fate and religious identity, while giving plenty of time for organizing temporal affairs.[36] The debilitating effects of the disease could be confronted as a sign of Christian fortitude, but conveniently consumption was not considered likely to cause much pain; rather a gentle decline was anticipated in which one faded away from the world of the flesh into that of the spirit. Consumption seemed to be a visible and material embodiment of the Christian dualist concept of the soul's victory over the body.

In the light of the tradition of the consumptive "good death" one can view *Tristram Shandy* as an extended and ironic meditation on this ideal.[37] Consumptive time, in the view of Fuller and Browne, is indeed a carefully composed religious narrative, culminating in the peaceful acceptance of the sick man into the kingdom of heaven. Tristram's experience of consumption is far from being orderly, as the fits and starts of the narrative in response to his apparently random lung haemorrhages suggest. At the end of volume 4, Tristram closes his two-volume set for another year with the distinctly disorderly comment: "I take my leave of you till this time twelve-month [...] (unless this vile cough kills me in the mean time)" (*TS* 4.32.402). The promise of controlled progression is rapidly undercut by the vital proviso of stable health for the author. Similar remarks are peppered throughout the novel with greater or lesser frequency, reminding the reader that the time of the narrative is fundamentally structured by the time of consumption and disease in general.

Thomas Keymer's work on *Tristram Shandy* as a serial publication has similarly made the case for recognizing its historicity: its responsiveness to the shifting times, the cultural and personal environments in which it was written, and the open-endedness of this textual process. Both Keymer's analysis and my own resist the notion that *Tristram Shandy* was planned as a finished entity in true formalist fashion from the moment of its inception. Sterne "set the wheels a-going," but was no more in control of the eventual outcome than any other serial writer subject to the general contingencies of life, and certainly no more than any other consumptive writer: Keats, to take the obvious example, was forced to stop writing a year before he died. Smollett, Sterne's contemporary and rival in the sphere of both novels and travel writing, was also consumptive and, like Sterne, was forced to travel for his health. "Smelfungus's" ill health actually inspired him to inaugurate a new genre of travel writing that combined both the cultural facts of the Grand Tour and also the medical information on climate, quality of air, lodgings, and so on that would be required by the consumptive seeking both health and cultural capital.[38]

Yorick and the End of Narrative

Despite the general logic of accidental and "diseased" narrative time, Sterne does seem to have attempted to imagine both a peaceful consumptive good death and an orderly narrative in the Yorick episode of the first volume, a point at which Sterne was still finding his *modus operandi* for *Tristram Shandy*. As R. F. Brissenden has observed, the death of Yorick and its build-up does not quite fit with the rest of the volume:

> The tone of the whole section is markedly different from the tone of the surrounding chapters—the style in general is more formal, more even and more restrained than it is elsewhere in Volume 1; it seems as if Sterne is at last trying to tell a straight story [. . .]. His portrait is sketched humorously, but the humor is of the grave, realistic, Cervantic sort.[39]

Yorick dies a largely symptomless consumptive death, "broken-hearted" at his treatment by the harsh world in parallel with Sterne's difficulties in local ecclesiastical politics after the publication of *A Political Romance*. Roy Porter has noted that earlier on Yorick suffers from a consumptive cough as he trots around on his emaciated horse.[40] Although Yorick is not entirely identified with Sterne, it is evident that some kind of wish fulfillment is occurring, especially at the point of Yorick's death. Brissenden states that "if the initial description of Yorick is realistic, the conclusion of his story is sheer fantasy," and goes on to argue that the Yorick episode shows Sterne's uncertainty concerning the on-going importance of characters in the novel, concluding that "the death of Yorick [. . .] has little meaning out of its local context" (pp. 263–64).

If one ignores the level of consumptive time in the novel, then this last conclusion is true, but for Sterne and the various char-acters that function as consumptive *alter egos*, consumption plays a major part in the entire book. Yorick's death combines the con-temporary sentimentality of the wounded innocent with the tra-ditional peaceful passing of the religiously resigned good man:

> *Yorick's* last breath was hanging upon his trembling lips ready to depart as he uttered this;—yet still it was utter'd with something of a *cervantick* tone;—and as he spoke it, *Eugenius* could perceive a stream of lambent fire lighted up for a mo-ment in his eyes;—faint picture of those flashes of his spirit, which (as *Shakespear* said of his ancestor) were wont to set the table in a roar!
>
> *Eugenius* was convinced from this, that the heart of his friend was broke; he squeez'd his hand,—and then walk'd softly out of the room, weeping as he walk'd. *Yorick* followed *Eugenius* with his eyes to the door,—he then closed them,—and never opened them more. (*TS*, 1.12.34–35)

Consumption was a convenient disease for a broken heart; the symptoms of lovers suffering from broken hearts traditionally overlapped with those of the consumptive, the generalized wasting away being common to both as Burton's *Anatomy of Melancholy* made clear in its descriptions of love melancholy.[41] Moreover, as eighteenth-century doctors pointed out, disturbances of the mind for whatever reason could occasion a consumption. George Cheyne is entirely representative when he states that "the *slow* and *lasting* Passions, bring on *chronical* Diseases; as we see in Grief, and languishing hopeless *Love*," while Richard Brookes noted that a consumption could be brought on by "unusual sadness or Mel-ancholy."[42] The "sheer fantasy" that is being played out here is that of Sterne imagining a good death updated by sentimentality, in which he is the sensitive suffering hero and object of the sympathy supplied by Eugenius and, by implication, the reader. Through Yorick Sterne revels in the idea of controlling the process and termination of his erratic disease while conveniently indulging in a certain amount of self-pity in the process.

The other fantasy, coterminous with the first, is that of narrative order and closure that, as Brissenden so acutely observes, seems to characterize the whole Yorick story. Of course death, for the individual, is the end of narrative time. The two black pages that signify Yorick's death also imply this. Sterne takes this opportunity to image his own death and that of his writing proleptically in ideal terms, but this perfect end to life and narrative is not to be had, as the reader quickly realizes when the novel restarts. Tristram's "vile" consumption torments him hellishly, rather than allowing him a heavenly respite. The fantasy of controlling disease and thus the time of the narrative in a serial publication remains precisely that: merely a fantasy. The narrative unity of the Yorick episode is enabled by an idealized and sentimental vision of consumption, a vision that could not be sustained in Sterne's own physical life, or in the textual existence of his extended *alter ego,* Tristram. As this chapter has shown, the time of consumption, whether realistic or imaginary, in many ways *is* the time and rhythm of the narrative: the two stark black pages signifying Yorick's death and the end of narrative time for the individual are merely visual proof of the thesis.

Notes

1. See, for example, Jean Jacques Mayoux, "Variations on the Time-Sense in *Tristram Shandy,*" in *The Winged Skull,* ed. Arthur H. Cash and John M. Stedmond (London: Methuen, 1971), pp. 1–20.

2. See A. A. Mendilow, *Time and the Novel* (New York: Humanities Press, 1965), pp. 166–278.

3. "Did Sterne Complete *Tristram Shandy?*" *Modern Philology,* 48 (1951), 172–83; for two rebuttals of Booth see Marcia Allentuck, "In Defense of an Unfinished *Tristram Shandy:* Laurence Sterne and the Non Finito" and R. F. Brissenden, " 'Trusting to Almighty God': Another Look at the Com-

position of *Tristram Shandy,*" both in *The Winged Skull,* pp. 145–53, and 258–69, respectively. See also Thomas Keymer, "Dying by Numbers: *Tristram Shandy* and Serial Fiction," *Shandean,* 8 (1996), 41–67; 9 (1997), 34–69.

4. See W. B. C. Watkins, *Perilous Balance: The Tragic Genius of Swift, Johnson and Sterne* (Cambridge: Boar's Head, 1939; repr. 1960), pp. 99–156, for one of the earliest studies of this type; more recent investigations include Daniel C. Furst, "Sterne and Physick: Images of Health and Disease in *Tristram Shandy*" (unpublished doctoral thesis, University of Columbia, 1974); Roy Porter, "Against the Spleen," in *Laurence Sterne: Riddles and Mysteries,* ed. Valerie Grosvenor Myer (Fulham: Vision, 1984), pp. 85–96; Roy Porter, " 'The Whole Secret of Health': Mind, Body and Medicine in *Tristram Shandy,*" in *Nature Transfigured: Science and Literature, 1700–1900,* ed. John Christie and Sally Shuttleworth (Manchester: Manchester University Press, 1989), pp. 61–84.

5. *Letters,* 257.

6. For details on Sterne's Cambridge incident see Arthur H. Cash, *Laurence Sterne: The Early and Middle Years* (London: Routledge, 1992), pp. 60–61; note 6 above provides ample proof of Sterne's medical knowledge; see also my own evidence on Sterne's need to understand his own condition in "Sterne, Edward Baynard, and *The History of Cold Bathing*: Medical Shandeism," *Notes and Queries,* 244, n.s. 46 (1999), 22–25.

7. Dorothy Porter and Roy Porter, *Patient's Progress: Doctors and Doctoring in Eighteenth-Century England* (Cambridge: Cambridge University Press, 1989).

8. See *A Catalogue of a curious and valuable collection of books, among which are included the entire library of the late Reverend and Learned Laurence Sterne* (1768), repr. in *Sale Catalogues of Libraries of Eminent Persons,* v: *Poets and Men of Letters,* ed. by Stephen Parks (London: Mansell, 1971). I have also taken for granted standard sources such as Chambers's *Cyclopaedia,* George Cheyne's major writings, and so on.

9. There are many medical histories of consumption and tuberculosis that encompass the eighteenth century; some notable examples include L. F. Flick, *Development of our Knowledge of Tuberculosis* (Philadelphia: Author, 1925); Lester S. King, "Consumption: The Story of a Disease," in Lester S. King, *Medical Thinking: An Historical Preface* (Princeton, N.J.: Princeton University Press, 1982), pp. 16–69; Walter Pagel, "Humoral Pathology: A Lingering Anachronism in the History of Tuberculosis," *Bulletin for the History of Medicine,* 29 (1955), 299–308.

10. For a useful summary of the received wisdom on consumption and its cognates, see Ephraim Chambers, *Cyclopaedia; or, An Universal Dictionary of Arts and Sciences,* 7th ed., 2 vols. (London: Innis and others, 1751–52), I,

entry on "Consumption"; and Ephraim Chambers, *A Supplement to Mr. Chambers's Cyclopaedia; or, An Universal Dictionary of Arts and Sciences,* 2 vols. (London: Innis and others, 1753), II, entry on "Phthisis."

11. See Chambers, *Supplement,* II, entry on "Phthisis."

12. *TS,* 1.5.8.

13. John Floyer, *A Treatise of the Asthma,* 3rd ed. (London: Wilkin, 1726), p. 17 (library sale catalog no. 1185).

14. *Richard Morton, Phthisiologia, or, A Treatise of Consumptions* (London: Innis and others, 1720), p. 212 (library sale catalog no. 1344); John Stephens, *A Practical Treatise on Consumptions* (London: Owen and Gretton, 1761), p. 78 (library sale catalog no. 1175).

15. See Stephens, *Treatise on Consumptions,* p. 165.

16. *TS,* 3.4.191.

17. Gerard van Swieten and Hermann Boerhaave, *Van Swieten's Commentaries upon the Aphorisms of Boerhaave,* abridged by Ralph Schomberg (London, 1762), p. 39.

18. *A Supplement,* II, entry on "Phthisis." Later it states, rejecting reported cases of cures, that "when the spitting of true purulent matter is come on, and is attended with colliquative sweats and a diarrhoea, there is no further hope for the patient; and in general, what is reported of the curing of consumptions, is founded on errors, and other cases have been mistaken for it."

19. *A Practical Dissertation on Bath-Waters,* 4th ed. (London: Leake, 1747), p. 93 (library sale catalog no. 1668).

20. *A Supplement,* II, entry on "Phthisis." Tristram's nature is well summarized by his observation on digressions: "If it is to be a digression, it must be a good frisky one, and upon a frisky subject too, where neither the horse or his rider are to be caught, but by rebound" (*TS,* 9.12. 761–62).

21. *TS,* 4.32. 401–2.

22. See Jean Jacques Mayoux, p. 14.

23. Sir John Floyer and Edward Baynard, *Psukhrolousia: The History of Cold Bathing, Both Ancient and Modern* (1706), 6th ed. (London, 1732); on Sterne's use of a late edition, see Melvyn New, "Sterne and *The History of Cold Bathing,*" *Notes and Queries,* 44 (1997), 211–12, note 3.

24. See my article "Sterne, Edward Baynard, and *The History of Cold Bathing*: Medical Shandeism."

25. Painted at Florence, between 18 December 1765 and 1 January 1766 (Jesus College, Cambridge).

26. Stuart Sherman, *Telling Time: Clocks, Diaries, and English Diurnal Form, 1660–1785* (Chicago: University of Chicago Press, 1996).

27. For the background to this see Lester S. King, "Consumption: The Story of a Disease"; and René and Jean Dubos, *The White Plague: Tuberculosis, Man and Society* (New Jersey: Rutgers University Press, 1992).

28. See *Letters,* p. 180; Cash, *Laurence Sterne: The Early and Middle Years,* pp. 60–61.

29. *TS,* 7.34.636.

30. I, entry on "Consumption."

31. Among the gloomy prognoses regarding the outcome of a consumption, for example, doctors were always ready to contradict themselves in the hope of selling themselves or their books. After his largely pessimistic attitude throughout most of his tome, Stephens (to name but one) proceeds to offer hope to his patients and readers by claiming that something can be done for the consumptive, while anticipating that he will be sneered at by his fellow physicians for such an assertion (*Treatise on Consumptions,* pp. 330–34).

32. *TS,* 3.8.196; see also *TS,* 3.6.192–93, for Walter's views on man, birth, and accidents.

33. Sir Thomas Browne, "A Letter to a Friend, upon the Occasion of the Death of his Intimate Friend," *Sir Thomas Browne: Religio Medici and Other Works,* ed. by L. C. Martin (Oxford: Clarendon Press, 1964), pp. 177–96 (p. 182).

34. *Sermon—Life out of Death,* cited in Robert Southey, *Southey's Common Place Book,* 4 vols. (London: Longmans, 1850), 4, 353. As Stephens put it in a more prosaic fashion: "The patient entertains those hopes of recovery from the dullness of his disease, which does not give him that degree of pain which he receives from other diseases" (*Treatise on Consumptions,* pp. 103–4).

35. "A Letter to a Friend," pp. 180–81; see also Katherine Ott, *Fevered Lives: Tuberculosis in American Culture since 1870* (Cambridge, Mass.: Harvard University Press, 1996), p. 15.

36. For the tradition of consumption and the good death, see Pat Jalland, *Death in the Victorian Family* (Oxford: Oxford University Press, 1996), pp. 41–46.

37. Thomas Keymer notes Tristram's consequent refusal to accept Death's courteous call by galloping away at high speed, the pun on "galloping consumption" presumably intended (*TS,* 7.1.577). See his "Dying by Numbers: *Tristram Shandy* and Serial Fiction (2)," *Shandean,* 9 (1997), 57.

38. See my paper with Akihito Suzuki, "The Disease of the Self: Representing Consumption, 1700–1830," *Bulletin of the History of Medicine,* 74. (2000), 258–94.

39. " 'Trusting to Almighty God,' " pp. 263–64.

40. Yorick is able to "compose his cough" on his weary steed (*TS,* 1.10.21); Roy Porter, " 'The Whole Secret of Health,' " p. 66.

41. Robert Burton, *The Anatomy of Melancholy,* 3 vols. (London: Dent, 1948), 3, pp. 133–84.

42. George Cheyne, *The English Malady* (1733), ed. Roy Porter (London: Routledge, 1991), p. xiii; Richard Brookes, *General Practice of Physic,* 2 vols. (London: Newbery, 1765), 1, 276.

PART IV

Narrative, Reading, and Meaning

Reader as Hobby-horse in
Tristram Shandy

HELEN OSTOVICH

◆ ◆ ◆

THE RELATIONSHIP BETWEEN Tristram and his reader is only superficially what the text calls at one point "conversation" (*TS*, 2.9.125). It might more properly be called dispute. As writer, Tristram sets upon his reader and draws him about, harassing, upbraiding, riding him like a temperamental jockey trying to manage a recalcitrant horse. This disputatious riding has for its object, not mere domination of the reader, but stimulation and provocation, the equal engagement of writer and reader in the creative journeying through the novel.

"The truest respect which you can pay to the reader's understanding," Tristram declares, "is to halve this matter amicably, and leave him something to imagine in his turn, as well as yourself." The writer's role in this creative partnership is to unburden himself; the reader's is to take up the burden of a vast quantity of apparently unsequenced and inconsequential detail, and simultaneously to attempt to find in it emotional, if not rational, coherence. The reader's ability to process this detail hinges on his growing emotional and intellectual response to the writer as the two progress from "slight acquaintance" to "familiarity" to "friend-ship," and on his willingness to accept the writer's aberrations. "As we jogg on, either laugh with me, or at me, or in short, do any thing,—only keep your temper" (*TS,* 1.6.10). So Tristram advises the reader. The ideal for both reader and writer is amused toler-ance, a "good-humoured acceptance of the inevitability of error and the likelihood of mutual responsibility for it."[1] Yet the near impossibility of keeping one's temper is what Tristram counts on. The reader's impatience carries Tristram forward in the story, while his ignorance backs Tristram into digressions that seem more tan-gential than explanatory. The resulting confusion is the cause of most of the reader-writer disputes in the novel, as well as the source of much of its liveliness.

The liveliest, most disputatious reader relationship in the novel is the one between Tristram and his female reader, Madam. Tris-tram usually treats Sir—his male reader—with casual indifference, and showers his mighty or fashionable readers, whether secular or clerical—your worships and your reverences—with genial con-tempt. He lumps the male readers together with other good, un-learned folks in his conception of the collective reader as recalci-trant hobby-horse. In his comparison of the novel to a painting, he states: "the dark strokes in the HOBBY-HORSE, (which is a secondary figure, and a kind of back-ground to the whole) give great force to the principal lights in your own [i.e., the reader's] figure, and make it come off wonderfully" (*TS,* 1.9.16). But Madam he treats as a special hobby-horse of his own—with all the ambi-guity the term implies. She is, like Rosinante, "the HERO'S horse . . . a horse of chaste deportment, which may have given grounds for a contrary opinion . . . —And let me tell you, Madam, there is a great deal of very good chastity in the world, in behalf of which you could not say more for your life" (*TS,* 1.10.18). This analogy suggests the complementary relationship between the ambiguous physicality of the horse and the extravagant imagination of the rider—between the mundane and the romantic. Man and hobby-horse, Tristram claims, are like soul and body: "Long journeys and much friction" create electric charges between the two that re-define both, so that ultimately "a clear description of the nature of the one . . . may form a pretty exact notion of the genius and character of the other" (*TS*, 1.24.86). That this interchange is beneficial can be proven only by experience: by getting on the hobbyhorse and riding it around. If the writer mounts with pleasure and the reader bears him well, then the experience provides its own answers. The sexual allusiveness enhances the reciprocal relationship because of the fertile creativity—physical, emotional, imaginative—inherent in the collaboration of writer and reader. Tristram sees it as a productive association: procreative (the book as child), recreative (the book as entertainment and as art), and generative (the book as proliferator of sensation and idea). Moreover, he implies that receptive and creative reading is both necessary and equivalent to writing. Both are activities that give meaning.[2]

Tristram plays persistently on the notion of Madam Reader as hobby-horse, setting off a number of associations which reverberate throughout the narrative. The hobby-horse was originally a kind of horse "such as Ireland breedeth" (*OED*, 1)—an amusing definition given Sterne's origins. It is also a traditional figure accompanying the morris dance. Wearing a wicker horse-like frame strapped to his waist, the dancer performs antics imitating a skittish horse: "jesting and frisking in the luxury of his nonsense" (*OED*, 2a, citing Milton). Hobby-horse, in this context, refers to the costume and the dance; Tristram is the dancer. The morris dancer traditionally wears a cap and bells (though not the jester's cap Tristram claims to sport) and performs in a group of nine, a consideration to bear in mind in looking at the nine volumes of the novel. At country mummings in the later seventeenth century, women danced the hobby-horse (*OED*, 2c), the dance clearly a fertility rite, another context for the significantly nine volumes of *Tristram Shandy*. Metaphorically, the hobby-horse is androgynous; not only a frivolous fellow or buffoon but also any lustful person, particularly a woman (*OED*, 3). In this latter context, "riding a hobby-horse" means fornicating. Concurrent with these definitions are the uses of the word as child's toy or adult's favorite pastime. The various literal meanings of the word have a way of backing up on one another in an ebullient compound of the erotic and the innocent. "The adult astride the child's toy," an apt description of Tristram's reductive games with the reader, "is a literary image of folly" and, combined with the sexually charged hobby-horse of the morris dancers, suggests rustic rites and "energies unrestrained by gentlemanly decorum"[3]—the license that warrants the Widow Wadman's "kick of both heels at once" (*TS*, 8.9.442), but that frightens Toby into retreat, and Walter into rigidly controlled monthly schedules. All of these meanings suggest the entertainment value of the hobby-horse, its association with either gender, and its ambiguous status as a provocation to the reader and a stimulus to respond to the writer at all possible interpretive levels.

Tristram's sly combination of indecorously overlapping meanings promotes a new kind of literary intercourse with the reader, one unrestricted by the staidly linear logic usually associated with male discourse. On the contrary, Tristram's discourse verges on the feminine in its free-form activity, tangentially seeking out a partner with whom and to whom he may relate his narrative with intimate and idiosyncratic abandon. By thus adopting an androgynous approach, he offers Madam Reader an alternative, on the one hand, to the convention of male writer addressing male reader in the kind of text that either "immasculates" or excludes women readers, and, on the other hand, to the decorum of the conduct book usually deemed appropriate for female readers.[4] In so doing, he allows Madam to interpret the writer's wit in ways consistent with her own femininity—that is, consistent with her independent judgment as a woman. Arguably, by subverting or distorting conventional male sexuality in the analogues to Walter's clockwork, Toby's war wound, Tristram's circumcision, even Phutatorius's hot chestnut and Diego's gigantic nose, Tristram is also rejecting the purely male perspective as farcically inadequate. Instead, Tristram proposes literary and sexual roles not hampered by strict notions of gender and performance, but played with and shared for mutual pleasure and whatever enlightenment comes with it.

Tristram's awareness of his reader as a physical being and of his book as a physical object provokes him to fill the book with appealing physical devices. The blank pages (to be drawn on by the reader, or filled in later by the writer), the black or marbled pages, the pointing fingers, the threats to rip out pages, the games with punctuation and chapter lengths, the crosses (for Catholics only), and the asterisks—all these are spurs and quirts to keep the hobbyhorsical reader trotting along. Any mental or physical activity is better than none: "so much of motion, is so much of life, and so much of joy—and . . . to stand still, or get on but slowly, is death and the devil" (*TS*, 7.13.593), says Tristram. Periodically he asks the reader to stand up, blow his nose, do research, walk behind a curtain, shut the door, shift the scenery, imagine the details, invent a curse—or simply wait impatiently until next year. In the complementary functioning of body and soul, reader and writer, Tristram hopes that "the judgment [will be] surprised by the imagination" (*TS*, 8.1.655) and believes that the resulting stimulation will be a good sign in itself, a vital mutuality.

Multiple meanings, particularly those with sexual overtones, intensify Tristram's and Madam's typically personal interchanges. Tristram consistently singles Madam out, first with gibes, later with special consideration for her receptivity and responsiveness. He teases her about the "various uses and seasonable applications of long noses" (*TS*, 3.36.267). Decrying the lewdness he has spurred her to imagine, he addresses her affectionately as "my dear girl" and then suggests that Satan is ravishing her imagination. But Satan is really Tristram himself, riding his reader into dispute. He offers her two contradictory roles to play at once: "unbacked filly" and "Tickletoby's mare"—that is, virgin and experienced lover— but both roles involve the same sexually explicit activity: "to frisk it, to squirt it, to jump it, to rear it, to bound it" until she throws her rider (Satan/Tristram). All this is both description and metaphor of the reader's responsive participation in the act—of sex or of reading. Whether Madam balks, or gives up "the reins of [her] imagination" into his hands, she is still "the sporting little filly-folly . . . an *any thing*, which a man makes a shift to get a-stride on, to canter it away from the cares and solicites of life" (*TS*, 8.31.716). The definition of the reader as hobby-horse implies a wide range of shared activity from the purely sexual to the purely fanciful: the combination of sense and nonsense that makes a hobby-horse worth riding.

Though she is his favorite, Madam is not the only horse in

Tristram's stable. Sir, the male reader, fails to comprehend this physical and spiritual connection. He asks, "And pray who was Tickletoby's mare?" Tristram warns, "Read, read, read, read, my unlearned reader! read," adding that if he lacks the knowledge to understand words so simple, he certainly will fail to "penetrate the moral" of the rest of the work (*TS,* 3.36.268). Madam, on the other hand, seems to have no difficulty in taking Tristram's meaning. Tristram can relate Slawkenbergius's tale directly to Madam, because, despite the complex detail and the implied scholarliness of the Latin text, the story of the affair between Diego and Julia is a simple hobbyhorsical matter of love and sexuality, soul and body, but blown up by observers into endless controversy—medical, civil, philosophical, religious, diplomatic, and commercial—all further obscured by abstruse Aristotelian terminology (*TS,* 4. "Tale"). These voluminous details only confuse the male reader. But the point of the story is that disputing lovers may be reconciled through sensuality and sentiment. The end is whispers and eye contact, and recognition that "There's often no good understanding" between heart and brain. Sympathetic "vibration in the strings, about the region of the heart" is the factor that permits a wordless resolution based on sensitivity to the other: "What is left, Madam, is not worth stooping for" (*TS,* 4.1.274–75).

Sterne's concept of reading and writing as dispute, as a play of complementary and active differences which—like sexuality— permits understanding when either thinking or feeling alone fails, works for the reader at several fictional levels. The novel is a set of various interposed plots: the fictions that apparently have little direct bearing on the Shandy history, like Slawkenbergius's tale or the tale of the Abbess and the Novice; the Shandy family fiction, including the integrated tales of the hot chestnut, Le Fever, and Trim's brother's marriage to the Jew's widow; and the procedural fiction of the writer's direct "conversation" with visiting readers in Tristram's study, while Jenny, Eugenius, and Garrick suggest the world beyond the study. Uniting these fictions is the fact of Sterne as author of the novel, and of ourselves as readers outside it.[5] Each fictional level stimulates and questions responses at other levels. Most emphatic are the responses to male–female relationships, ambiguously designated as "conversation," which, like "intercourse," marks the intersection of verbal and sexual exchange. Dispute over sexual roles centers on the physical-metaphorical confusion over who is riding whom—or which is the hobby-horse. This is the focus of the Madam–Tristram "conversation." Other relationships exist largely as topic of and excuse for the Tristram–Madam "conversation." That Sterne is generalizing about male–female roles is clear in Tristram's references to his two favorite women: Madam, the social mode of address to women; and Jenny, the generic colloquial term for any female animal (like jenny-wren). Janatone, the name of the innkeeper's sexually permissive daughter, is French for jenny-ass. This naming is particularly instructive for the outside reader because Sterne seems to imply that there is a sense in which all writers are male, "going backwards and forwards to keep all tight together in the reader's fancy" (*TS,* 6.33.557–58), and all readers female. What is a distinctively female reader? According to the feminist critic Patrocinio Schweickart, "men define themselves through individuation and separation from others, while women have more flexible ego boundaries and define and experience themselves in terms of their affiliations ... with others." That is, although men value autonomy, women value relationships and, in order to maintain those relationships, are eager to negotiate between opposing needs, "up to and including a symbiotic merger with the other."[6] The suggestion, then, that the author is male, the reader female, however reductive, is intrinsic to the whole context of Sterne's sexualization of disputing opposites: soul and body, reason and sensibility, and especially wit and judgment. Wit begins as a self-defining mechanism, one that separates the autonomous writer from the dependent reader. As the masculine prerogative, a sign of intellectual potency at least, wit is Tristram's forte, whether in translating Slawkenbergius, or quoting Walter, or goading Madam, or showering the reader with logos, or galloping into digression and frustrating expectation by showing interest only in the incongruous. Judgment appears to be the feminine prerogative, a role of the reader: being receptive to the writer's probing wit, and to analogies between one level of fiction and another, one idea and another, one character and another. To the extent that Madam's critical judgment represents gravity and prudery, it is the polar opposite of Tristram's exuberant wit.[7] But this concept of wit and judgment is not, like Locke's, built upon "operations differing from each other as wide as east is from west" (*TS,* 3. "Preface." 227)—that is, not a rigid dichotomy splitting and labeling sexual roles. It is instead something like Pope's, in which

> . . . Wit and Judgment often are at strife
> Tho meant each other's Aid, like Man and Wife.
> ("Essay on Criticism," lines 82–83)

As Tristram points out in a more androgynous comparison that suggests the folly of such gender antagonism, just as "farting and hickuping" are two different means of venting the body, so wit and judgment are simply two different means of venting the brain. Judgment may coincidentally provide a base for wit's acid, or apply restraint to wit's exuberance, but chiefly their combination keeps up "that just balance between wisdom and folly, without which a book would not hold together a single year" (*TS,* 9.12.761). Together, they create, through their beneficial coexistence, "the proper ballance" (*TS,* 3. "Preface." 231), however precarious, for understanding.

Tristram explores this partnership between wit and judgment by linking Madam's role in the procedural fiction (vis-à-vis the writer) to Mrs. Shandy's role in the Shandy family history (vis-à-vis Walter). The association between the two women is made clear from the opening chapters of volume 1, when Mrs. Shandy's disruptive, "Pray, my dear . . . have you not forgot to wind up the clock?" is soon followed by Madam's embarrassing, "—But pray, Sir, What was your father doing all December,—January, and February?" (1.4.7). Madam may even be the questioner at the end of chapter 1: "Pray, what was your father saying?" The return journey of the Shandys from London allows for another analogy. Walter becomes obsessed with Mrs. Shandy's apparent weakness of judgment, "which led his imagination a thorny dance, and, before all was over, play'd the duce and all with him" (1.16.48), as he contemplates other kinds of weakness, wondering, like Leontes in *The Winter's Tale,* whether

> My wife's a hobby-horse, deserves a name
> As rank as any flax-wench that puts to
> Before her troth-plight.
>
> (I.ii.276–78)

Walter's hypersensitivity about Mrs. Shandy's sexuality and his own contempt for or fear of sexual activity are pervasive motifs in every volume of the novel. He flies into a rage at Toby's suggestion that Mrs. Shandy has refused Dr. Slop's services because "she does not choose to let a man come so near her ****" (*TS*, 2.6–7.116–17). Later he pointedly accuses Mrs. Shandy of prurience because she wants to observe Toby and the Widow Wadman through a keyhole: "Call it by it's right name, my dear, quoth my father" (*TS*, 8.35.729; and *TS*, 9.1.735). He denigrates sexual passion ("ass"), calls lovers "the most egregious fools and coxcombs . . . that ever was let loose in the world" (*TS*, 8.26.709), curses pregnant women ("Duce take 'em all" [*TS*, 4.12.340]), and is—defensively—offended by jokes about paternity, hornworks, and curtins. Tristram's nose-crushing birth and later his baptismal misnaming send Walter out to stare into the fish pond (*TS*, 4.17.350 and *TS*, 31.394). Is he wondering, like Leontes, if "his pond [has been] fish'd by his next neighbour" (*Winter's Tale*, I.ii.195)?[8] Like Leontes, though much more obliquely, he tries and condemns his wife on the basis of a hypothesis; like Leontes, he loses one child to an untimely death (Bobby-Mamillius) and apparently loses in the other (Tristram-Perdita) the hope of future generations—an untimely fall of a sash-window cutting them off, as it were, by "phimosis" (Slop's diagnosis, 5.39). Like Leontes, one moment he "holds his wife by th'arm" and believes "Physic for't there's none / It is a bawdy planet" (*Winter's Tale*, I.ii.93, 200–201); and the next, "his conscience [smites] him":

> My mother was then conjugally swinging with her left arm twisted under his right, in such wise, that the inside of her hand rested upon the back of his—she raised her fingers, and let them fall—it could scarce be call'd a tap; or if it was a tap—it could have puzzled a casuist to say, whether 'twas a tap of remonstrance, or a tap of confession: my father, who

was all sensibilities from head to foot, class'd it right—Conscience redoubled her blow—(9.1.735–36)

As the physical, the moral, and the logical intertwine, Walter recognizes his own folly in his wife's cool appraisal. His fanciful wit is
grounded by her judgment, his ebullient soul confused by the
"temperate current of blood" in her "orderly . . . veins"; his physical sensations of shame remind him that "REASON, is half of it,
SENSE" (*TS,* 4.13.593).

Tristram shows a similar hypersensitivity to Madam's sexuality
by constantly alerting her to bawdy or potentially obscene elements in the narrative, often pretending that his is the innocent
mind, and hers the prurient imagination. His protest that noses
are merely noses is the most obvious example. In his mentions of
Jenny, he implies that only Madam's gutter-fancy could believe
their relationship to be primarily sexual, rather than sentimental:
"Surely, Madam, a friendship between the two sexes may subsist,
and be supported without—Fy! Mr. Shandy—" (*TS,* 1.18.56–57).
When he argues that eloquence as a token of masculine potency
of mind and body was lost when orators stopped cloaking themselves in flowing mantles and took to wearing short coats, he adds:
"We can conceal nothing under ours, Madam, worth shewing" (*TS,*
3.14.218). He insists, again purely for Madam's benefit, " 'That both
man and woman bear pain or sorrow (and, for aught I know,
pleasure too) best in a horizontal position' " (*TS,* 3.29.254). When
he mentions that Toby's scarlet breeches ripped between the legs,
he cautions: "Yes, Madam—but let us govern our fancies" (*TS,*
9.2.739). This teasing is no *Winter's Tale* obsession; it is more like
Petruchio's "riding" of Kate, whom he calls "my horse, my ox, my
ass, my anything" (*The Taming of the Shrew,* III.ii.249). Kate is "tamed"
because she learns to share a joke, to enter into the spirit and
humor of a man whom she grows to love, and who does "all . . .
in reverend care of her" (IV.i.202). Kate participates in his nonsense,
calling the sun the moon, and an old man a "Young budding
virgin, fair and fresh and sweet" (IV.v.45), because she gains in
affectionate understanding every time she increases the distance
between the old Katherina, the "shrew," and the new Kate, the

"merry mistress." Petruchio's wit—and his re-creating of Kate (read "cate") as his delicacy, his dainty, his *fancy*—entices her into growing in judgment, cleaving her judgment to his wit, and ultimately arriving at a creative understanding of their relationship. In Tristram's terms, this is the understanding achieved when "the judgment is surprised by the imagination." It blossoms as Madam comes to an affectionate acceptance of the "Mr. Shandy" who so annoyed her in the opening volumes. He becomes simply "Tristram" and their repartee becomes shared nonsense:

—Pray reach me my fool's cap—I fear you sit upon it, Madam—'tis under the cushion—I'll put it on—

Bless me! you have had it upon your head this half hour.—There then let it stay, with a

Fa-ra diddle di
and a fa-ri diddle d
and a high-dum—dye-dum
    fiddle——dumb-c.

And now, Madam, we may venture, I hope, a little to go on. (*TS,* 7.16.616)

Whether as judges of conscience or judges of nonsense, Mrs. Shandy and Madam have much in common as readers of situations. Both are, for the most part, silent readers, not verbalizers. They are both, because of the contextual set-up, seemingly passive, in that they inspire verbal activity in their partners while remaining largely silent themselves. But both are active manipulators of the verbal play around them, not merely silent receptors. Mrs. Shandy's silence provokes Walter's flights of speculation, and forces him to invent both sides of an argument to which she acquiesces by repeating whatever he suggests. The beds-of-justice conversation (*TS,* 6.18.526–29) gives a clear illustration of Mrs. Shandy's method of being deliberately and "maddeningly agreeable"[9]—a method Tristram draws Madam's attention to as writer and reader eavesdrop behind the bedroom curtain: "only to hear in what kind of manner my father and my mother debated between themselves, this affair of the breeches—from which you may form an idea, how they debated all lesser matters" (*TS,* 6.16.523). The dispute that follows illustrates the "significance of the apparent tension between Mrs. Shandy's inherent strength and her husband's and to lesser extent her son's denigration of her."[10] Walter's denigration of Elizabeth seems to arise out of his frustration at not being able to control that silent other. It is indirectly an admission of his defeat in face of the unexpected and perhaps superior resilience of his wife. Elizabeth Shandy's ready and apparently sympathetic acquiescence frustrates Walter's attempts to rouse her to an argument over Tristram's breeches; by agreeing with every side of his argument, she diverts his desire to argue into a quibble that angers Walter without unduly discomposing herself. She has the satisfaction of knowing that, if she has confused convenience with pleasure in the matter of ordering Tristram's breeches, he has reduced pleasure to convenience in the matter of their Sunday night sexual and post-sexual conversation. Madam's silence has the same effect on Tristram. He moves back and forth in his narrative, progressing and digressing, in an effort to answer Madam's unspoken questions or to relieve her unexpressed boredom, ultimately to redefine her critical reception of his life and opinions.

In the larger context of writer and reader, the analogy also holds. A reader of a book cannot argue effectively with the writer of it, because, as Georges Poulet defines their relationship, the reader becomes the host to thoughts parasitically bred in him by the writer. The reader is thus "on loan to another,"[11] and finds himself responding to the writer only as a postulated "mock-reader" (like Madam, Sir, or one of your worships and your reverences) whose identity may not be compatible with the real reader's notion of himself.[12] Sterne deliberately provokes the real reader by transforming him into a mock reader, putting him into unflattering positions, and then jeering at him. The reader's only effective recourse is to accept the travesty as a tease and, by laughing, defuse it. The reader may question or echo the writer's words, but the reader can influence the writer only through the writer's ability correctly to forecast reader interest and reader expectation. Even limiting this analogy to the reader of a work-in-progress, as

Tristram Shandy originally was, the reader's opportunity to "talk back" to the writer and alter the content is curtailed to periods between the publication of one volume and the next. The separation of writer and reader and the fact of publication make response to what is already written merely academic. Even the most receptive and astute of readers can enforce nothing more than a draw—a coexistence of two opposing points of view.

Both Mrs. Shandy and Madam do, on occasion, talk back in this way: not routing the opponent, but achieving a stand-off. Take, for example, the Shandy's argument over hiring a male or female midwife. Walter has already won the point that the child be delivered at Shandy Hall, the legal consequence of Mrs. Shandy's false pregnancy of the year before. He now attempts to win a second point: that the midwife be Dr. Slop. Although Walter, "almost at his wit's end," argues from so many positions that he seems to have the advantage "seven to one," Mrs. Shandy's "small reinforcement of chagrine personal" balances the dispute "with so equal an advantage,—that both sides sung *Te Deum*" (*TS,* 1.18.55). The face-saving expedient is to summon both midwives, with the understanding that the female will attend the birthing, while the male will merely attend. In this quibbling stand-off, female practical judgment seems to hold witty male complication at bay, but Mrs. Shandy reckons without the intervening factor of the male child breached in her womb. Ultimately, she is forced to yield to Walter's "knotted" logic, which has taken new shape in Dr. Slop's bag of obstetrical tools,[13] not because of the superiority of either male midwifery or male argument, as Walter would have it, but simply because of the obstinate accidental wedging of a little male in the female ****: another absurd equipoise in which "male" and "female" strike an uneasy temporary balance.

Tristram's argument with Madam over his mother's religion follows the same pattern. Madam's response to Tristram's prodding is spirited: "Papist! You told me no such thing, Sir . . . Then, Sir, I must have missed a page . . . Then I was asleep, Sir. . . . Then, I declare, I know nothing of the matter—" (1.20.64). Once Madam has turned back to reread chapter 19, Tristram talks about her behind her back, criticizing her "vicious taste . . . of reading straight forwards, more in quest of adventures, than of . . . deep erudition." But when the "fair lady" returns, she is not chastened. She snaps at Tristram: "Not a word like it!" Like Walter, he is forced into a quibble (here, on the hidden logic of baptism in the womb) and, to redress the balance between himself and Madam, generalizes "from her example" his hope "that all good people, both male and female, . . . may be taught to think as well as read" (*TS,* 1.20.66).

That both Mrs. Shandy and Madam cause argument to break down into quibble is a clue to their practical purpose in the narrative as deflaters of witty extravagance, representatives of the "comic irreverence" of reality,[14] reminders of our absurd physicality, fragile and vulnerable no matter how high the spirit flies. Sometimes the women seem simply not to comprehend a witticism, as in Madam's comment: "I did not apprehend your uncle *Toby* was o'horseback," which flattens Tristram's joke that Toby was forced to dismount his hobbyhorse in face of Walter's annoyance— not that he had been on a horse at Namur (*TS,* 3.3.189). Mrs. Shandy constantly frustrates Walter by refusing to ask—or perhaps rather like the outside reader by being unable to ask—for direct explanations: "That she is not a woman of science, my father would say—is her misfortune—but she might ask a question" (*TS,* 6.39.569). Walter's comment is, of course, typically hyperbolic. Mrs. Shandy asks questions he does not want to hear about practical concerns such as, "Only tell us . . . what herbs" (*TS,* 5.27.459), when she sees Walter consulting folio volumes immediately after Tristram's sash-window circumcision; or "Lord! . . . what is all this story about?" when Walter spins out an incoherent analogy after refusing to accept the fact that the Shandy bull is sterile (*TS,* 9.26.615).

This ellipsis in cause and effect, characteristic of Shandean thought patterns, seems to be a consequence of the quibble. For Walter, the spontaneous quibble is both the result of his frustrations and his relief from them. For example, when he discovers that his favorite mare has produced a mule instead of the longed-for part-Arabian riding-pad, he berates Obadiah: "See here! you rascal, . . . what you have done!—It was not me, said *Obadiah.*— How do I know that? replied my father. Triumph swam in my father's eyes, at the repartee——" (*TS*, 5.3.420–21). The quibble becomes a means of redressing the balance. In the same way, quibble and ellipsis govern Tristram's tangential structuring of his life and opinions: "I write a careless kind of a civil, nonsensical, good-humoured *Shandean* book, which will do all your hearts good——And all your heads, too,—provided you understand it" (*TS*, 6.17.525). Tristram's elaborate carelessness is a facet of his wit. Mrs. Shandy's carelessness about asking questions or listening to hypotheses is a facet of her judgment. Her critical responses to Walter or Toby are always just, immediate, and coherent. When Walter's fantasy of being "an Asiatick monarch," delegating his procreative duties in the harem to Toby, seems to veer too closely to his actual unhappy household practice ("and I would oblige thee, *nolens, volens,* to beget for me one subject every month——"), Mrs. Shandy injects her own comment on "the system of Love and marriage" by taking a pinch of snuff. Her sniff is an expressive if understated prelude to the rebuke she subsequently articulates in her defense of natural love (*TS*, 8.33.719–21). And when Toby confuses Walter's metaphorical "ASSE" with the blister on his arse, she joins the general laughter before redirecting Walter's comment more comprehensibly: "Every body, said my mother, says you are in love, brother Toby—and we hope it is true" (*TS*, 8.32.717–18). Her attitude to the community gossip about the Widow's problem with Toby is equally sensible: "she saw nothing at all in it, to make the least bustle about" (*TS*, 9.32.804). In Tristram's words, she is "careless about it, as about every thing else in the world which concerned her;—that is,—indifferent whether it was done this way or that,—provided it was but done at all" (*TS*, 6.20.533).

Mrs. Shandy simply believes in action, not ideas: what Tristram distorts in Madam as the "vile pruriency for adventures in all things" (*TS*, 1.20.65). Tristram, echoing Toby's and Walter's fastidiousness, argues that too much emphasis on the physical—"the gross and most carnal parts"—negates the spiritual and moral elements. Mrs. Shandy's implied argument is that too much of the cerebral negates the physical and moral relevance of life.[15] Trim's concrete application of the fifth commandment in supplementing his parents' income, his story of his brother's marriage, his own experience with the Beguine, and his activities with Susanna and Bridget, all seem to celebrate this same point of view: that respect for physical needs leads to enriched understanding and appreciation of the wholeness of life. Men are neither mere insensate "stocks and stones" nor "angels," but are "cloathed with bodies" (*TS,* 5.7.431–32), and whatever they comprehend of imagination or spirit comes to them most eloquently, like the dropping of Trim's hat, through physical agency. Mrs. Shandy makes this point most clearly when she passes judgment on Walter's theory that *rational* love, "desire of philosophy and truth," is superior to *natural* love, "*desire,* simply" (*TS,* 8.33.721). "—To be sure, said my mother, love keeps peace in the world—." Walter attempts to belittle her statement with his correction: "In the *house*—my dear"; but Mrs. Shandy, supported by Yorick, will not submit: "It replenishes the earth." For that reason, she enjoys observing the progress of the Toby–Widow Wadman love affair and hopes they will marry and have children. This, for her, is what life is all about: not using "a hard word" correctly—"*cuvetts,*" after all, "are foolish things" (*TS,* 9.11.758–59). The fact that the Shandy children do not provide "amusement" (*TS,* 6.39.569) for their parents, or live to procreate families of their own, does not make Mrs. Shandy abandon her philosophy, any more than Walter considers abandoning his system of Sunday nights, even though it results in neither true discourse nor satisfactory sexual activity.

Mr. and Mrs. Shandy have tried to ensure the propagation of the Shandy line and failed, but ironically the measure of their failure is also the measure of their success as formative influences on Tristram and Madam his reader. The measure is the extent to which heart and brain can coexist in toleration and ultimately in affection, despite and even because of daily friction. This paradoxical complementarity is at work in the Shandys' dispute over whether the Widow Wadman will "persuade" Toby to impregnate her:

—Though if it comes to persuasion—said my father—Lord
have mercy on them.
Amen: said my mother, *piano.*

Amen: cried my father, *fortissime.*

Amen: said my mother again—but with such a sighing cadence of personal pity at the end of it, as discomfited every fibre about my father—he instantly took out his alman-ack . . .

The first Lord of the Treasury thinking of *ways and means,* could not have returned home, with a more embarrassed look. (*TS,* 9.11.760)

This interchange suggests the several apparently irreconcilable problems of the Shandy marriage: Walter's system of Sunday nights is now in the context of unfortunate "persuasion," dampening what might have been the warmth of conjugal union achieved when both spouses are ready and willing; Mrs. Shandy's repeated Amen seems to express partly her boredom at Walter's lovemak-ing,[16] partly her private sorrow, both perhaps the result of allowing Walter's calendar to take precedence over her own biological clock, and partly compassion for Walter's angry disappointments; Walter's embarrassment is partly an apology, partly a feeling he has hoisted himself by his own petard. Their sensitivity to the impact of each one's attitudes on the other becomes a mollifying, if not modifying, factor in their marriage.

This responsiveness, Tristram discovers in his affair with Jenny, compensates for a great deal. A relationship need not be embittered or discontinued, as Toby's is with the Widow Wadman, simply on the basis of sexual dysfunction, when another "method of book-keeping, at least with the disasters of life," may adjust the balance:

'Tis enough, said'st thou, coming close up to me, as I stood with my garters in my hand, reflecting upon what had not pass'd—'Tis enough, Tristram, and I am satisfied, said'st thou, whispering these words in my ear, **** ** **** *** ******;___**** ** **** ———any other man would have sunk down to the center———. (7.29.624)

Similarly, when a chapter of digressive intercourse with Madam is over, he pens his "sad signature of 'How our pleasures slip from under us in this world'" and Madam responds with ambiguous sympathy to the writer's quest for comprehensive and permanent connection: "What a strange creature is mortal man!" (*TS,* 9.15.767). Both the signature and the response suggest the elusive and inconclusive sentiments that can temporarily resolve dispute. They suggest further that dispute, as a mode of communication, need not be intolerant or divisive. Even in the gentle friendship between Toby and Trim, dispute is a positive factor:

> Now if I might presume, said the corporal, to differ from your honour—
> —Why else, do I talk to thee Trim: said my uncle Toby, mildly——. (*TS,* 8.28.712)

This responsiveness to and acceptance of shifting sensitivities Tristram has already explained: "Attitudes are nothing, Madam—'tis the transition from one attitude to another—like the preparation and resolution of the discord into harmony, which is all and all" (*TS,* 4.6.331):

> But mark, Madam, we live among riddles and mysteries— the most obvious things . . . have dark sides which the quickest sight cannot penetrate into; and even the clearest and most exalted understandings amongst us find ourselves puzzled and at a loss . . . —yet we find the good of it . . . —and that's enough for us. (*TS,* 4.17.350)

The lesson Tristram applies to his relationship with Madam Reader he has learned through careful observation of the successes and failures of Toby, Trim, and the Widow Wadman, of himself and Jenny, and especially of his parents. Walter and Elizabeth Shandy "find the good of it" in the moments of wordless affection that arise from the exasperations, vexations, and griefs of their marriage.

For Tristram, with death tagging at his heels throughout the narrative, the propagation of the line takes on new meaning in the writer–reader relationship. The process of writing and reading *Tristram Shandy* becomes a fruitful collaboration outliving the last of the Shandys. Madam the reader, as hobby-horse, eventually gives up the "reins of [her] imagination" into the writer's hands with the same laudable carelessness that characterizes Mrs. Shandy's indifference to how and why, and her sane concern for natural love. Madam's reward for thus permitting herself to be ridden is "the greatness of gusto" in the ride. If there is a price to be paid for such an exhilarating journey, "for heaven's and for your own sake, pay it—pay it with both hands open" (9. "Invocation." 781). Generosity of feeling is the talisman against despair and bewilderment. It offers "a comic vision strong enough, not to ward off impending evils, but to allow one to live with them when they turn up."[17] The metaphorical intercourse at all levels between the reader and writer, as the symbolic basis for communication, corresponds vividly to the generosity of feeling that activates the narrative. The Tristram–Madam relationship elevates what is worthwhile in the Walter–Mrs. Shandy marriage and makes of it the basis for a perpetually creative process of stimulating wit and sympathetic judgment.

Notes

1. Mary S. Wagoner, "Satire of the Reader in *Tristram Shandy*," *Texas Studies in Literature and Language* 8 (1966): 344.

2. John Preston, *The Created Self* (London: Heinemann, 1970), pp. 161–65. See also Wolfgang Iser, "The Reading Process: A Phenomenological Approach," *Reader-Response Criticism: From Formalism to Post-Structuralism,* Jane P. Tompkins, ed. (Johns Hopkins University Press, 1980), p. 51. Two articles in Valerie Grosvenor Myer, ed., *Laurence Sterne: Riddles and Mysteries* (London: Vision Press, 1984), interpret the basis of this active reader participation: Jacques Berthoud's "Shandeism and Sexuality," pp. 24–38, describes it as the voyeurism of the dirty joke, the writer as pimp provoking the reader to uncover salacious meaning; Bruce Stovel, "Tristram Shandy and the Art of Gossip," pp. 115–25, sees it as the titillation of gossip, provoking the reader to pry into and chortle over other people's embarrassing secrets. Frank Brady, "*Tristram Shandy*: Sexuality, Morality, and Sensibility," *ECS* 4 (1970): 46, describes the reader–writer relationship as "seduction." Robert Alter, "*Tristram Shandy* and the Game of Love," *American Scholar* 37 (1968): 316–23, gives another view of reader–writer intercourse.

3. See David Oakleaf's extended discussion of such word associations in "Long Sticks, Morris Dancers, and Gentlemen: Associations of the Hobby-horse in *Tristram Shandy*," *Eighteenth-Century Life* (1987): esp. 63, 67.

4. See, for example, Susan Schibanoff, "Taking the Gold out of Egypt: The Art of Reading as a Woman," p. 91, and Kathryn Shevelow, "Fathers and Daughters: Women as Readers of the *Tatler*," p. 114, in Elizabeth A. Flynn and Patrocinio P. Schweickart, eds., *Gender and Reading: Essays on Readers, Texts, and Contexts* (Johns Hopkins University Press, 1988).

5. Preston, pp. 181, 205.

6. "Reading Ourselves: Toward a Feminist Theory of Reading," in Flynn and Schweickart, p. 55. Schweickart is referring to the closeness between feminist reader and female text, but her contention also applies to the whimsical sexuality binding Madam and Tristram, and the satisfying complementarity they find in each other.

7. Melvyn New, in "Sterne, Warburton, and the Burden of Exuberant Wit," *ECS* 15 (1982): 245–74, argues that Sterne wages a war of wit against the stodginess of eighteenth-century judgment, as epitomized by Warburton. See especially pp. 246–47, 268–69.

8. For the analogy between Shakespeare's dark comedies and Sterne's humor, see, among others, Ben Reid, "The Sad Hilarity of Sterne," *Virginia Quarterly Review* 32 (1956): 107–34.

9. Ruth Faurot, "Mrs. Shandy Observ'd," *SEL* 10 (1970): 581. See also A. R. Towers, "Sterne's Cock and Bull Story," *ELH* 24 (1957): 26, describing Mrs. Shandy's tactic of "good-natured apathy."

10. Leigh A. Ehlers, "Mrs. Shandy's 'Lint and Basilicon': The Importance of Women in *Tristram Shandy*," *South Atlantic Review* (1981): 61. I am indebted to Professor Melvyn New for drawing my attention to this article.

11. Georges Poulet, "Criticism and the Experience of Interiority," in Tompkins, pp. 44, 46.

12. Walker Gibson, "Authors, Speakers, Readers, and Mock Readers" in Tompkins, pp. 2, 5.

13. Ehlers, pp. 67–68.

14. Henri Fluchère, *Laurence Sterne: From Tristram to Yorick* (London: Oxford University Press, 1965), p. 143.

15. For a related view of the emphasis on physicality, see Andrew Wright, "The Artifice of Failure in *Tristram Shandy*," *Novel* 2 (1969): 217.

16. Valerie Grosvenor Myer, "Tristram and the Animal Spirits," in Myer, p. 109.

17. Susan Auty, *The Comic Spirit of the Eighteenth-Century Novel* (Port Washington, N.Y.: Kennikat Press, 1975), p. 125.

Sterne and the Narrative
of Determinateness

MELVYN NEW

◆ ◆ ◆

The reader who demands to know exactly what Sterne
really thinks of a thing . . . must be given up for lost.
—FRIEDRICH NIETZSCHE, *Human,*
All Too Human

I WILL BEGIN WITH a seemingly noncontroversial observation by
a recent critic of *Tristram Shandy,* anonymous simply because it is
the sort of comment any one of a hundred might write today:
"Sterne's point," he asserts, "is clear enough: life is a confused
muddle of intent and accident." It is the sort of generalization
many have accepted at least since E. M. Forster in 1927 declared
"muddle" to be the God ruling over the work.[1] However, a closer
examination of this particular formulation, not a jot different from
that of countless others, might suggest an interesting problem.
Simply put, if the point of *Tristram Shandy* is *clear,* then the work
must be significantly divorced from the life—defined as a "confused muddle of intent and accident"—it portrays. Or, from another perspective, critics who find Sterne's point "clear enough"
are themselves divorced from a work they argue is a muddle—
and from a life that also does not allow the *clarity* they believe it
can have in *Tristram Shandy.* Can one reformulate the observation?
Perhaps we might say that "Sterne's point is obscure and muddled;
life is a confused muddle and so I, as a reflective reader, become
muddled when I try to understand his imitation of that muddle;
it is seemingly successful as an imitation, although I cannot be
quite clear on that point either." Frankly, I do not foresee this

becoming the new mode of critical discourse. In this I would like to suggest why not, drawing on what I believe to be Sterne's own encounter with the paradox of the interdeterminate text in human hands.

Using *Tristram Shandy* as my model, I specifically want to explore a key means by which its narrative, while pretending to suspend judgment about itself (to remain muddle), simultaneously reminds us of the impossibility of reading without judgment; we are unable to refrain from seeking the definitive statement of what is *clear* about the work. Since the narrative of *Tristram Shandy* is nowadays taken as a prime illustration of disruptive, fragmented, open, disjunctive narrative,[2] it helps us at times to keep our attention not on any particular interpretation, but more broadly on the contrasting "stories" people tell about the work, the narratives they initiate in order to organize or possess or subdue Sterne's mysterious text. In brief, while these modernist readers insist that *Tristram Shandy* is an open narrative, they all impose strategies of closure and *clarity* in their own writing upon it.[3]

Sterne had anticipated just such efforts in the characters of Walter and Toby Shandy, both of whom ride very hard the hobby-horse of explication and explanation. What Toby wants to do on the bowling green is to make very *clear* to the observer exactly what happened during the muddle of a real-life battle; what Walter wants to do with his theories, his consultations, his documents, is to find very *clear* solutions to the muddle of a real life. In addition, the text of *Tristram* contains numerous interwoven narrative subtexts that serve as commentaries upon the primary narrative—the marriage contract, the Memoire of the Sorbonne doctors, the sermon, Ernulphus's curse, passages from Burton and Rabelais, Montaigne and Chambers's *Cyclopædia,* and on and on.[4] These "narratives" restage the narrative strategies of the reader/critic, since they are almost always reifications, efforts to organize and control the flux of events and attitudes ("the life and opinions") by narrating them into a fixed (that is, a clear and explicable) order and arrangement. What Sterne shows us, I suggest, is that the instinct or desire to order the story is always more powerful than our capacity to rest in muddle, to celebrate disorder without a contrary urge to tidy up the place. Hence, for both character and reader, the interpolated narrative is almost always considered part of the larger narrative, a relevant commentary (limitation) upon it, rather than a further dislocation or random interference.

Sterne's technique is tied, I believe, to the classical doctrine associated with the skeptic Sextus Empiricus, concerning the inner suspension of judgment (ἐποχή) about the conformity of appearance to reality, that is, the meanings of narrative representations.[5] Like Hume, Sterne seems to suggest that such suspension, while highly desirable and useful, is not often within the human being's capacity—we cannot refrain from believing in the truth of our own perceptions, our own narratives.[6] As Terence Penelhum comments rather wryly in *God and Skepticism*: "Neither the plain man nor the philosopher can refrain from believing that they are veridical. We cannot make our own assertions *un*dogmatically."[7] *Tristram Shandy* explores the delusions of the undogmatic, indeterminate narrative, even while denying its possibility.

If Sterne embraces many strategies of indeterminacy as part of his general skeptical embrace of the mysteries and riddles of experience,[8] he is equally attracted to—indeed, fascinated by—the narrative instinct, the "art" of storytelling, as an emblem of that divine harmony to which he seems to have remained committed. Our narratives are "truths" in so far as they make life possible for us. The inner compulsion not to contradict these truths, the instinct to narrate our stories to some useful conclusion would seem inbred in our use of language; we *are* this instinct, since our being is our narrative. But where twentieth-century philosophy strives to keep our eye fixed always on the naiveté of assuming such narratives are true (the epistemological issue), Sterne's interest was at least equally focused on the comic and tragic impotence that results from insisting they are not—ultimately, an ontological issue. In particular, Sterne seems intent upon ridiculing those critics and nonbelievers *determined* to practice modes of *indeterminacy* and blind to the paradox of doing so.

Several years ago, in the course of a short essay on the process of annotating *Tristram Shandy*'s bawdy, I asked:

Is there, then, nothing for the annotator to do with Sterne's game of sexual discovery? Is all such mediation an unwarrantable intrusion between the reader and the text, most especially so when the reader's capacity to "get" the text is the game being played? Sterne confronts the problem in the first volume ... when he sends madam back to reread a chapter, punishment for having missed a clue concerning intrauterine baptism. Here the author plays his own annotator or mediator, forcing all his readers to "get" a text I am certain all will miss on first reading. Sterne's humour depends on requiring from his readers a knowledge they could not possibly be expected to have.[9]

Jonathan Lamb, a recent exuberant proponent of the indecipherable text of *Tristram Shandy* (as his recent book-length explication makes *absolutely clear*),[10] takes me to task for these comments in this manner: "The annotator [argues New] does his duty by 'forcing all his readers to "get" a text I am certain all will miss on first reading.' ... the absolute jostling [of] the reader in that sentence seems at odds with the relativising tone [New] adopted elsewhere" (p. 3). It is indeed at odds, since the "jostling" reflects Sterne's humorous "theory" of annotating, the "relativising" my serious response to its unacceptibility. Lamb, however, is in no mood for such subtle distinctions: "I think it is a pity to strip initiatives from readers in this way, especially in view of the great lengths taken by Sterne to extend them" he laments (p. 3).

I present this exchange between Lamb and my own text not in order to defend the Florida volume of *Notes,* which proved quite useful to him in the course of his study despite his quarrel with its editor, but to argue against his fundamental premise, that Sterne goes to "great lengths" to extend the "initiatives" of the readers. Certainly that is not true in the present instance: Madam is given absolutely no choice but to read the text in one way—Mrs. Shandy was not a papist, and the documentation for that reasoned conclusion is provided—signed, sealed, and delivered—in French *and* English. Does the reader have a choice? Can it be somehow argued that the text (the Sorbonne's, Sterne's, Madam's) remains undetermined at this point? But the very issue being discussed by the Sorbonne is an emblem of absolute determinacy; not a scintilla of doubt will be able to survive the work of the doctors. Every question, every doubt, every possible avenue of uncertainty, will be put to rest, brought to a satisfying conclusion, canonized into law; doubt will be turned into certainty before it is allowed to leave the womb.

The world that Sterne represents may be a muddle as has been suggested, but it is peopled by multitudes (inside the book *and* holding the book) with brooms and pens, *petites canulles* and swords, diagrams and models and paradigms, all intent on tidying up the place, making it neat and *clear.* There is, in short, no sufficient difference between the learned doctors of the Sorbonne and the learned doctors of today's academy. All work to establish the laws, the principles (the "double principle," in Lamb's case) that will make the muddle of life and its literature *clearer* and hence—no slight benefit—keep the proponents of such principles in positions of authority and acclaim. Sterne celebrates this tendency in Toby and Walter, in the doctors of the Sorbonne, in encyclopedists, in classical and theological scholars, in men like Obadiah Walker[11] and Bishop Warburton.[12] His book celebrates them all, but the appreciation is tempered by his jealous rivalry with their seemingly boundless energies; and by his chastising reminders—satiric and Christian—that human wisdom is a constant dupe to its own aspirations.

The pattern of indeterminacy being put to rest by one means or another is, to my mind, as prevalent in *Tristram Shandy* as the opposing tendency, undeniably present, of shattering certainties into fragments of ambivalence and belief. The modern critical agenda, however, focuses all its interest on the second tendency. There is not a serious work of literature, from Homer to Dante, from Shakespeare to Joyce, that has not been shown to be indeterminate, a uniformity which alone might give wisdom pause, as might the absolute *sameness* with which the prevalence of *difference* is everywhere celebrated. Such paradoxes hover at the edges of Sterne's particular plan to confront us with our inability to remain in "uncertainties, mysteries, doubts, without any irritable reaching after fact and reason."[13] And from the very beginning Sterne offers us a series of documents within *Tristram* that mimic—in their absoluteness and totality, their clarity, their principles of elucidation and discovery—the discourse of criticism that has accompanied Sterne's work from the beginning; the cant of criticism—a wonderful pun—he calls it at one important point.[14]

We are told, by Tristram and others, that this is the most cooperative book ever written, that we are joint sharers in its creation, half and half with its author.[15] But surely in the instance of the Sorbonne doctors, we have no such creative freedom. Even if we refuse to return with Madam to reread the passage, I do not think a similar option is available to deny Tristram's purpose in introducing the Memoire (1.20.67–69), namely, to document certainty, not induce uncertainty. Such moves are seen everywhere in *Tristram,* beginning perhaps in chapter 4 of the first volume, where Tristram consults a "memorandum in my father's pocketbook" concerning his whereabouts in the months prior to his son's conception. Then, in chapter 15, we are given, verbatim, the article in the marriage settlement that defines Mrs. Shandy's movements—and the codicil offered by Toby which slams shut the one slight evasion she might have exercised. Moreover, these documents do work. They confront issues which are undecided, and they decide them. Would we want to enter into a dispute with the Sorbonne doctors concerning the legitimacy of their findings? Are we invited to question the authorship of Walter's memorandum? Are we tempted to challenge the marriage settlement in court? Clearly Sterne is here not sharing his storytelling with the reader, but, quite the contrary, setting out one boundary at which language does serve human purposes—authorization, communication, control.

To be sure, these documents are parodies of the real things— or real documents in parodic situations, as is the case with the major interpolated document in volume 2, the "Abuses of Conscience" sermon. For ultimately, Sterne is not putting his faith in human language as the ultimate source of certitude; no one, not Locke in his much misunderstood (among Sterneans) *Essay Concerning Human Understanding,* or even Swift, with his maligned acad-

emy, believed in such a possibility, the eternal contradiction between "human" and "certitude" being essential to a religious
construct all three accepted. But neither does Sterne put his faith
in gesture, sentiment, or sympathy, the popular answers of the
Shaftesburian "evasion," the fallacies of which the "Abuses" sermon directly addresses.[16]

Nor, finally, does he seem quite at home, this rural Anglican
clergyman, in the indeterminate, existential, absurd, phenomenological, solipsistic universe where we nowadays seem to find him.
Rather, the documents interpolated everywhere into the world of
Tristram Shandy seem to me overt examples of one of Sterne's richest
observations: the human being produces such texts, in one form
or another, *endlessly, necessarily, inevitably.* The copy of *Tristram* we hold
in our hands is one such document, Walter Shandy's *Tristrapædia* is
another, Slawkenbergius's tome and this brief essay are also examples, and the works of Rabelais and Montaigne and Burton,
whose texts reappear in *Tristram* as part of its "documentation," are
all restagings of the instinct, the drive to order and comprehend
through our language whatever is not yet our language. The urge
not merely to begin but to *complete* the narrative of ourselves is
evident everywhere in *Tristram Shandy.* That we fail to do so could
easily be explained for Sterne within the Christian narrative of sin
(human limitation) and death (its consequence). Why we nonetheless continue to *essay* to "tell all" (and it is Montaigne who most
clearly literalizes this urge), to make absolutely, positively certain
that we have found the fullest measure of explanation and definition, the ever replenishing cornucopia of endless discourse, that
is a question less easily answered and the one I believe particularly
fascinated Sterne.[17]

I believe I could make my point with the "Abuses" sermon; or
with Ernulphus's curse (a memorial to the urge for closure and
the resourcefulness of language); or with "Slawkenbergius's Tale,"
perhaps Sterne's most extended analysis of the noise and dangers
of endless commentary.[18] Indeed, almost all Sterne's interpolated
documents respond to what I have defined as a quest for certainty
and determinacy (documentation), perhaps because their received
form as "supporting evidence" is the outcome of our own need to

define, explain, and comprehend. Can we imagine, for example, a discussion of the "Abuses" sermon that suggests it has absolutely nothing to do with *Tristram Shandy?* Could we substitute another sermon in its place (perhaps by Sterne, perhaps by Donne) and argue that it would not matter? Such hypothetical silliness can often serve to test the more serious absurdities of our present critical environment.

I would like to focus attention, however, on two interpolated documents rarely commented upon among Sterneans, the first, Rubenius's *De Re Vestiaria Veterum,* which Walter is said to consult for the breeching of Tristram in volume 6; and the second, Spencer's *De Legibus Hebræorum Ritualibus,* which comes into play in chapter 28 of volume 5 after Tristram's accident with the window sash.

Albert Rubens (1614–57) catalogs the clothing of the ancients in a large quarto that wavers between the old style of learning and the new, between the universal citing of past authorities in the hope that truth would emerge from the welter of contrary opinions, and the beginnings of a more scientific orientation that accumulates and catalogs data as the foundation for further generalization. As such, *De Re Vestiaria Veterum, Præcipue de Lato Clavo (Of the Clothing of the Ancients, Particularly of the Latus Clavus,* 1665) is typical of late seventeenth-century learning, and Sterne seems brilliantly to have caught its genius in his reduction of Rubenius to lists, the cataloging of knowledge in a manner that suggests above all the growing importance of distinction and difference. For example, Sterne lists eighteen different types of shoe, beginning with

> The open shoe.
> The close shoe.
> The slip shoe.
> The wooden shoe. . . . (*TS,* 6.19.531)

This listing, with its vertical presentation—an echo, perhaps, of similar lists in Rabelais—is of especial interest because Walter cannot find in it or in the various other lists of *De Re Vestiaria* the advice concerning breeches that he is looking for. What he does find is a wealth of argumentation, the concentration of energy into a single point upon which the learned of the world converge in their determination to settle a point—absolutely, definitively, and with the greatest clarity possible, namely, the identification of the *Latus Clavus*:

> *Rubenius* told him, that the point was still litigating amongst the learned:—That *Egnatius, Sigonius, Bossius Ticinensis, Bayfius, Budæus, Salmasius, Lipsius, Lazius, Isaac Causabon,* and *Joseph Scaliger,* all differed from each other,—and he from them: That some took it to be the button,—some the coat itself,—others only the colour of it. (*TS,* 6.19.532)

Walter—and indeed Rubens before him—finds in this collection of data not a point of certainty but simply another list, this time of a community of scholars, a source of comfortable companionship that enables Walter to proceed with his life, whatever obstacles he encounters. Moreover, if the first list suggests to us the elusiveness, indeed impossibility, of the quest for "truth," for "the key," the second list just as certainly and dramatically indicates the refusal of the human mind to surrender to that impossibility.[20] The great satirists of scholastic learning who preceded Sterne—Rabelais and Swift—share with him an ambivalence toward learning that perhaps only the best ironists (and best skeptics) can have.

We must, however, qualify the list of authorities in two ways. In the first place, Sterne informs us that "the great *Bayfius,*" listed among the disputants, in reality "honestly said, he knew not what it was,—whether a fibula—a stud,—a button,—a loop,—a buckle,—or clasps and keepers" (*TS,* 6.19.532). In a disputatious world of thesis and antithesis, statement and counterstatement, the admission of "ignorance," of "doubt," gives particular weight to the word *honestly.* But Walter's response, typical of the learned world in general, indicates that "doubt" is simply not a satisfactory resting place for the restless mind: "——My father lost the horse, but not the saddle——They are *hooks and eyes,* said my father——and with hooks and eyes he ordered my breeches to be made" (*TS,* 6.19.533). The sceptical moment of ἐποχή, the suspension between equally interesting alternatives, is unsustainable because "interest," a word weighted with theological as well as moral meaning in the eighteenth century,[20] denies us the pleasure and satisfaction we might otherwise take in stasis. For Sterne, the idea is embodied most often in the concept of the hobby-horse. To be thrown from one's horse, like Dr. Slop in volume 3 or Walter in this passage, is typical of the Shandy world; to dismount, as Bayfius appears to have done, is an heroic moment rarely encountered—except in the important normative actions of Yorick.

Second, and surely of no small significance to our present discussion, it is to be suspected that Sterne's discussion of clothing is indeed not from Rubens, that his citation is a false one. The Florida *Notes* suggests that while the list of authorities might have been gleaned from the first chapter of *De Re Vestiaria,* Sterne's other lists and the language of his discussion follow much more closely Lefèvre de Morsan's *The Manners and Customs of the Romans. Translated from the French* (1740). This is a handbook of Roman costume probably intended for schools; and precisely its commonplace nature suggests that Sterne may have used not it but a similar "textbook" as yet undiscovered.[21] In rather stark contrast to the "honesty" celebrated in Bayfius, we have here a seeming instance of basic scholarly dishonesty: deliberate miscitation. Walter's authorization to move forward collapses, the cited author and his text disappear, the determinations and absolutes of the learned prove to be indeterminate after all. Here, perhaps, is the muddle that Forster identified, the loss of "author(ity)" that makes *Tristram Shandy* seem so modern a work. I suggest, however, that the discovery upon which this collapse depends is not something Sterne could—or would—count upon. Indeed, quite the opposite. The annotator here creates an indeterminacy (two hundred years after the work's appearance) that Sterne made every effort to foreclose in a most time-honored manner—by citing learned authority. It seems important to Sterne's conception of Walter that he participate in the community of scholars represented by Rubenius, that his researches be thorough and his consultations authentic; at the very least, there is nothing in the text that serves as a clue to the imposition of Rubenius upon unsuspecting readers.[22] One might argue, of course, that none of Sterne's citations is to be trusted, that the unreliability of Tristram as a narrator is constructed from the materials of false learning, but this is precisely to confuse the ontological question with the epistemological.

Sterne's point depends upon the reality of his documentation, the fact that the Sorbonne Memoire, the "Abuses" sermon, Ernulphus's curse, all actually exist; how true they are to the reality they attempt to define is a quite separate matter. But while it serves Sterne's purpose for the reader to recognize, for example, Tristram's attack on plagiary at the opening of volume 5 as a "steal" from Burton,[23] here his purpose seems best served by the sense of closure and determinateness produced in Walter after his consultation with "authority." Or again, where we are not asked to think of Slawkenbergius as anything other than a fabrication, here we are quite directed to the narrator's learning, not his invention, as a source of knowledge. Such distinctions are vital to our reading of Sterne because they indicate a more balanced perspective on, among other things, the documentation that is so inherent a part of the *Shandy* text itself. It is, indeed, no wonder that Tristram and his annotators should so often cross paths, since he, like them, expends much energy in the pursuit of authority, documentation, and closure; unfortunately, in this instance, the annotator may have opened a door (extended an "initiative" in Lamb's terminology) that Sterne had gone to "great lengths" to close.

Unlike the other disasters that befall Walter and Tristram, the falling window sash finds the father quite prepared. He does not write about it, as we might assume—that response is reserved for Tristram, who "*completes*" (my emphasis) the *Tristapædia* with his own chapter on sash-windows and chamber pots (*TS,* 5.26.458–59). Rather, he turns to his library, to some heavy folios, while Mrs. Shandy runs for the "lint and basilicon." What is Walter looking for in these tomes, and specifically in John Spencer's *De Legibus Hebræorum Ritualibus* (*On the Ritual Laws of the Hebrews*), published twenty years after Rubenius on Roman costumes? Not simply consolation or curatives, for he has not proceeded very long before he is deep in controversy, a war of words, the futility and frustration of both history and language.

The parodic use of the documents we noted before is especially apparent here, because of both the subject matter and Yorick's guiding presence. Most important, Yorick knows the text beforehand, and the learning represented by four Greek footnotes is in response to his familiarity with Spencer's learned work. Hence, when Walter is about to let us know just what the theologians have debated, Yorick interrupts: "Theologically? said *Yorick,*—or speaking after the manner of apothecaries?—statesmen?—or washer-women?" (*TS,* 5.28.461). The three groups are footnoted, Sterne (Yorick) responding to phrases he found in Spencer, one having to do with disease (anthrax), another with population, a third with cleanlinesss.[24] Yorick's position is significantly ambivalent, however; he knows the text (as did Sterne, obviously),[25] but he can wish he did not, and when Toby suggests it is all "*Arabick to*" him, Yorick chimes in, "I wish . . . 'twas so, to half the world." At this point, Walter's reading lapses quite into controversy. Having more or less ignored the opportunity to discuss whether the Jews or Egyptians practiced circumcision first (which certainly occupies pages of Spencer and would occupy Bishop Warburton among many others),[26] he finds himself suddenly on the shoals of Ilus's identity and the controvertists' "two and twenty reasons" for his circumcising his entire army—a question which, significantly, immediately involves Toby's "determinate" nature as well: "Not without a court martial?" (*TS,* 5.28.462). Perhaps Spencer, perhaps Walter's obvious enjoyment of the controversy, leads Yorick to an attack on polemic divines: "I wish there was not a polemic divine . . . in the kingdom;—one ounce of practical divinity—is worth a painted ship load of all their reverences have imported these fifty years" (*TS,* 5.28.462); and in the next chapter, he reads Rabelais's description of Gymnast and Tripet's riding competition (another document!—and one that Yorick keeps in his coat pocket),[27] which serves to pin down in all our minds, exactly and definitely and determinately, Yorick's attitude toward the cavortings of the intellectual community. Yet Yorick's "familiarity" with Spencer suggests as well his community with that world of books and words. Significantly, it is the same community that Walter looks for when he seeks in *De Legibus* a consolation for the maiming of Tristram:

> Nay, said he, mentioning the name of a different great nation
> upon every step as he set his foot upon it—if the EGYPTIANS,—
> the SYRIANS,—the PHOENICIANS,—the ARABIANS,—the CAPA-
> DOCIANS,——if the COLCHI, and TROGLODYTES did it——if
> SOLON and PYTHAGORAS submitted,—what is TRISTRAM?——
> Who am I, that I should fret or fume one moment about the
> matter? (*TS,* 5.27.460)

Whether it is the link that Sterne forges with Rabelais at the end
of this scene, the link with Shakespeare inherent in the naming of
Yorick, or the link with a world of past scholars and churchmen,
and the lost cultures of the past (and we must remember that
volume 5 opens with a somewhat parallel passage, again an interpolated document, Cicero's consolatory letter to Sulpicius, by way
of Burton's *Anatomy of Melancholy*),[28] one has here, I suggest, an answer to the question posed earlier: why do we continue to talk
and write and exercise our language in the pursuit of knowledge,
definition, unattainable clarity, and wisdom?

The real community of *Tristram Shandy* is not, as is so often said,
simply that of the Shandy brothers; rather, it is represented by all
the authors and books, all their documents and cultures and artifacts, all that illustrates to us what it means to live in a world
written by God, and hence always approximated by the same human endeavor. At times the documents are necessarily ludicrous,
as is so much human effort in the face of the infinite, but at other
times they are useful and perhaps even profound, as human effort
can also be. Sterne keeps us aware of both possibilities, and aware
above all that while every attempt to create a world of certainty
and truth will fail, the attempt is what ties us to the community
of humanity, what offers us the equivalent of communion with
our legacy, and, in the end, allows us to create, if not God's world,
then our own world in imitation of His. Writing seems to have
been an activity Sterne delighted in, not as an epistemological experience, but an ontological one. Sterne's "documents" suggest to
me that the present emphasis in narrative theory on the epistemology of indeterminacy is a tendency he might have predicted

but never have succumbed to. Sterne's fiction arises, to the contrary, in the ontology of the human urge to speak the truth.

That that urge so often takes the shape of fiction and folly is nothing that was not explained to him by his faith, and redeemed by it as well. Nietzsche is one of his few readers who seems fully to appreciate Sterne's ontological bent: "His antipathy to seriousness is united with a tendency to be unable to regard anything merely superficially. Thus he produces in the right reader a feeling of uncertainty as to whether one is walking, standing or lying: a feeling, that is, close to floating."[29] Classical skepticism might call it hovering between all possibilities, but I suspect Nietzsche, Sterne, and Sextus Empiricus each had a nicely muddled idea (*clarity* would not suffice) of approximately the same thing.

Notes

1. "Obviously a god is hidden in *Tristram Shandy* and his name is Muddle, and some readers cannot accept him," *Aspects of the Novel* (New York: Harcourt, 1927), p. 146.

2. See, for example, J. Hillis Miller, "Narrative Middles: A Preliminary Outline," *Genre* 11 (1978), 375–87; Ralph Flores, "Changeling Fathering: *Tristram Shandy,*" in *The Rhetoric of Doubtful Authority: Deconstructive Readings of Self-Questioning Narratives, St. Augustine to Faulkner* (Ithaca, N.Y.: Cornell University Press, 1984), pp. 116–44; and Jonathan Lamb, *Sterne's Fiction and the Double Principle* (Cambridge: Cambridge University Press, 1989).

3. The most glaring instance is Wolfgang Iser's *Laurence Sterne: "Tristram Shandy"* (Cambridge: Cambridge University Press, 1988), where the reading of *Tristram* as an indeterminate text turns Sterne into both a forerunner and strict proponent of Iser's own critical theories. See also Robert Markley, "*Tristram Shandy* and 'Narrative Middles': Hillis Miller and the Style of Deconstructive Criticism," *Genre* 17 (1984), 179–90, an attempt to justify Miller's obfuscations while at the same time "translating" them into what might pass for a transparent (i.e., a *clear*) expository prose.

4. This structure of borrowings is apparent on almost every page of *Tristram Shandy: The Notes,* ed. Melvyn New, with Richard A. Davies and W.G. Day, vol. 3 of *The Florida Edition of the Works of Laurence Sterne* (Gainesville: University Presses of Florida, 1984), cited hereafter as *Notes;* one need only

compare these notes with those required for Fielding's or Smollett's fictions (excepting *Adventures of an Atom*) in the Wesleyan and Georgia editions respectively to realize a fundamental difference between Sterne and the novelists with whom he is most often grouped.

5. See the very fine essay by Donald R. Wehrs, "Sterne, Cervantes, Montaigne: Fideistic Skepticism and the Rhetoric of Desire," *Comparative Literature Studies* 25 (1988), 127–51.

6. See David Hume, *An Enquiry concerning Human Understanding,* ed. Antony Flew (La Salle, Ill.: Open Court, 1988), pp. 189–90 (section 12, part 2): "For as, in common life, we reason every moment concerning fact and existence, and cannot possibly subsist, without continually employing this species of argument, any popular objections, derived from thence, must be insufficient to destroy that evidence. The great subverter of *Pyrrhonism* or the excessive principles of scepticism is action, and employment, and the occupations of common life. These principles may flourish and triumph in the schools; where it is, indeed, difficult, if not impossible, to refute them. But as soon as they leave the shade, and by the presence of the real objects, which actuate our passions and sentiments, are put in opposition to the more powerful principles of our nature, they vanish like smoke, and leave the most determined sceptic in the same condition as other mortals." See the essays by M. F. Burnyeat ("Can the Skeptic Live His Skepticism?") and Robert J. Fogelin ("The Tendency of Hume's Skepticism") in *The Skeptical Tradition,* ed. Myles Burnyeat (Berkeley: University of California Press, 1983), especially pp. 118–21, 398–404.

7. *God and Skepticism: A Study in Skepticism and Fideism* (Dodrecht: D. Reidel, 1983), p. 124.

8. Sterne uses the phrase "riddles and mysteries" twice in *Tristram Shandy* (4.17.350, 9.22.776) and once in his *Sermons* ("Felix's behaviour towards Paul," 19.182; but see also a close variant of this passage in "The ways of Providence justified to man," 44.415). In the original version of this essay (published in 1992), I deplored the tendency of critics to follow Martin Battestin "in asserting that the phrase indicates a secular worldview: the Shandy world is 'inexplicable even when it appears most obvious, overwhelming in its multiplicity, unpredictable in its contingencies, it bewilders and eludes them all' " (*The Providence of Wit: Aspects of Form in Augustan Literature and the Arts* [Oxford: Clarendon Press, 1974], p. 245). As Wehrs points out (see esp. 145–46), Christian fideism paints exactly the same picture of the mundane world, but leading *toward* rather than *away* from faith. Happily, the source of Sterne's "riddles and mysteries" has now been

recovered, in John Norris, *Practical Discourses upon Several Divine Subjects: Volume Two* (1691), p. 238: "We live among Mysteries and Riddles, and there is not one thing that comes in at our Senses, but what baffles our Understandings; but though (as the Wise Man [Wisdom 9:16] complains,) *hardly do we guess aright at the things that are upon Earth, and with labour do we find the things that are before us.*" See *Notes to the Sermons,* pp. 218–20 (n. to 19.182, lines 21–30) and pp. 447–48 (n. to 44.415, lines 1–14); also New, "The Odd Couple: Laurence Sterne and John Norris of Bemerton," *Philological Quarterly* 75 (1996): 361–85. Norris (1657–1711), often considered the last of the Cambridge Platonists, and certainly a Christian theologian and philosopher in his own right, may seem, indeed, an "odd" source for Sterne, but "oddity" is often merely a riddle we have not yet made *clear.*

9. " 'At the backside of the door of purgatory': A Note on Annotating *Tristram Shandy,*" in *Laurence Sterne: Riddles and Mysteries,* ed. Valerie Grosvenor Myer (London and Totowa, N.J.: Vision Press and Barnes and Noble, 1984), p. 17.

10. The title of Lamb's book, *Sterne's Fiction and the Double Principle,* contains its own statement of the problem I am exploring, namely, the human inability to confront "doubleness" without reducing it to a "principle"—to oneness. Only once, to my mind, does Lamb come close to recognizing this paradox (p. 104: "The lesson for the reader, you or me, comes unsettlingly close"); far more telling is the fact that not only Sterne but Cervantes and Montaigne as well are found to conform to Lamb's "double principle." Reductiveness, even in the pursuit of indeterminacy, is no virtue.

11. The author of *Of Education,* from which Sterne borrowed, verbatim in many instances, his discussion of auxiliary verbs at the end of volume 5; see *Notes,* pp. 392–94, n. to 484.11ff.

12. See my "Sterne, Warburton, and the Burden of Exuberant Wit," *Eighteenth-Century Studies* 15 (1982), 245–74 for a full discussion not only of Sterne's borrowings from Warburton, but of his mixed response to Warburton's great (if hobbyhorsical) learning.

13. Herbert Read, an astute reader of Sterne, was perhaps the first to connect Sterne and Keats: "We know that Keats was familiar with *Tristram Shandy,* and it may be that his notion of *Negative Capability* ('which Shakespeare possessed so enormously') owes something to Sterne's character of Yorick—in any case, Sterne was certainly also 'a man . . . capable of being in uncertainties, Mysteries, doubts' " (*The Contrary Experience* [London: Faber and Faber, 1963], p. 330). Keats outlined his idea in a letter to his brothers dated 21 December 1817.

14. *Tristram Shandy,* 3.12.214: "Of all the cants which are canted in this canting world———though the cant of hypocrites may be the worst,—the cant of criticism is the most tormenting!"

15. See, for example, *Tristram Shandy,* 2.11.125: "The truest respect which you can pay to the reader's understanding, is to halve this matter amicably, and leave him something to imagine, in his turn, as well as yourself." Perhaps the favorite incident for those critics who take such comments literally as the shaping spirit of the work is Tristram's invitation in volume 6, chapter 38, to draw the widow Wadman in the blank page provided for our fancy. Yet surely, even here, Sterne's point is far more determinate than indeterminate, since his work depends not at all upon the reader actually taking pen and ink in hand (and I have never found a single copy of *Tristram Shandy* in which the offer was accepted), but upon grasping the humor of Tristram's distinction between wife and mistress. That women might not find the passage humorous at all indicates precisely how overdetermined Sterne's joke is at this point.

16. Interesting recent discussions of Sterne and Shaftesburian sensibility include Robert Markley, "Sentimentality as Performance: Shaftesbury, Sterne, and the Theatrics of Virtue," in *The New Eighteenth Century: Theory, Politics, English Literature,* ed. Felicity Nussbaum and Laura Brown (New York and London: Methuen, 1987), pp. 210–30; and John Mullan, *Sentiment and Sociability: The Language of Feeling in the Eighteenth Century* (Oxford: Clarendon, 1988), pp. 147–200. See also *Notes,* pp. 180–81, n. to 157.14ff.

17. Montaigne's own embrace of Pyrrhonic skepticism, most especially in the "Apology for Raimond de Sebonde," leads I think to his often stated love of self-exploration. See, for example, "Of the Resemblance of Children to their Fathers": "I do not hate Opinions contrary to my own. I am so far from being angry to see a Disagreement betwixt mine and other Men's Judgments . . . that on the contrary . . . I find it much more rare to see our Humours and Designs jump and agree. And there never was in the World two Opinions alike, no more than two Hairs, or two Grains. The most universal Quality, is *Diversity*"; and "Of Repentance": "Could my Soul once take footing, I would not essay, but resolve; but it is always learning and making trial. Every Man carries the entire Form of [the] human Condition" (*Essays,* trans. Charles Cotton, 6th ed. [London, 1753], 2:521; 3:20). In September 1760 Sterne confirmed a correspondent's guess that Montaigne was a favorite author: " 'for my conning Montaigne as much as my pray'r book'—there you are right again" (*Letters,* p. 122).

18. I explore this aspect of *Tristram Shandy* in "Swift and Sterne: Two

Tales, Several Sermons, and a Relationship Revisited," in *Critical Essays on Jonathan Swift,* ed. Frank Palmeri (New York: G. K. Hall, 1993), pp. 164–86.

19. An interesting confluence of Sterne's interest in the learned community and his life as an Anglican clergyman may be seen in a popular clerical manual like John Wilkins's *Ecclesiastes: or, A Discourse Concerning the Gift of Preaching,* which reached its ninth edition by 1718. Wilkins's efforts are primarily bibliographical, pages upon pages listing works to consult on such topics as "Scripture-Philosophy," "Scripture-Geography," "Scripture-Measures and Weights," then on individual books of the Bible, usually at least twenty sources for each, and finally on topics such as "Independency" or "Communion and Schism," each list divided into "pro" and "con." This vast accumulation of learning, when thus cataloged, is at once an impressive commentary on human endeavor and human folly; perhaps Wilkins sensed the ambiguity when he warns the clergy in his introduction to "beware of that vain affectation of finding something new and strange in every text, though never so plain. It will not so much shew our *parts* . . . as our *pride* and wantonness of wit" (p. 16).

20. See, for example, Isabel Rivers, *Reason, Grace, and Sentiment: A Study of the Language of Religion and Ethics in England, 1660–1780* (Cambridge: Cambridge University Press, 1991), pp. 70–88.

21. See *Notes,* pp. 417–22, n. to 529.17ff.

22. There is good evidence, indeed, that Sterne wanted to pass as more learned than he really was; see my "Sterne, Warburton, and the Burden of Exuberant Wit" (cited above, n. 13), for one possible explanation. The single instance where he most successfully achieved an unearned reputation may be his borrowings from Locke; twentieth-century critics have often discovered in Sterne a profound commentator on the *Essay Concerning Human Understanding,* although they remain undecided as to whether Sterne supports or criticizes Locke. In fact, Sterne's citations of Locke repeat the most common notions associated with him and might easily derive from popular sources, for example Chambers's *Cyclopædia.*

23. Sterne gives ample indication that Burton's *Anatomy of Melancholy* is on his mind, from the two mottoes on the title page of the first edition of volume 5 to borrowings from Burton in both the Whiskers episode (see *Notes,* p. 342, n. to 412.5ff.) and Walter's funeral oration (*Notes,* p. 345, n. to 418.8–12, etc.).

24. See *notes,* p. 374, n. to 461.16–17.

25. Spencer's *De Legibus Hebræorum Ritualibus* appears twice (items 303 and 810) in *A Facsimile Reproduction of a Unique Catalogue of Laurence Sterne's Library*

(London: James Tregaskis, 1930); Rubenius appears as item 828. The catalog is not an accurate representation of Sterne's library (other libraries were grouped in the sale), but the appearance of Rubenius and Spencer in a 1768 sale catalog of private libraries helps to make one essential point of this essay. There was a community of learned lay readers (with a capacity for Latin, to be sure) in mid-eighteenth-century England whose libraries were well stocked with arcane learning from the seventeenth century.

26. See *Notes,* pp. 372–73, n. to 460.9–11.

27. Sterne borrows from Rabelais. See *The Works of Francis Rabelais, M.D.,* trans. Thomas Urquhart and Peter Motteux, with notes by John Ozell, 5 vols. (1750), 1:35; see *Notes,* pp. 376–78, n. to 463.1ff.

28. See *Notes,* pp. 348–50, n. to 421.17 to 422.28. That Warburton had used a similar parody of the letter by Scarron to attack the "wits" of the age (see the "Dedication to Free Thinkers" in his *Divine Legation of Moses*) was almost certainly on Sterne's mind; and perhaps, as well, a parody of Cicero's letter by Swift. To suggest that such a text, then, is somehow open and indeterminate and that the annotator who directs attention to these relationships limits the reader's freedom strikes me as absurd; indeed, I might suggest, instead, that the reader who does not hear Cicero, Burton, Scarron, Swift, and Warburton in this passage is exiled from the community of *Tristram Shandy,* much as Toby "frees" himself by this literal interpretation: "My uncle *Toby* had but two things for it; either to suppose his brother to be the wandering *Jew,* or that his misfortunes had disordered his brain" (*TS,* 5.3.423). Toby is at this point a very poor reader of his brother's text.

29. Nietzsche, *Human, All too Human,* trans. R. J. Hollingdale (Cambridge: Cambridge University Press, 1986), p. 239.

PART V

Politics and History

Sterne and Irregular Oratory

JONATHAN LAMB

◆   ◆   ◆

L AURENCE STERNE HAS always been considered the least rule-
bound of the British eighteenth-century novelists, and his *Tristram Shandy* is generally cited as the most eccentric production
within the already varied collection of narrative types of
eighteenth-century fiction. The common method of assimilating
his work to the new province of novel writing is to assume that
the digressions, apostrophes, typographical outrages and zany time
scheme that make it so unaccountable are the result of a thoroughgoing parody of the conventions of realism established during
the previous decade by Richardson and Fielding. Accordingly,
when Sterne is not sporting with the immediacy encouraged by
the epistolary novel by intimately addressing the reader, accu-
mulating heaps of pointless minutiae, or confounding real time
with narrative time, he is taking Fielding's modified neoclassicism
to absurd conclusions by invoking the principle of selectivity to
justify his missing chapters, or using that principle to authorize
wild appeals to the reader about what to include and what to leave
out, and by wickedly clever misapplications of the rule of *ut pictura*

poesis (a poem should be like a speaking picture) in the shape of marbled and blackened pages, and waving lines intended to represent the flourish of a stick or the digressions of his story.[1]

That this sort of parody might not be construed as irresponsible trifling (as F. R. Leavis called it), critics such as Sigurd Burckhardt and John Traugott have assumed that Sterne is clearing away the debris of verisimilitude in order to celebrate the sudden and natural communion one soul shares with another when the mediation of art is sidestepped—such sympathy being Tristram Shandy's sole plot as a narrator who is determined to treat his readers as friends with whom he expects to "so manage it, as to convey but the same impressions to every other brain, which the occurrences themselves excite in my own."[2]

This recuperation of Sterne's more spectacular irregularities as means to spontaneous communication between narrator and reader reflects his own taste for reprocessing texts (such as his favorite source of arcana, Burton's *Anatomy of Melancholy*) as well as his opinions concerning the detestable effects of imposture and the value of an open heart; but at a price. For one thing, such stabilizing of Sterne's text depends on an improbable estimate of the dominance of the novel's realism, as if it were well enough established by the 1750s for its parody readily to be undertaken and appreciated: for another, this approach demands a rather naive view of Sterne's naturalism and of his valorization of sensibility, as if the appearance of spontaneity itself were not always mediated by art. Virginia Woolf, one of the first to read Sterne's fiction as a critique of realism, uses it to illustrate an argument about modernism and its relation to the last great realist novelists such as Bennett and Galsworthy.[3] These arguments in favor of Sterne as sentimental protomodernist largely ignore questions of the motives for composition and the reception of his fiction in the eighteenth century.

In this chapter I want to consider *Tristram Shandy* (and to a lesser extent *A Sentimental Journey*) as fictions embedded in a definite cultural milieu, responsive to determinate and particular moments of political and social pressure, and ambitious to exert real power over their readers. This involves taking seriously what Sterne himself said about his first novel, namely that it was a satire, and as such alive to the current practices of churchmen, lawyers, politicians, medical experts, and soldiers, as well as writers. If we take Sterne's work seriously as social and cultural critique, it is possible to discover how his radical modification of his satiric enterprise, and his improvement of its side effects into a success of a different kind, involves his engagement with the public sphere on terms that emphasize not the satirist's monitory guardianship of society's rules and norms, but the importance of an individual's eloquence in determining the power relations that govern both the private "world" of Shandy Hall and the world at large. Furthermore, I hope to show that Sterne's eloquence (which is both the subject of his novels and their governing style of presentation) requires from the reader a reconceptualizing of narrative so that it is neither sentimental nor satirically instructive. Instead of thinking of Sterne's novels as fables from which the moral is to be deduced— that is, stories with a meaning that eventually becomes clear by means of interpretation[4]—it is more accurate to think of Sterne's narratives as an unstable series of seized initiatives, designed not for interpretive symmetry but for local practical advantages in the engagement with the reader. What may look like an invitation to share moral agency with the author is in fact more likely to be a tactical immobilization of the reader's resistance to what is being proposed.

In this chapter I shall draw an extensive parallel between Sterne's narrative practice and the political eloquence recommended by thinkers such as Lord Bolingbroke and David Hume, an eloquence shortly to be exploited to devastating effect by William Pitt, leader of the war ministry when Sterne began writing *Tristram Shandy* (1759–67) and the patron to whom that novel is twice dedicated. I shall rely to a great extent on the work of Jonathan Clark and John Pocock, historians who have recently contributed to a fundamental reconsideration of politics in midcentury Britain, and who have also based their reassessments on what they see as a recurring set of narratives in the political and ideological discourse of the age. Their work offers to explain why and how Pitt exploits the principles of the disinterested patriot out of motives that are not principled and for purposes that are self-interested. This tactical eloquence of the politician and Sterne's redeployment of satiric techniques share a common ground in their provisional and expedient adaptations of normative language. I propose to approach Sterne's adaptations as practical narrative, like the politician's speeches rather than as the narrative form of a definite interpretable meaning.

In *Tristram Shandy* the narrator's father, an autodidact with pediatric ambitions along the lines of Cornelius Scriblerus (one of a set of characters invented by Pope, Swift, and their friends to satirize pedantry), is conceived as the occasion for a variety of satirical attacks on rigid principles of reasoning and belief whose validity is simply assumed, never tried. Walter Shandy is the type of thinker who shelters untested hypotheses and prescriptions behind a screen of jargon and abstraction. His implicit belief in the value of a priori rules governing childbirth, Christian names, noses, and auxiliary verbs is compared during the first part of the novel with French theoreticians, Dutch commentators, and inquisitorial torturers in the ferocity of its attachment to the conjectural foundations of "an argument *a priori*" (*TS*, 2.17.166). When Walter's arguments are overwhelmed by empirical facts and practice, he is inconsolable until he can fashion (as in the case of his child's accidental circumcision by a falling window sash) an a priori rule out of an a posteriori breach of the order he wants to prevail. At the end of the fourth volume, however, Tristram intervenes to beg that his stories not be mistaken for satirical analogues ridiculing the bigotry of systematic thinking:

> In the story of my father and his christen-names,—I had no thoughts of treading upon *Francis* the First—nor in the affair of the nose—upon *Francis* the Ninth—nor in the character of my uncle *Toby*—of characterizing the militiating spirits of my country . . . nor by *Trim*,—that I meant the duke of *Ormond*—or that my book is wrote against predestination, or free will, or taxes. (*TS*, 4.22.360)

As for Walter's character, initially the vehicle of the satire against a priori systems, it develops a freestanding versatility and unexpectedness that Tristram expects his reader to find more and more sympathetic and interesting, and less and less generically ridiculous.

The displacement of what appears initially to be a satiric plan by the strengthening impulse to value oddity for its own sake results in descriptions whose particularity generates a self-subsistent comedy, presenting characters who are uninterpretable in any other sense than that that of their own indisputable singularity, involves two tricky renegotiations of the original satiric position. Characters such as Walter are not simply represented as generic—the pedant, as Didius is the lawyer or "your reverence" is the prelate. He and the others in the Shandy family develop profiles whose interest lies not in their conformity to any norm, but rather in their freedom from all types and precedents. Talking of the unaccountable diversity of his father's whims, Tristram warns the reader, "Be wary, Sir, when you imitate him" (*TS,* 5.42.484). At the same time, the novelty of such characters cannot be so pure as to defeat all methods of recognizing and appreciating them. The growing inimitability of hobbyhorsical eccentricity, evinced in Toby's "unparallel'd modesty" (*TS,* 1.21.74) or the baffling unpredictability of Walter's reactions to events (*TS,* 5.24.456), requires this assimilation of private singularity to the terms of public and sentimental approval if it is not to disappear into pointless elaborations of irregularity and anomie. This double shift, from the public standards of satire to the privacies of unparalleled minds, and then back from these private particulars to their recognizably public value, is achieved by the persuasive force of eloquence.

Sterne first experimented with this double shift in his satire on the ecclesiastical politics of York, *A Political Romance* (1759). Delivered in two parts, the first telling the story of Trim and the watchcoat, which runs parallel with the row between John Fountayne and Francis Topham over the control of minor ecclesiastical offices in Yorkshire, the second offering the "Key," in which the satirical allegory is variously interpreted by a political club, the satire evolves into a dramatization of the reading it provokes in this particular audience. The point at issue ceases to be the real events represented by the allegory in that "a good warm watch coat" stands for the church offices that were being contested, and becomes instead the contradictory particularity of its interpretations:

> Thus every Man turn'd the Story to what was swimming uppermost in his own Brain;—so that, before all was over, there were full as many Satyres spun out of it, and as great a Variety of Personages, Opinions, Transactions, and Truths, found to lay hid under the dark Veil of its Allegory, as ever were discovered in the thrice-renowned History of the Acts of *Gargantua and Pantagruel*.[5]

The risible failure of reading as a decisive interpretive act leads to a narrative whose stake is no longer an accurate decoding of signs, but the plausible representation of a series of scenes which dramatize the comic futility of thinking that there is one correct reading. By making the point of ridicule the search for meaning rather than the meaning *tout court,* Sterne's assault on the a priori falls not on the fantastic claims of church lawyers (the ostensible object of the exercise) but on the reader who claims to understand it as such. The a priori is now the assumption behind the act of reading and interpreting rather than the governing assumptions behind what is read about; and this strategy leaves the field of narrative particulars free from all normalizing interventions. The story is what it is, not another thing, and all its purposes are served in triumphantly revealing to the reader that it has none. For his part, the narrator enjoys the emancipation of his skills—a satire on the interpretation of satire—that is derived from self-reference. The more he can incorporate interpretation as the primary material of his story, the less the reader is free to interpret it. The index of this swing of choices in the narrator's direction is his reflexive grasp on the capacity of narrative to include within its purview its own effects, and to make its own genesis, development, and consumption the legitimate objects of representation.

Sterne shifts from the public object of satire to the private foibles that make impossible the unveiling and stripping away characteristic of satirical discourse, and that involves a parallel shift from the reader's competence based on his ability to interpret signs to the author's own narrative freedom based on representational self-reference. So, in *Tristram Shandy* Tristram defends the unimpeachable singularity of his characters against readers who might like to judge them according to an objective criterion. After his apostrophe to his Uncle Toby, who has almost killed himself trying to find in calculus the secret of projectiles, Tristram tackles the reader. He explains that "the best plain narrative in the world" would have been "cold and vapid upon the reader's palate" after "the last spirited apostrophe" (*TS*, 2.4.104). He fills up the space between the apostrophe and the next piece of narrative with an instructive maxim, namely that an author is like a painter in deeming it "more pardonable to trespass against truth, than beauty." A truth laid down like this in defiance of literal truth presents no problems for Tristram, who goes on to show that the truth of what he has said lies solely in its timing: "As the parallel is made more for the sake of letting the apostrophe cool, than any thing else,—'tis not very material whether upon any other score the reader approves of it or not." The truth of this kind of "truth" at the expense of an objective truth is determined by the circumstances and the rhetorical effects of its telling, not what it tells. Sterne's narrative does not offer the reader a prescriptive standard, moving in advance of the story and designed as a reference point in the critical estimate of its execution, but the narrative serves rather as a mirror in that the narrator may plume himself at the reader's expense. Here the a priori that is to be demolished is not belief, truth, or even the aestheticization of truth, but the reader's assumption that any rule or standard of objective accuracy might have priority over narrative practice. The self-referential skill of the narrator allows him to convert rule and principle into further narrative material—to represent the theory of representation as part of the story—so that what comes behind is always in advance of what goes before. The strange time scheme of *Tristram Shandy* is inseparable from this unsettled relation of the moral to the fable. An event can be narrated only after a set of rhetorical choices has been made, and in narrative therefore the world being represented is subordinated in every sense to the demands of persuasively representing it.

The story of the conception and delivery of the infant Tristram is Sterne's largest experiment in narrative self-reference, and it works by constantly incorporating metaphors of representation as the substance of the narrative. The technique is based on the analogy between eloquence and childbirth. The best orators are like mothers or accoucheurs in the deft production of a small child:

> When a state orator has . . . hid his BAMBINO in his mantle so cunningly that no mortal could smell it,—and produced it so critically, that no soul could say, it came in by head and shoulders,—Oh, Sirs! it has done wonders.—It has open'd the sluices, and turn'd the brains, and shook the principles, and unhinged the politicks of half a nation. (*TS,* 3.14.218)

The bambino in Tristram's tale is of course himself; and like other by-products of systemic ways of thinking, he is both the object and channel of a stream of eloquence directed ultimately at the world at large, represented by the reader. When he draws another analogy between his mother's retentive womb and Dr. Slop's bag, so tightly knotted by Obadiah that it cannot easily be delivered of its instruments of delivery, and wonders which shall emerge first, the bambino or the forceps, he postpones all accounts of himself "till I am got out into the world" (*TS,* 3.8.196). To get out into the world is to make the transition from the muteness of infancy to the passionate practice of oratory by acquiring the powers "which erst have opened the lips of the dumb in his distress, and made the tongue of the stammerer speak plain" (*TS,* 6.25.545). These are the same "exquisite powers" already apostrophized as David Garrick's (*TS,* 4.7.333), and in Tristram's case they are acquired when the instruments and the objects of delivery become indistinguishable as items of narrative interest. When forceps double up as the infant they are to deliver, and when the agency of representation (the orator producing a baby from his mantle) doubles up as the object of representation (the baby born in the third volume of the novel), narrative power is generated. Tristram does not sentimentalize this power. It has practical effects often indistinguishable from the confusion Walter has always seen on the far side of the a priori, such as the mangled body which Ernulphus's tremendous imprecation (an actual Roman Catholic curse or Latin sentence of excommunication by Ernulf, bishop of Rochester from 1114 to 1124, that

Walter finds amusing and that Sterne inserts in the text) seeks to create, or the unhinged politics and shaken principles which it is the aim of ancient oratory to provoke. Hume points out in his essay "Of Eloquence" that the greatest achievements in oratory are contemporary with the worst kinds of disorder and violence.[6]

Tristram is committed therefore to acting as the deliverer of his own delivery, thereby controlling and directing the destructive and unsettling effects of eloquence. Like the tautologous relation existing between the womb and the bag of instruments, or a midwife and an orator, Tristram's relation to his genesis is closely implicated in the instrumentality of the eloquence that will make it known to the world. Whatever comes before, in the sense of being historically prior, finds its value solely in what comes after, in the sense of that narration of it which is rhetorically posterior. Hence the equivocation on the right and wrong ends of Mrs. Shandy, suggestive of the fact that young Tristram has come foremost into the world by a hindmost route. He has made his way forward backward; he owes his rise to a bottom, and so on. Tristram plays with these paradoxes, which are both comic and profound in their implications.

Tristram and his author cling to this reversible metaphor through thick and thin: a hypothesis (especially a hypothesis about childbirth) is like a fetus, for "when once a man has conceived it . . . it assimilates every thing to itself as proper nourishment" (*TS,* 2.19.177); an abortion occurs when, after a sound conception, a man is forced to "go out of the world with the conceit of it rotting in his head" (*TS,* 1.22.80). Sterne told Stephen Croft that it was in Ireland that "my mother gave me to the world," and it is by a parallel act of motherhood that he attempts to give his own children to the world: "I am going to ly in of another child of the Shandaick procreation, in town—I hope you wish me a safe delivery." But sometimes he is unlucky: "I miscarried of my tenth Volume by the violence of a fever . . . I have however gone on to my reckoning with the ninth, of wch I am all this week in Labour pains."[7] A perfect circularity, or at least a consistent nonpriority, exists between all aspects of his work. Both end and instrument of what he fashions, Tristram exactly resembles the state orator's baby, so indistinguishably presented as the object and impulse of rhetoric that no soul can say he comes in by head or shoulders. All his audience knows for sure is that either as cause or effect of eloquence, Tristram's is an unhinged and unhinging case. Tristram makes no bones about this. He apostrophizes the force as power: "O ye POWERS! (for powers ye are, and great ones too)—which enable mortal man to tell a story worth the hearing" (*TS*, 3.23.244). Tristram salutes the great actor Garrick's art as power, and he several times warns his reader not to take it lightly; after all, it is confusing and politically dangerous: "O my countrymen!—be nice;—be cautious of your language;—and never, O! never let it be forgotten upon what small particles your eloquence and your fame depend" (*TS*, 2.6.166).

His most eloquent reflection on the dangers of eloquence follows Trim's remarkable speech on death. Trim ornaments a self-evident truth: "Are we not here now, and are we not gone! in a moment." But he does this not with a bambino but a hat, dropped so dextrously halfway through the citation that its triteness is transformed into a stunning practice, a deathly gesture on the topic of death:

> The descent of the hat was as if a heavy lump of clay had been kneaded into the crown of it.—Nothing could have expressed the sentiment of mortality, of which it was the type and fore-runner, like it,—his hand seemed to vanish from under it,—it fell dead,—the corporal's eye fix'd upon it, as upon a corps. (*TS*, 5.7.432)

Then Tristram turns eloquently to the world Trim's eloquence has revealed, and apostrophizes it as follows:

> Ye who govern this mighty world and its mighty concerns with the *engines* of eloquence,—who heat it, and cool it, and melt it, and mollify it,—and then harden it again to *your purpose*—
>
> Ye who wind and turn the passions with this great windlass,—and, having done it, lead the owners of them, whither ye think meet—

> Ye lastly, who drive—and why not, Ye also who are
> driven, like turkeys to market, with a stick and a red clout—
> meditate—meditate, I beseech you, upon *Trim*'s hat. (*TS,*
> 5.7.433)

What does such a meditation bring? Not, certainly, an impression
of a comfortable intimacy with the force of eloquence, which is
shown to flow through the most public parts of the actual world,
as well as in the text we are presently reading, toward ends that
are manifestly not altruistic, principled, or even safe. Whom then
might Tristram have in mind as he talks of the governor of this
mighty engine? Garrick is always associated with eloquence in
Sterne's writing, but his power is limited to the theater. It is hard
not to think that Tristram is alluding to an orator thought by
many of his contemporaries to be the modern equal of Demos-
thenes and Cicero, the friend of Garrick who, by Garrick's good
offices, was to become the patron of the aspiring comic author[8]—
namely William Pitt, to whom *Tristram Shandy* is twice dedicated, a
state orator whose eloquence in the House of Commons was by
this time legendary, and whose power was then at its height. I
want to explore the connection between Tristram's paradoxical and
comic reflections on eloquence and the leading Patriot politician
of the day by unpacking from the two dedications the themes we
have been following through the novel.[9] In the first, "the Author"
addresses the secretary of state from a thatched house in "a bye
corner of the kingdom," asking him not to protect the book but
to read it when he himself goes into the country. The Patriot
subtext is not difficult: A marginal figure with an ambition to "get
out into the world" addresses a politically central figure who nevertheless idealizes the integrity associated with the retirement from
which the aspiring author speaks. Pitt's politics were nurtured at
Stowe, the great estate and country house of one of his political
mentors, the earl of Cobham, and he loved a country life. He wrote
to his sister Ann as "her gentle loving shepherd," and to his brother
John he confessed, "I long to be with you kicking up my heels—
and looking like a shepherd in Theocritus."[10] The "Country" ideology locates the disinterested man, and even the disinterested

book (which "must protect itself" and not be slavishly dependent), in a topographical and temperamental remoteness from the run of politicians, who are so busily scheming at court that they cannot enjoy the happiness that the author claims to share with the statesman. The dedication, composed as Sterne was beginning the third and fourth volumes of his novel, sets satire aside in order to praise the decent isolation from which an honest individual may speak to a sympathetic figure in the world.[11] The singularity of the man who loves privacy guarantees in him an equilibrium that nothing can upset or corrupt, because it is disinterested, unmortgaged to party or faction, and freely emanating in public spirit. Such an individual resembles a Shandean humorist, whose singularity coincides with integrity, and whose isolation is the guarantee of an innocence that can not be violated by the interpretation of the public, or a readership, not inured to the privacies of practical virtue.

The second dedication is very different, coming as it does after Pitt, the "Great Commoner" as he had been called, has accepted not only a peerage as the earl of Chatham in 1766 but also a large pension from the Crown. When Obadiah has to tell Walter that he cannot ride the horse Patriot because "Patriot is sold" (*TS*, 5.2.416), and when Yorick tells the Comte de B— that "Our court at present is so full of patriots, who wish for *nothing* but the honours and wealth of their country [that] there is nothing for a jester to make a jest of" (*SJ*, 115), it is plain that Sterne is not blind to the pressures exerted upon individual integrity once it has got out into the world. The difference between Pitt and the earl of Chatham he recognizes as in some way analogous to the difference between a priori and a posteriori: that is, between an untested principle and the practice of power.

> Having, *a priori*, intended to dedicate *The Amours of my uncle Toby* to Mr. ***—I see more reasons, *a posteriori*, for doing it to Lord *******.
>
> I should lament from my soul, if this exposed me to the jealousy of their Reverences; because, *a posteriori*, in Court-

latin, signifies, the kissing hands for preferment—or any thing else—in order to get it. (*TS,* 9. Dedication. 733)

Tristram notes without bitterness the passage from the ideal of retirement, which he claimed to share with Pitt in the 1750s, to the murkier reaches of power politics in which he now locates the state orator. The rural figure that the author cut in first greeting the Country party politician is now remodeled as "some gentle Shepherd," the sharpest antithesis to pensioners and Patriots he can think of, "Whose Thoughts proud Science never taught to stray, / Far as the Statesman's walk or Patriot-way" (*TS,* 9. Dedication. 734). However, it is evident that the gentle shepherd is not the author, and that the transition he marks from the simple patriotism of the first dedication to the compromised political positions of the second, is not the occasion for a reintroduction of the satiric project at Pitt's expense.[12]

The key terms "a priori" and "a posteriori" are brought into play to mock, if anything, the naive valorization of the singular private life that Sterne once thought could be brought into the world without any danger of confusion or corruption. The lesson he has learned is that the eloquence which reproduces the private oddity as a public performance depends upon a power that is dangerous both to the orator and the audience, in that it shakes principles, generates confusion, and arouses ambition. But he has not learned this simply by following and interpreting Pitt's career. The process of writing and publishing his fabulously successful book has kept pace with Pitt's acquisition of power, involving modifications to the cultivation of the singular and the particular until the risks involved in getting into the world are undeniable, embodied in Sterne's practice of a narrative manner that has overwhelmed all constraints and all readerly resistance and made him rich and famous.

In Britain of the 1750s the party distinctions of Whig and Tory had been discredited.[13] Walpole's administration, which ended in 1742, and the Jacobite rebellion of 1745 were cited as instances of the wicked extremes to which party principles could carry people.

More realistically, it was understood that high politics was such a pragmatic and quotidian negotiation between the king and the House of Commons that the conventional language of revolution and liberty was too rough to distinguish the subtle differences between ambitious men who, although they would all call themselves Whigs, were divided by the means each pursued in getting power, not by the objectives to be pursued once it had been obtained.[14] The chief architect of this state of affairs was Henry St. John, Viscount Bolingbroke, the man addressed in Pope's lines in praise of the gentle shepherd that Sterne cites in his second dedication to Pitt. Bolingbroke had succeeded simultaneously in persuading the public that power such as Walpole's, exercised self-interestedly and without restraint, was corrupt and corrupting, and that a parliamentary opposition, founded on steady principles of public spirit, not only gave the politically marginal figure a public voice but also entered on his behalf a plausible claim for political office. The first fruit of the opposition led by Henry Pelham was the administration of his brother, the duke of Newcastle, who practiced the art of the possible unhindered even by notional loyalties to founding ideals. Bolingbroke's advocacy of principles transcending private interest, combined with his recommendation of parliamentary oratory capable of a practical "force and authority,"[15] was soon to be embodied in the career of Pitt, an orator remarkable for eloquence whose transcendent qualities carried him above all definable commitments to principle and fed an ambition that was limitless.

Sterne's early enthusiasm for Pitt did not include approval of Patriot political theory in general, or of Bolingbroke in particular. His political journalism in the 1740s defended Walpole's policies, even after his fall, and was couched in the language of Hanoverian Whiggism. In the *York Gazetteer,* he attacks the scandal and invective of Pelhamites, raked out of "the Kennels of Craftsmen and Journalists" and sedulously spread about once again by Caesar Ward in the pages of the *York Courant.*[16] The noise of "the CRAFTSMAN and COMMON SENSE" is the cacophony of "false Invective and false Panegyrick." "*True Patriots* are good for nothing but to sit safely in their closets and attaque the tender Characters of Men,"[17] while

maneuvering for the plunder they deplore. Of Patriot rhetoric during the aftermath of Walpole's fall, when the mayor and aldermen
of London were pressuring their MPs to hasten their dilatory pros-
ecution of Walpole, Sterne writes, "Nothing can give a reasonable
Man, a meaner or more despicable Idea of the Citizens of London,
than to hear them, in the midst of the most abandon'd Venality
and Corruption, perpetually declaiming against Venality and Corruption" (*York Gazetteer,* "Sterne's Politicks," 99). Although Sterne
confessed that he wrote these paragraphs to please his powerful
Uncle Jaques and to gain preferment, there is a thread running
through all his work that twitches in response to the scandalizing
of a vulnerable reputation. His own suffered at the hands of this
same Uncle Jaques who, angered when his nephew refused to write
any more paragraphs in defense of vulnerable politicians, had it
put about York that Sterne had preferred to let his mother be
lodged in the poorhouse rather than give her a subsistence.[18] Parson
Yorick's blighted career (as summarized in the opening volume of
Tristram Shandy) represents in its most acute form everything Sterne
felt was most opprobrious and unjust about this sacrifice of in-
nocents for the sake of an outraged public virtue. Such vengeful
hypocrisy he seems to have considered the speciality of contemporary Patriotism, "For I make no Doubt, that a great Part of the
Opposition and OutCry against standing Armies, &c. for some time
past, has proceeded from a Jacobite Party, under Pretext of Patriots.
. . . Glorious Patriots indeed! *O my Soul, enter thou not into their Secrets.*"[19]

As for Bolingbroke, he seems to have represented for Sterne the
type of a spoiled political idealism. In one of his letters, Sterne
plays at arranging antithetical pairs ("Our Sydenhams, and San-
grados, our Lucretias,—and Massalinas"), ending with "our Som-
mers, and our Bolingbrokes," (*Letters,* 88) setting the true Whig
against the false Patriot. The reason for such pointed hostility lies
in the difference Sterne marks in the *York Gazetteer* between the
language of opposition and the practical calls of political office.
The Pelhamites now in government, "who before were the only
True Patriots of our Country," find themselves the objects of the
same vituperation that was previously reserved for Walpole, "which
shews how widely *Opposition* differs from Patriotism, and that Places

will always make Men appear Criminal: As if Government cou'd exist without Places, and Men to fill them, or a Man was less a Patriot for taking a Place in a Ministry which he approves" (*York Gazetteer*, "Sterne's Politicks," 92).

J. G. A. Pocock and J. C. D. Clark have drawn attention to the anomalous nature of Bolingbroke's commitment to principle.[20] In his *Letters on Patriotism*, Bolingbroke constantly links the marginalized figure—the scorned and exiled sacrificial victim whom Sterne had no trouble identifying with[21]—to the systematic array of principles that Sterne associates with an unacceptable faith in the a priori. According to Bolingbroke, opposition is a process of reasoning "on principles that are out of fashion," "a moral system of the world," "a system of conduct" (3, 12, 59). Such a system avoids, or at least pretends to avoid, the least taint of a posteriori application. As the German political theorist Jürgen Habermas has pointed out, and as Sterne divined, the rhetoric of Patriot opposition could enter the public sphere only on condition that it equated powerlessness with integrity, and place with corrupt influence.[22] This is the dream language of the political exile, designed to embarrass those whose place he cannot take. With none but the most oblique claim on practice, patriotism and its inventor perpetrate, as far as Sterne is concerned, the worst betrayal of political practice by blackening the names of those who dare to act. And this scandal is spread with the authority of an impossible rule of conduct. From Sterne's point of view, Bolingbroke is describing himself when he characterizes continental philosophers like this: "Rather than creep up slowly, a posteriori, to a little general knowledge, they soar at once as far, and as high, as imagination can carry them. From whence they descend again, armed with systems and arguments a priori."[23]

With this degree of skepticism about patriotism, how can Sterne salute Pitt in the language of Country ideology? The short answer is that Pitt, like so many politicians of the midcentury, married the language of principle to adroit interventions into practical politics. Sterne's two dedications comprehend the a priori and the a posteriori of Patriot possibilities, from the language of exile to what Clark calls "the tactical implications of principled rhetoric." Once that marriage is made, there is (as Clark also points out) "no clear, mutually exclusive difference between the sincere and the insincere assertion of principles. . . . Assertions of policy and principle have their place in a theory of the explanation of conduct only in the more general sincerity of a common ambition" (Clark, *The Dynamics of Change,* 151, 19). There is the gentle shepherd who kicks up his heels, like a swain in Theocritus, and the gentle shepherd desperate not to lose his political influence, like George Grenville. If Pitt understood and exploited from the outset of his career the advantages of principled language in the day-to-day maneuvering for the prime objective—power—then Sterne came to understand the convenient alignment of invoked principle to practice in the process of writing his book, where the double shift from satire to particularity, and from particularity to public value, requires that the language of narrative principle be deployed for the ends of eloquence, not of authentication. In *Tristram Shandy* each triumph over the reader's desire to interpret a story or to judge a character marks a narrativization of the a priori. That is to say, Sterne's main narrative strategy is the self-referential conversion of occasions of judgments into opportunities for a brilliant delivery.

When he finds the language of Garrick electrifying because it acquires its power by going beyond the rules of grammar (*TS,* 3.12.213) he begins to apprehend the qualities in Pitt's delivery that Horace Walpole declared "would have added reputation to Garrick," and which always shone most brightly when he was "exposing his own conduct: [and] having waded through the most notorious apostacy in politics . . . treated it with an impudent confidence, that made all reflections upon him poor and spiritless."[24] The collapse of an interpretable satiric allegory that eventually resolves itself into the rhetoric of Tristram's self-indulgent and erratic history of his life runs parallel to the instrumental eloquence Pitt finds in Bolingbroke's exilic dream language once he has emptied it of its meaning. The narratives each then goes on to produce have much in common in terms of that circular or tautologous symmetry characteristic of state oratory. Choice and power stand in a direct ratio to self-reference, such as the delivery of delivered infancy, the satire of satiric interpretation, eloquence upon eloquence, reflection upon reflection.

An example of Pitt's delivery of a bambino occurs in a speech on the Scottish magistracy that Horace Walpole instances as one of his finest. He paraphrases it in the third person:

> When master principles are concerned, he dreaded accuracy of distinction: he feared that sort of reasoning; if you class everything, you will soon reduce everything into a particular; you will then lose great general maxims . . . He would not recur for precedents to the diabolic divans of the second Charles and James—he did not date his principles of the liberty of this country from the revolution: they are eternal rights: and when God said, *let justice be justice,* he made it independent.[25]

Only on reflection can we see that Pitt has invented, or conceived, this originary establishment of justice and the donation of rights purely on his own account. In the passion of delivery it comes with all the self-evidence of the *fiat lux,* from which it is no doubt derived, in order to blind the audience to the absence of any objective principle either in the theme or the conduct of the oration. You cannot tell how "eternal rights" come in, whether by head or shoulders. All the audience is told is that rights are rights because justice has been announced as justice; and all they discover is that rights belong to the man whose voice so eloquently and magisterially produces and, in producing, legitimates them. The language of "great general maxims" and revolution principles is a stalking horse for this invention of right, and the figure of illegitimacy—"the diabolic divans of the second Charles and James"— serves like the bend sinister on the coat of arms on the Shandy coach simply as the detectable outside of an arbitrary act of conception and delivery.

Like the Shandean reduction to narrative and rhetorical manipulation of the principles needed to decipher signs and to make judgments, Pitt's speech includes principles as a further theme of oratorical practice, citing the a priori in order to emancipate the a posteriori from its control. Just as Sterne's undermining of narrative referentiality disturbs the verisimilitude of his novel, so Pitt's eloquence unsettles the relation of political agency to ethical imperatives by transforming his indicators of probity into the figures of his oratory. As J. G. A. Pocock says: "We must beware of supposing that the actors in high politics were motivated by the things they said, and we must beware of supposing that the categories of ideological rhetoric necessarily furnish either reliable description or reliable evaluation of the way the institution of high politics worked."[26] Pocock is responding to Clark's summary of the politics of the 1750s as *narrative:*

> Narrative is the mental language of political action appropriate to men who, in real situations, refrain from basing their actions on a generalised view of their predicament . . . Narrative . . . involves a submission to the partial blindness dictated by events evolving successively in an order which, if a sequence, is not necessarily a pattern, and to which "pattern" is ascribed in retrospect in a great variety of ways . . . Narrative reflects an order given to events by an actor in them in order to take the next step: it displays the coherence, the sequence, the significant selection which the actor adopts as the substitute explanation (no full, ideal explanation being attainable) of his own next action.

It follows that "actions are intelligible only if they can be narrated" and that narrative is the spur for subsequent activity.[27] Narrative is what happens when the stream of history runs backward as eloquence, and the discourse of generalized views obedient to a priori principles is gutted for an essentially pragmatic a posteriori rhetoric that both precipitates and justifies actions that are convenient and opportune. Pitt's genealogy of eternal right is just such a narrative, in which the illusion of priority is served by a circular argument. *Tristram Shandy* is another. Narrative is the state orator's and the autobiographer's sleight of hand that delivers and legitimates the bambino in the one recursive flourish.

In writing histories of a decade in which narrative came into this new relation to practice, Horace Walpole and William Godwin were prone to reproduce the improvisational, circumstantial, and personal rhetoric that has so often been claimed as Sterne's peculiarity. Confronted with "this chaos of politics" and of administrations "unprincipled and disunited, made up of the deserters of all parties," Godwin has recourse to a dense particularity: "A thousand additional circumstances attract us, in the present case."[28] Walpole is likewise determined by one factor in writing his *Memoirs*: "They are the minutiae of which I have observed posterity is ever most fond"; his aim being, "to relate our story with exact fidelity to the impressions it made on me" (*Memoirs*, 111.92; 111.47). What but a redaction of this narrative position is Tristram's maxim of situational relativity: "The circumstances with which every thing in this world is begirt, give every thing in this world its size and shape" (3.2.187), and Sterne's confession, "I am governed by circumstances—so that what is fit to be done on Monday, may be very unwise on Saturday" (*Letters*, 194). It is an impossible simplification to assume that this circumstantiality is a serious, or even a parodic, contribution to the realism of the emergent novel. Similarly, to interpret Tristram's and Walpole's plan of striking the reader with their own impressions of circumstances as a straightforward exercise in provoking sympathy is to neglect the apperception of the power of narrative on which it is based.

Ian Watt assigns Sterne's "very careful attention to all the aspects of formal realism: to the particularization of time, place and person; to a natural and lifelike sequence of action; and to the creation of a literary style which gives the most exact verbal and rhythmical equivalent possible of the object described" to his reconciliation of Richardson's "realism of presentation" with Fielding's "realism of assessment."[29] This judgment does scant justice to Sterne's exploitation of the energies that arise from the subversion of accurate presentations and assessments. Similarly, Michael McKeon's summary of the midcentury novel as "a form sufficient for the joint inquiry into analogous epistemological and social problems" seems to be less urgent than novels such as *Tristram Shandy* deserve. More appropriate to them are his remarks on travel writing, in which the first person singular is engaged in a calculated act of persuasion, based on "hearsay reports mediated through narrative style," in which attention is eagerly focused on "the very instrument of mediation, within the shape of the style itself."[30] The versatile narrative shared by Pitt and Sterne/Tristram develops three connected aspects: a factitious identity in the narrator; a taste for tautologous phrases and self-referential turns; and a desire for self-presentation so unbounded that the story of it cannot end. The child (Tristram) who escapes the definitions of a priori pediatric systems in order that he might bring himself into the world in his own way, the orator whose delivery is successful precisely because he has "only passions to sacrifice, not principles," are uniquely unrestricted by previous models and precedents. They are singular, or, to use Godwin's term for Pitt, "unresembled" (*History of Pitt,* 237) in proportion as they are self-authorizing and self-produced, conceivers and deliverers of their own selves. William Warburton wrote of Sterne, "As now everyone *makes himself,* he chose the office of common jester to the many" (*Letters,* 96 n6). His close political associate, the earl of Shelburne, accused Pitt of making himself: "What took much from his character was that he was always acting, always made up, and never natural." Good as his parts were, he was afraid to trust to them,[31] and was "a complete artificial character."[32] Significantly it is to Garrick, in the same letter in which he acknowledges his obligations to Pitt, that Sterne reports an event which gave him the hint for what later he called "Shandying it," and doing "a thousand things which cut no figure, *but in the doing*" (*Letters,* 157): " 'Twas an odd incident when I was introduced to the Count de Bissie, which I was at his desire—I found him reading Tristram" (*Letters,* 151). The queer sensation of being introduced to the man reading your book as the chief character in it—"ce Chevalier Shandy" (*Letters,* 157)—provides the basis for the scene in *A Sentimental Journey* where the same Comte de Bissy cannot tell the difference between the Yorick who has appeared in front of him and the Yorick in the pages of his Shakespeare to which the other Yorick points. It provides Sterne with the opportunity simultaneously to mock the French and Warburton for acting on the belief that the difference between the natural and the artificial man is worthy of discrimination and surprise.[33] It also allows him to show, both here and in the Parisian sections of that novel, that artificial characters are the only ones to be met with in circles of political and social influence. Gentle shepherds and pastoralizing Yoricks may pretend otherwise, fashioning themselves simple identities whose very simplicity is intended as a reproach to artifice, but this posing is always a perilous simplification. Tristram is still uncertainly negotiating these issues when he meets an officer of the king's posts in France, and has his expostulation cut short: "As sure as I am I—and you are you—And who are you? said he.—Don't puzzle me; said I" (*TS*, 7.33.633).

The self-measurement of things and qualities has already been evident in satire upon satire, delivery upon delivery, reflections upon reflections, and so on. These tautologies are expressive of the narrative incorporation of all regulatory judgments, and of the triumph of selfish eloquence. Like the apparition of the "real" Tristram in front of the reader of the fictional one, tautologies proclaim the ever-widening circle of a self-justifying narrative to a reader experiencing growing difficulties in determining its boundary. Sterne's "Shandying it" in Paris is justified in no other terms *"but in the doing."* Just as political narrative revolves between the arbitrarily chosen events that it articulates and the actions that such articulation legitimates, so Shandean logic produces the duplicate of the "unresembled" thing as both its warrant and example. Considering the self-generating possibilities of the narrative he is engaged upon, the furthest Tristram ventures into language that reveals his awareness of this solipsism is to observe, "I shall lead a fine life of it out of this self-same life of mine; or, in other words, shall lead a couple of fine lives together" (TS, 4.13.342).

If such tautologies are expressions of that circular or iterative form by which Sterne's narrative and Pitt's eloquence of the mid-century empower themselves, then something like interruption or aposiopesis (a figure of speech in which a thought or sentence suddenly breaks off) is the appropriate figure for political ambition which, as it has no authoritative source, can have no definite end. Godwin talks of Pitt's ambition as uncommon in its disinterestedness and inexhaustibility, "The mere possession of power was not calculated to gratify it." At the same time, Pitt's ambition is so importunate as to introduce that "feebleness and versatility" into his story which makes it impossible to wind up satisfactorily (Godwin, 73, 150). If Pitt's story turns and turns and gets nowhere owing to his growing fascination with the institution of Bolingbroke's dream language as a political reality, the parallel with Tristram Shandy's "life" is to be found in the effects of a vision as imperial, in its own way, as Pitt's.

Such dissatisfaction with the actual world on the part of novelist and politician stems from the self-proselytizing tendency evident among eloquent individuals. The power they establish over their audience, which is measured in terms of extensive worldly success commanded by their tongues, eventually washes back over them, committing them to a quixotic attachment to an improbable and unnarratable ideal. The moment of eloquence is triumphant but transitory, since it aims at nothing but an immediate and vivid effect rather than at an assertion of a solid reference to an external world. When Tristram announces that he aims to do nothing but write his life to the end of his life, he has arrived at the first stage of literary empire (*TS,* 4.13.342); and when he says he will read no book but his own as long as he lives, he has come to the second (*TS,* 8.5.661). His narrative is fully tautologized as a self-delivery that will give both *Life* and life, in which he will function as the fascinated reader of his own writing and his audience will be forced to cooperate with that self-enclosure. Interruption such as dominates every page of *Tristram Shandy* guarantees, paradoxically, the continuity of eloquent self-delivery as a nonoriginary and nonteleological activity concerned with virtualities and effective artifice. Contrariwise, the overinvestment in *Life* as *life*—a translation of the self-fashioned self into a naturalistic and biological existence improbably extending far into the future such as we expect novelistic narrative to deliver—is fated to encounter interruption as a guarantee of nothing but mortality. *Tristram Shandy* is thus profoundly antinovelistic, since it values the moment of joyous individual eloquence as the revelation of personality (*Life*) and rejects with horror the narrative of a "life" as it is lived as merely a tracking of the inevitabilities of death and dissolution. As long as Sterne's first-person narrators remember that, their self-deliveries a posteriori will never be mistaken for true births, and their bambini will never be trapped in a narrative that dispatches them from a beginning to an end.

Notes

1. This view has found its most influential expression in Ian Watt, *The Rise of the Novel* (Berkeley: University of California Press, 1957), 290–91. Its fullest theoretical airing is to be found in a formalist consideration of Sterne's use of the estrangement effect in Victor Shklovsky, "A Parodying Novel: Sterne's *Tristram Shandy*," reprinted in John Traugott, ed., *Laurence Sterne: a Collection of Critical Essays* (Englewood Cliffs, N.J.: Prentice Hall, 1968), 61–79.

2. F. R. Leavis, *The Great Tradition* (New York: Doubleday, 1948), 10–11n; Sigurd Burckhardt, "Tristram Shandy's Law of Gravity," *ELH*, 28 (1961): 70–88; John Traugott, *Tristram Shandy's World: Sterne's Philosophical Rhetoric* (Berkeley and Los Angeles: University of California Press, 1954); *TS*, 4.32.400.

3. Virginia Woolf, "Sterne," in *Granite and Rainbow* (London: Hogarth, 1958), 167–75; and "The 'Sentimental Journey, " in *The Common Reader: Second Series* (London: Hogarth, 1932), 78–85.

4. As in contemporary accounts of verisimilitude, such as Samuel Johnson's *Rambler,* 4, Edward Young, a close collaborator with Richardson, defines the verisimilitude of his long poem *Night-Thoughts,* and, incidentally, of Richardson's longer novel *Clarissa,* as follows: "It differs from the common modes of poetry which is from long narratives to draw short morals. Here, on the contrary, the narrative is short, and the morality arising from it makes the bulk of the poem." *The Correspondence of Edward Young,* ed. Henry Pettit (Oxford: Clarendon, 1971), 349.

5. *A Political Romance* (York, 1759; reprinted Menston: Scolar, 1971), 45.

6. "It may be pretended, that the disorders of the ancient governments, and the enormous crimes, of which the citizens were often guilty, afforded much ampler matter for eloquence that can be met with among the moderns." Although Hume affects to dispute this argument, he does not contest its associated proposition, namely that eloquence flourishes in proportion as laws are few: "The multiplicity and intricacy of laws is a discouragement to eloquence in modern times." David Hume, "Of Eloquence," in *Essays Moral, Political and Literary,* ed. Eugene F. Miller (Indianapolis: Liberty Classics, 1987), 106, 103.

7. *Letters,* 250, 290, 294. Subsequent references are in brackets in the text.

8. In a letter to Garrick acknowledging his help, he seems to include another debt of gratitude to him when he adds, "I am under great obli-

gations to Mr. Pitt, who has behaved in every respect to me like a man of good breeding, and good nature." *Letters,* 152.

9. "Patriot" (along with "Country," as opposed to those who favored the "Court" interest) was the general name applied to those who thought of themselves as the opposition to the long (and corrupt) dominance of English politics by Robert Walpole from 1721 to 1742. As a term that signified political opposition on "patriotic" rather than self-interested grounds, the word lingered into the 1760s.

10. See Jeremy Black, *Pitt the Elder* (Cambridge: Cambridge University Press, 1992), 7, 17.

11. During his first trip to London after the publication of *Tristram Shandy,* Sterne is struck with the patriotic vigor of the new king, whom he applauds in the same terms as he salutes Pitt. He seems, he tells Stephen Croft, "resolved to bring all things back to their original principles, and to stop the torrent of corruption and laziness . . . the K[ing] gives every thing himself, knows everything, and weighs every thing maturely, and then is inflexible—this puts old stagers off their game." *Letters,* 126.

12. The person aimed at seems to be George Grenville, Pitt's cousin, who earned the contempt of his more eminent relative when, in 1763, he stayed on in Bute's administration, and was active in support of raising fresh revenue. In the midst of a speech where he kept plaintively asking his colleagues where, where, he was going to lay new taxes, Pitt interrupted him by whining the refrain of a popular song, "Gentle Shepherd, tell me where!" After that the name stuck, and Grenville was known as the "Gentle Shepherd." See *Macaulay's Essays on William Pitt,* ed. R. F. Winch (London: Macmillan, 1898), 92–93.

13. To Stephen Croft, Sterne wrote, "We shall be soon Prussians and Anti-Prussians, B[ute]s and Anti-B[ute]s, and those distinctions will just do as well as Whig and Tory—and for aught I know serve the same ends." *Letters,* 126.

14. Although Pitt's clarion call "Not men, but measures" was offered as a corrective to expediency, Burke shows how it presents opportunism in a different form: "When people desert their connections, the desertion is a manifest *fact,* upon which a direct simple issue lies, triable by plain men. Whether a *measure* of government be right or wrong, is no *matter of fact,* but a mere affair of opinion." That is to say, it escapes all *"leading general principles of government." Thoughts on the Present Discontents,* reprinted in *Edmund Burke on Government, Politics, Society,* ed. B. W. Hill (Glasgow: Fontana, 1975), 115–16.

15. Bolingbroke, *Letters on the Spirit of Patriotism* (London: A. Millar, 1752), 51–56. In Hume's opinion, Bolingbroke himself is a fine specimen of what is desiderated in the modern orator: "Lord BOLINGBROKE's productions, with all their defects in argument, method, and precision, contain a force and energy which our orators scarcely ever aim at." Hume, "Of Eloquence," 108.

16. *York Gazetteer*, 16 November 1742; reprinted in Kenneth Monkman, "Sterne's Politicks, 1741–42," *Shandean*, 1 (1989): 100. Monkman gives his reasons for assigning the piece to Sterne.

17. *York Gazetteer*, 2 November 1742, reprinted in Kenneth Monkman, "Sterne's Politicks," 92.

18. See *Letters*, 32–41; and Arthur H. Cash, *Laurence Sterne: The Early and Middle Years* (London: Methuen, 1975), 236–40.

19. *An Answer to a Letter Addressed to the Archbishop of York* (Edinburgh, 1745), reprinted in Kenneth Monkman, "Laurence Sterne and the '45," *Shandean*, 2 (1990): 72. The ascription of this piece to Sterne is less certain than the articles in *York Gazetteer*, but the political opinions it expresses are close to Sterne's.

20. "In the *Craftsman* period he made the historical reality of principles a cardinal doctrine." J. G. A. Pocock, *The Machiavellian Moment* (Princeton: Princeton University Press, 1975), 482. "Bolingbroke . . . was atypical in his willingness to express his political stance in general terms." J. C. D Clark, *The Dynamics of Change: The Crisis of the 1750s and English Party Systems* (Cambridge: Cambridge University Press, 1982), 8.

21. "I will not say, like SENECA, that the noblest spectacle which God can behold, is a virtuous man suffering, and struggling with afflictions: but this I will say, that the second Cato, driven out of the forum, and dragged to prison, enjoyed more inward pleasure, and maintained more outward dignity, than they who insulted him." *Letters on Patriotism*, 330–31. See also *Reflections upon Exile*: "Your name is hung up in the tables of proscription, and art joined to malice endeavours to make your best actions pass for crimes, and to stain your character." *Letters on the Study and the Use of History etc.* (London: Alexander Murray, 1870), 165.

22. Jürgen Habermas, *The Structural Transformation of the Public Sphere*, trans. Thomas Berger (Cambridge, Mass.: MIT Press, 1989), 64.

23. "A Letter to Mr. Pope," in *A Letter to William Windham etc.* (London: A. Millar, 1753), 471.

24. Horace Walpole, *Memoirs of King George II*, ed. John Brooke (New Haven: Yale University Press, 3 vols., 1985), 2:111; 1:64.

25. *Memoirs,* 2:39.

26. J. G. A. Pocock, *Virtue, Commerce, and History* (Cambridge: Cambridge University Press, 1985), 244.

27. Clark, *The Dynamics of Change,* 17–18.

28. William Godwin, *The History of the Life of William Pitt, Earl of Chatham* (London: G. Kearsley, 1783), 146, 181, 283.

29. Watt, *The Rise of the Novel,* 291.

30. An argument congenial to this is Michael McKeon, *The Origins of the English Novel,* 1600–1740 (Baltimore: Johns Hopkins University Press, 1987), 410, 104, 109. The argument most congenial to mine is John Sitter's concerning the effects of the speed of the midcentury's shifting premises. Satire gives way to "the melodrama of momentary intensities," "a program for thinking to the moment: a willingness to take any felt certainties which came one's way regarding 'particular points' " at a "particular instant," including a renewed interest in the sublime and other examples of language "in which the gap between word and deed had been closed." John Sitter, *Literary Loneliness in Mid-Eighteenth-Century England* (Ithaca, N.Y.: Cornell University Press, 1982), 26, 229, 68.

31. Walpole on Temple, *Memoirs,* 2:184.

32. Cited in J. C. D. Clark, *The Dynamics of Change,* 283.

33. "Now whether the idea of poor Yorick's skull was put out of the Count's mind, by the reality of my own, or by what magic he could drop a period of seven or eight hundred years, makes nothing in this account—'tis certain the French conceive better than they combine—I wonder at nothing in this world, and the less at this; inasmuch as one of the first of our own church, for whose candour and paternal sentiments I have the highest veneration, fell into the same mistake in the very same case.——'He could not bear,' he said, 'to look into sermons wrote by the king of Denmark's jester' " (*SJ,* 112; see also 341). See also Jonathan Lamb, "The Job Controversy, Sterne, and the Question of Allegory," *Eighteenth-Century Studies,* 24, I (Fall 1990): 19.

Tristram Shandy and the
Appositeness of War

MADELEINE DESCARGUES

◆　◆　◆

> I am not insensible, brother *Shandy*, that when a man,
> whose profession is arms, wishes, as I have done, for
> war,—it has an ill aspect to the world;——and that,
> how just and right soever his motives and intentions
> may be,—he stands in an uneasy posture in
> vindicating himself from private views in doing it.
> —LAURENCE STERNE, *Tristram Shandy*
> (6.32.554)

T HE MOTTO TO THIS article is the opening sentence of Uncle
Toby's three-page-long *"apologetical oration,"* a problematic passage set in the sixth volume of *Tristram Shandy*. The sources of the
uneasiness are several. There is of course the moral and political
judgment one may pass on Toby-as-character's "private views" despite his attempt at vindicating himself from them. Then there is
the philosophical and ethical problem posed by the oration, i.e.,
the ambivalence of Toby's figure as Everyman, a compound of
Christian "goodness" and "excellency," celebrated by his nephew
Tristram (*TS*, 3.34.265), when taken with his more sanguinary ap-
petites. Also the composition of the oration, a criss-cross of intertextual references, makes it a puzzle set for the reader. Only the
working out of this may eventually suggest an interpretation of
this apology for war as such and within the narrative structure of
Tristram Shandy.

In order to pave my interpretive way, I wish first of all to reflect on the significance of Toby and Trim, ersatz soldiers and emblems of Christian charity in *Tristram Shandy*, then to examine the inscription of Toby's apology for war in its satirical intertexts, in particular Burton's *Anatomy of Melancholy*. Further still, one has to confront the ambiguity of this stage in the narration where the reader encounters the deadpan presentation of contradictory rhetorical discourses—an implicit attack on war and an explicit defense of it—and is left without any gloss at all from the otherwise voluble narrator, Tristram. What is the meaning of the aporia here? War is not easily disposed of in *Tristram Shandy*, even though man's warring drives, the novel seems to indicate, can be satisfied through conflicts and games that need not always be bloody.

Toby and Trim in the Historical Context

One of the most important couples of the Shandy household is that formed by Uncle Toby, officer of the British army, and Corporal Trim, his friend more than his servant. Their quasi-conjugal pairing speaks for the strength of the bond of suffering and support acquired throughout the hardships of war, a favorite conversational topic throughout *Tristram Shandy*. Trim's feelings for his friend and master, "fidelity and affection" (*TS*, 2.5.109), are rewarded by love: "My uncle *Toby* loved the man in return" (ibid.). Not that those two are only happy to play war games in each other's company exclusively. They also conjugate the verb *to love* in the active form among their fellow beings in a way that establishes the two disabled soldiers as the very emblems of sympathy in the Shandy world.[1] The edifying story of Le Fever, another "poor gentleman . . . of the army" (6.6.500), in volume 6, gives Trim the opportunity to challenge Yorick's curate on the subjects of charity and prayer: "I thought, said the curate, that you gentlemen of the army, Mr. *Trim*, never said your prayers at all" (*TS*, 6.7.505). To which Trim, showing effective concern for the relief of Le Fever's son, soon to become an orphan, and observing the curate's detachment in the circumstances, hotly replies: "I believe, an' please your reverence, said I, that when a soldier gets time to pray,—he prays as heartily as a parson,—though not with all his fuss and hypocrisy" (*TS*, 6.7.506).

The hint of sarcasm in the curate's observation nevertheless reminds us of the disrepute commonly enjoyed by soldiers, even in those years during which John Bull's aspiration to relief from the war effort was qualified by his mercantile appetite and accompanying distaste for his French neighbor. For all their warm humanity, Toby and Trim were really—and still are—the fictional embodiment of those inactive soldiers who found it difficult to adapt themselves to civil life and could be perceived as retrograde ideologically, or a social burden. Of course they are not concerned with the war which was contemporaneous with the publication of *Tristram Shandy,* i.e., the Seven Years War with France, which had begun in 1756 over colonial territories. Theirs were the wars fought under King William and Queen Anne, the wars of the League of Augsburg and of the Spanish Succession, the latter being concluded by the Treaty of Utrecht in 1713—the year of Sterne's birth, forty-six years before the publication of the first volumes of his novel. This has the consequence of blurring issues. Through inaction or feebleness of both body and mind, Toby and Trim, the soldiers of *Tristram Shandy,* are made innocuous. This allows them to retain their military flavor, while contributing to the general impression that war is put at a distance, when war was in fact still being pursued, albeit in distant places. The preference for domesticity, in *Tristram Shandy* as in most later eighteenth-century fiction, is ambiguous. While it seems to turn away from war, Sterne's novel endorses feelings of unquestioned loyalty in the good old wars of William and Anne.

Toby's claim in the oration is that his and Trim's war was fought "upon principles of *liberty,* and upon principles of *honour* [. . .] to keep the ambitious and the turbulent within bounds" (*TS*, 6.32.557). One could probably argue that the wars waged under William, from 1689 to 1697, and including the siege of Namur in 1695 (during which Toby gets his wound in the groin), took place at a time when the resistance to France was an English national imperative. But England's part in the other war, that of the Spanish

Succession, from 1701 to 1713, during the reign of Queen Anne, was another story. Since the Treaty of Utrecht sealed the supremacy of Great Britain, it is difficult to believe that Marlborough and his epigons were only trying then to keep "the ambitious [. . .] within bounds." And it was this offensive rather than defensive war which Toby and Trim, both incapacitated by their wounds, had to be content with emulating virtually on their bowling green with their model sieges and fortifications. Thus *Tristram Shandy* tends to present its readers with a picture of impotent harmless military men, but it never sets out explicitly to question the validity of Toby's somewhat bellicose aspirations.

In fact Sterne dedicated the first installment of *Tristram Shandy* to William Pitt the Elder, at a time when his popularity was greatest, owing precisely to his leadership and victories in the Seven Years War with France, mentioned above. This dedication may well have been a matter of opportunism more than conviction; yet it does not absolve its author from sharing probably in the national pride of his compatriots over the British successes in the Seven Years War, as observed by Susan Staves, with the following remark: "While relishing the comic incongruities between Toby's pacific goodness and his military enthusiasm, Sterne, like almost all his contemporaries, avoided pressing such contradictions as far as they might have been pressed."[2] At any rate, the text of *Tristram Shandy,* whatever ironies are involved in the treatment of Toby and Trim, does not propose one clear discourse concerning war. On the contrary: because it originates in war, it is bound to make the issue confused, on account of the obscurity generally attached to origin. For one thing, Toby's fictional being is rooted in the historical context of wars.[3] His famed hobby-horse springs from the necessity to distract his mind from the wound in his groin, which it does felicitously, as it turns out to provide a symbolic and even, to a certain degree, a practical remedy. For another, many a sigh of his—"[t]o the end of his life he never could hear *Utrecht* mentioned upon any account whatever [. . .] without fetching a sigh" (*TS,* 6.31.552)—is caused precisely by the signing of the Treaty of Utrecht, putting an end to the need for war. The unpalatable truth about Toby is that his peaceful game with model fortifications enrolls warring energies he would have preferred to use otherwise. The sense of unease this may cause is certainly not dissipated by the apologetical oration.

The Character of Toby and the Intertexts of Satire

Sterne had tried his skill at satire, siding in the press with a Whig candidate against his Tory opponent, before he wrote *Tristram Shandy*. His correspondence shows him in July 1742 characteristically more flippant than bitter at the realization that he was being used by politics (and by his own uncle, as the case stood) more than he could use them (*Letters*, 21):

> I find by some late Preferments, that it may not be improper to change Sides; therefore I beg the Favour of you to inform the Publick, that I sincerely beg Pardon for the abusive Gazeteers I wrote during the late contested Election for the County of York, and that I heartily wish Mr. Fox Joy of his Election for the City.
>
> > Tempora Mutantur, & nos mutemur in illis.
> > I am, Sir, your Penitent Friend and Servant.
> > L. S.

Then in 1758, just before *Tristram Shandy*, he had written *A Political Romance*—very much in the spirit of Swift's *Tale of a Tub*[4]—which he more or less regretted publishing afterward on the grounds that he had, firstly, written it for an ungrateful person, and secondly that he had "hung up [someone], in the romance—in a ridiculous light—wch. upon my Soul I now doubt, whether he deserves it—" (*Letters*, 147). Subsequently, he reactivated satirical strategies in *Tristram Shandy*, never forgetting to claim his Swiftian heritage.[5]

This can particularly be felt in the polyphony of the text where characters as vectors of criticism always fall under their own attacks, where the satirical aspersion in the end is itself railed and relativized. For example, Walter, Toby's brother, happens to be his most pugnacious and uncompromising opponent concerning war.

He is, in the words of Melvyn New, "the demagogue of language [. . .] [who] does not have the cannons"[6] and a typical target of Swiftian satire whose elaborate rhetoric (only defective in whatever practical aspect it applies itself to) and verbal thrusts are a brilliant illustration of the warring principle at work in the language of persuasion. So his attacks on war and on Toby's military obsessions are to be taken with a grain of salt in *Tristram Shandy*.

Further, the vision of the world at the heart of Swiftian and Sternean satire is inspired by what Kathleen Williams identifies as "the traditional Renaissance view of man as a limited creature in whom mind and body are at odds and must be, as far as possible, reconciled."[7] Both writers aim at striking a middle chord between passion and reason. Toby's dominant passion, which inspires his hobby-horse, cannot be eradicated any more than man's warring drive in general, a translation of self-love. Yet reason, the manifestation in man of God's revelation, demands that we should obstinately endeavor not to yield to passion, that we should not only identify chaos but take responsibility for it and for our attempts to compose it into meaning:

> man [is] the creature of self-love whose passions lead him astray but who yet, if he recognizes and uses these passions, may become more actively and usefully and fully virtuous than the passionless Stoic can ever be; man who is no longer innocent but can become good if he recognizes himself for what he is.[8]

The balance between humility and pragmatic resolution owes a lot to the Pauline influence, reminding man of the impotence of his reason, when he forgets it is a gift of God. It belongs to the philosophical tradition of skeptical fideism, enabling its proponents to resist the wish to reconcile through dogmatism irreconcilable contraries and to work out instead a compromise between hardly compatible tensions.[9]

The central part given to paradox in these conceptions enables one to interpret the character of Toby-as-fool by the light of Paul's foolishness-in-God.[10] The oxymoronic quality of the peaceful soldier's personality has indeed always reverberated through readers' appreciation of *Tristram Shandy:* "[t]he episode of Le Fever," wrote a reviewer in 1762,

> is beautifully pathetic, and exhibits the character of Toby and his corporal in such a point of view, as must endear them to every reader of sensibility. The author has contrived to make us laugh at the ludicrous peculiarity of Toby, even while we are weeping with tender approbation at his goodness of heart.[11]

As narrator, Tristram is disposed to make a very affectionate portrait of his uncle:

> Peace and comfort rest for evermore upon thy head!—Thou envied'st no man's comforts,——insulted'st no man's opinions.——Thou blackened'st no man's character,——devoured'st no man's bread: gently with faithful *Trim* behind thee, didst thou amble round the little circle of thy pleasures, jostling no creature in thy way;——for each one's service, thou hadst a tear,——for each man's need, thou hadst a shilling. (*TS,* 3.34.265)

This homage, one might argue, is double-edged in its depiction of the two heroes as ductile horses patiently harnessed to the mechanical repetition of a humble task, within a limited circle indeed of pleasure and ambition. The word *service* being possibly loaded with "bawdy implication" (*Notes,* 265), Toby's potential goodness, which will not enable him to serve Widow Wadman's turn, otherwise than in lachrymose commerce, is signally presented as also made up of imbecility.

But the flatness of his stupidity is just what defines the total outwardness of his disposition. In comparison, Tristram advises "[his] dear girl," Madam reader, not to be ill-advised by Satan when reading about "the various uses and seasonable applications of long noses" (*TS,* 3.36.267) and he reproaches her, a few volumes later, for being too knowledgeable:

> There was, Madam, in my uncle *Toby,* a singleness of heart [. . .]; you can—you can have no conception of it: with this,

there was a plainness and simplicity of thinking, with such
an unmistrusting ignorance of the plies and foldings of the
heart of woman;——and so naked and defenceless did he
stand before you, (when a siege was out of his head) that you
might have [. . .] shot my uncle *Toby* ten times in a day,
through his liver, if nine times in a day, Madam, had not
served your purpose. (*TS* 6.29.550)

The appeal of such exposed vulnerability is patent in Tristram's
feelings, described elsewhere as "the warmest sentiments of love
[. . .] that ever virtue and nature kindled in a nephew's bosom"
(*TS,* 3.34.265). Hence his promise: "[w]hilst there is a rood and a
half of land in the *Shandy* family, thy fortifications, my dear uncle
Toby, shall never be demolish'd" (*TS,* 3.34.265), a declaration inviting
us to read *Tristram Shandy* as written *in memoriam* Toby Shandy as much
as Parson Yorick, despite his black page.

Toby is after all a tender fly-loving brute and a wise fool. Because
the sentimental soldier is inadequate, his charitable and military
exploits can appositely convey an ideal of Christian charity. Such
a definition of his character also makes him fall into place as a
particular literary item in a series of sentimental soldiers, emblem-
atizing man's folly in the satirical discourse from the Antiquity to
the Renaissance and the Augustan age. David McNeil, reflecting
on the grotesque apropos the treatment of war, brings in Toby in
his argument, for being a paradigm of "martial benevolence."[12] For
McNeil precisely, the aesthetic experience of the grotesque is informed by a "relaxation-tension paradox," one which would allow
Toby to be a site of contraries, providing comic relief out of the
tragedy of war.[13]

But there is more to Toby's grotesqueness than an aesthetic
definition. In his oration, he tries to cope with Walter's and even
more Yorick's critical comment on war: "Need I be told, dear *Yorick,*
as I was by you, in *Le Fever*'s funeral sermon, *That so soft and gentle a
creature, born to love, to mercy, and kindness, as man is, was not shaped for this?*"
His defense is feeble and politically questionable, as already noted:
'But why did you not add, *Yorick,*——if not by NATURE——that
he is so by NECESSITY?' (*TS,* 6.31.557). He prefers to address the

argument emotionally and to leave aside the complex question of war's "unnaturalness," as argued by Yorick in the wake of Erasmus's, then Burton's attacks against war.[14] If it seems logical that Toby should not share such ideas, it is more of a surprise that he should nevertheless borrow the words used by their authors, Burton in particular, in their diatribes against war.

Burton's expostulation against the " 'brute persuasion of false honour,' as Pontus Huter in his Burgundian history complains" places him in a line of historians and satirists denouncing the vain cruelty of war and the illusion of the soldiers:

> leaving their sweet wives, children, friends, for sixpence (if they can get it) a day, prostitute their lives and limbs, [...] marching bravely on, with a cheerful noise of drums and trumpets, such vigour and alacrity, so many banners streaming in the air, glittering armours, motions of plumes, woods of pikes, and swords, variety of colours, cost and magnificence, as if they went in triumph.[15]

Now Toby's plea for the soldier echoes this very passage in "Democritus to the Reader," when he cries out:

> ———'Tis one thing, brother *Shandy,* for a soldier to hazard his own life—to leap first down into the trench, where he is sure to be cut in pieces [...] and march bravely on with drums and trumpets, and colours flying about his ears [...] and 'tis another thing to reflect on the miseries of war. (*TS,* 6.32.556)

Similarly, his description of the siege of Troy may owe something to Burton's in the same passage. It is problematic that Toby should be using the words of a satirical text against war, when he himself is speaking in its defense: "Toby's oration is similar to Quixote's in tone, but it is from Burton's introduction to the *Anatomy* that Sterne borrows specific passages, and it may be important to remember that Burton is here delivering his famous diatribe *against* war," note the editors of the Florida *Tristram Shandy* (*Notes,* 432). Certainly the distorting prospect implied in this particular "quoting" operation is an element worth pondering. Is the reader supposed to recognize

Toby's misquoting of Burton's text and to enjoy a peaceful scholarly laugh? More disturbingly, how is the meaning of the text
affected by Toby's perversion of it? What sense does Toby's
(mis)quote make?

The very structure of the oration's piecemeal rhetoric, its mus-
tering of fragmented arguments with divergent possible interpretations, subverts any consistent message about and against war.
Toby is ill-informed enough to dismantle his own arguments by
quoting from satirists who would not support his views but, in
doing so, he enlists them in the unending game of war—harm-
lessly practiced by the Shandy brothers within the safe fictional
limits of the Shandy household; the same game that frames the
satirical activity. "Burton's moral system is consistent and com-
pelling, but Toby's, however generous in impulse, is patently illogical," H. J. Jackson remarks. "At times both parties—both 'patterns'
in the verbal illusion which Sterne created by repeated reference
to the *Anatomy*—become objects of mockery."[16] In this example of
ventriloquism, Sterne takes the skeptical questioning of meaning
to its most destabilizing consequences, when nobody or nothing
seems a fixed point of reference any longer, even by convention.
But he also exposes the satirist to an awareness of the fallibility of
the satirical strategy in general. In this respect, Toby's oration proposes an exercise in skeptical doubt which contains a constructive
lesson in reading and interpreting.

The Character in the Narrative Structure

If the oration is perplexing for its incongruity per se and in its
reference to satire, it is even more so for the way it works in the
narrative structure of *Tristram Shandy* and relates the characters in
the plot, for the reader's comprehension of the story. In the preceding chapter, Walter has made Toby his satirical butt, by ironically pressing the point that Toby needs the continuation of war,
this far from harmless human activity, to pursue his hobbyhorse,
played in model fortifications with Corporal Trim: "never mind,
brother *Toby,* he would say,—by God's blessing we shall have an-

other war break out again some of these days; and when it does,—
the belligerent powers, if they would hang themselves, cannot keep
us out of play" (*TS*, 6.31.552). Yet it is Walter who copies out Toby's
oration, so "highly pleased" (*TS*, 6.31.553) is he with it. As for the
narrator, Tristram, he "give[s] it to the world, word for word (in-
terlineations and all) as [he] finds it" (*TS*, 6.31.554), thereby giving
no evidence that he either approves of Toby's bellicose aspirations
or is unconcerned by them and making himself obtrusively absent
in the form of a missing gloss. Having considered the self-critical
import of the subversion of satirical discourse, we may now wonder
why it is the narrator's task to lead the reader to yet another form
of aporia in the story.

The context in which Toby proposes his "justification of his own
principles and conduct in wishing to continue the war" (*TS*,
6.31.553) is the ongoing argument at Shandy Hall about the sensitive historical matter of the Treaty of Utrecht, the first point to
which Richard Lanham attends, in his analysis of the oration:

> The Utrecht treaty that Toby thought base, made precisely
> the point Toby addressed himself to—that war was not nec-
> essary, was being continued for the reasons of honor that,
> Toby confesses, are really what gratify him. One can, I think,
> safely conclude that Toby disproves—and we are intended
> to see (though Tristram does not see) that he disproves—his
> own argument.[17]

Certainly, the more Toby seeks to exonerate himself, the weaker
his arguments stand, in this his only articulate speech in the whole
of *Tristram Shandy*—a counterpart to his more elliptic general response to situations that bewilder him, that is, the whistling of
Lillabullero. Well aware of the unattractiveness of his cause, he can
only invoke nature's own design: "If, when I was a school-boy, I
could not hear a drum beat, but my heart beat with it—was it my
fault?—Did I plant the propensity there?——did I sound the alarm
within, or Nature?" (*TS*, 6.32.555). And he confesses to the ambivalence of his heart—his strongest point indeed: "because, brother
Shandy, my blood flew out into the camp, and my heart panted for
war,—was it a proof it could not ache for the distresses of war

too?" (*TS*, 6.32.556). The rest—the intellectual content of the argument on war proper—may be dismissed, as I have argued above, as a weak attempt at disguising the truly selfish motivations of (his) war.

If this needs confirming, a later statement clinches the matter, and exposes the social prejudices hidden behind the "innocence" of Toby and Trim's puffing and warring activities, with pipes in lieu of cannons:

> I hope, Trim, [. . .] I love mankind more than either [glory and pleasure]; and as the knowledge of arms tends so apparently to the good and quiet of the world——and particularly that branch of it which we have practised together in our bowling-green, has no object but to shorten the strides of AMBITION, and intrench the lives and fortunes of the *few*, from the plunderings of the *many*——whenever that drum beats in our ears, I trust, Corporal, we shall neither of us want so much humanity and fellow-feeling as to face about and march. (*TS*, 9.8.753)

This injunction to humanity and fellow-feeling precedes Toby's walk to Widow Wadman's house and the final misunderstanding that puts an end to their idyll. The two words, *few* and *many*, italicized by Sterne, "place war where it truly belongs," notes New, "among privilege and inequity and the preservation of property and wealth."[18] There again, the weakness of Toby's arguments exposes his sentimental nature as a mere instrument in the hands of strategists. It is a case of unconscious double language through which the man of feeling's inconsistency is revealed. But I would argue that there are other ironies in the oration and its narrative surroundings than those which demythologize Toby's sentimentalism; and that the mockery of Toby's disposition reflects on the very narrative act through which the author Sterne uses a perplexed narrator to present a perplexing view.

What the narrator's silence is supposed to elicit from the reader is now at stake. For Lanham "we are intended to see (though Tristram does not see) [. . .] that [Toby] disproves his argument." He further explains:

It is not always easy, in *Tristram Shandy,* to separate Sterne from Tristram, and I do not think Sterne kept or wanted to keep a constant distance between them. Here [the context of the oration] they seem some way apart [. . .] [Toby] turns a fight into a game. Here is his naïveté, a naïveté his brother cannot understand. Toby remains consistent within his own terms and Tristram accepts these, presumably, and applauds them. At least he never really brings the two opinions together, whereas Sterne, I think—or the novel if you will—insists that we do.[19]

Certainly it is not easy to separate Sterne from Tristram when the dynamics of the text depends on the superimposition of the narrator's storytelling and the author's writing, when the dramatic force of the narrator's story of conception, birth and life, with his introductory "I Wish" gets energized time and again by the inaugural gesture of the author's writing—"I am now writing this book for the edification of the world,—which is *March* 9, 1759," "And here am I sitting, this 12th day of August, 1766," etc. The text of *Tristram Shandy* functions rather as if the author's desire were to make his existential self and his narrator coincide, as if he were never prepared to give up his story to the reader, therefore never finishing it, always interrupting, on the contrary, at the point of closure.[20] A complex set of devices is therefore mobilized in the flexible narrative technique of *Tristram Shandy,* including illustrations and a marbled leaf, dashes, a blank page, a real sermon and a pseudo-oration, all enlisted alike to make one's reading live by the fictive presence of the author as much as by the story related by the narrator: as if the author did not want to stop writing his text as he also wanted it written, a creative version of having one's cake and eating it. Or of fixing meaning through a story and at the same time wanting the possibility to change it.

Which is why authorial discourse in *Tristram Shandy* is particularly unstable, because balking at the risk of fixed meaning in things once said, a realization that throws some suspicion on what "Sterne—or the novel if you will—insists that we do." Rather, the reader's determination to invest the text with meaning is here at stake, in a moment when the text itself frustrates this desire. In *Tristram Shandy,* the reader gets at once more and less than he expects: less in the sense that in this unfinished story, the seriousness guaranteed by the singleness of meaning is denied, more because the existential illusion that runs through the fiction provides an imaginary dialogue with the inspirer of the story. It is as if reader and author's desire worked in agreement, a mostly gratifying fantasy, enabling one to justify, place, and meet one's desire and quest for meaning in the author's. Supposing one can identify a Sternean discourse, no way is it an authority presiding over the narrator and speaking above his head to the reader. One of Tristram's best roles in fact is to mime the author's reluctance to have said, once and for all, and to have finished saying. He shows himself in general comically aware of the disjunction between the two aspects, which can linguistically never coincide, and dramatically aware as well of the necessity of dialogue, however flawed with misunderstanding it may be, to make sense.

For Donald Wehrs, Sterne does not believe in the idea that "mimetic, plausible narrative could secure inductively certain interpretation": His narrative actually subverts this theory of interpretation "by offering multiple inductive possibilities, proliferating connotations, and thus dramatizing the reader's role (perhaps guilty, lazy, presumptuous) in manufacturing a form of coherence."[21] Sterne's own image of the several handles in *Tristram Shandy* gives an apposite metaphor for the task of reading.[22] "By providing grounds for multiple interpretations," adds Wehrs, "Sterne transposes into narrative the rhetorical techniques of classical skepticism." He has his narrator contrive "skeptical suspense," by presenting readers with conflicting possibilities of interpretation, which may entail aporia.[23] But what if the reader feels empty-handed, with no possibility left in the text to pursue meaning? What if the act of saying and the thing which is said are effectively disjuncted, in the operation of meaning, and if consequently the coincidence of the narrator's, the author's, and the reader's intentions and desires reveals itself to be a delusion?

In the case under examination, Tristram is anxious to present the oration as transcending judgment, drawing the reader's attention to the contradiction inherent in Toby's position by pretending it to be unproblematic—a form of paraleipsis:

> I may safely say, I have read over this apologetical oration of my uncle *Toby*'s a hundred times, and think it so fine a model of defence,—and shows so sweet a temperament of gallantry and good principles in him, that I give it to the world, word for word, (interlineations and all) as I find it. (*TS*, 6.31.553–54)

The narrative is supposed to interrupt itself for a text that claims its autonomy from it, a familiar device in *Tristram Shandy*,[24] also one which creates a double-bind situation in its narrative system. Because we follow Tristram, we cannot follow him. As readers, bound to be in the text, enjoying the squabbles between the dramatis personae and, most of all, the fiction of a dialogue with the actual author, thanks to the protean and ubiquitous quality given to the narrator, we are urged in disarray and helplessness to reestablish ourselves as readers *of* this text by means of an omission of the gloss Tristram is in other circumstances so willing to provide. Just as the white page insists that we cease for a while to trust the referential power of the fictional text and confront ourselves with the difficulty of producing a referent for beauty, the ambivalence of satire and Tristram's uncharacteristic speechlessness make it our unresolvable problem to define a consistent moral and intellectual position. At this stage, no authorial voice can pretend to make up for the narrator's silence.

Certainly this is a self-reflexive moment when the readers' attention is forcibly drawn to the conditions of the very performance of the act of reading, in accordance with Robert Alter's remark that in *Tristram Shandy,* an "early but ultimate instance of self-reflexive fiction, the many mirrors of the novel set to catch its own operations also give us back the image of the mind in action."[25] Tensions are unresolved in Sterne's fiction, which reminds readers of their responsibilities in the order of moral or political judgment. But more specifically, what happens here, in this complex pattern of proximity (implied by the engagement with the arguments) and distance (owing to the self-consciousness involved), has to do with poetic justice, rewarding the good and punishing the bad (readers). In *Tristram Shandy,* readers have to resist the trap of the fictive dialogue of kindred minds, the seduction game played by the author's own desire not to separate from his text. If they don't, they may be caught up in the existential illusion of the author's self, which hinders their quest for meaning. Or, which amounts to the same, they may wish to undertake the misguided effort of working out the dead author's "real" mind on the subject, in a vain attempt at biographical explication.[26] The set-up of Toby's apologetical oration, in which Toby's defective rhetoric is followed by no corrective discourse and no viewpoint, would therefore seem to have a cautionary value in that it displays the narrative strategy of *Tristram Shandy* at its most intricate and emphasizes the need to decode satirical conventions and intertextual reference. Last but not least, the very uneasiness of the passage signals the conspicuous absence of the author, which is mimed by the silence of the narrator. As a result, the problematic apology for war can be said to condense the formidable energies of Sterne's text, and for the best of reasons: "———Endless is the Search of Truth!" (*TS,* 2.3.103)—all to make the reader more present to his own act of interpretation.

Notes

1. See Melvyn New, *Tristram Shandy: A Book for Free Spirits* (Twayne, 1994), 85–87.

2. Susan Staves, "Toby Shandy: Sentiment and the Soldier," in *Approaches to Teaching Sterne's Tristram Shandy,* ed. Melvyn New (MLA, 1989), 85. The Seven Years War lasted from 1756 to 1763. The first two volumes of *Tristram Shandy* were published in 1759.

3. Biographical studies would tend to see Sterne's own father, Roger Sterne, a lieutenant in the English army, as a possible source for uncle Toby. As an example, here is the description Sterne makes of his father in his "Memoirs": "he was in his temper somewhat rapid, and hasty— but of a kindly, sweet disposition, void of all design; and so innocent in his own intentions, that he suspected no one; so that you might have cheated him him ten times a day, if nine had not been sufficient for your purpose" (*Letters,* 3).

4. See Laurence Sterne, *A Sentimental Journey through France and Italy by Mr. Yorick* with *The Journal to Eliza* and *A Political Romance*, ed. Ian Jack (Oxford University Press, 1968), 195–96.

5. Swift is a frequent reference in Sterne's letters, as in the following case, in defense of *Tristram Shandy*: "—I deny it—I have not got as far as Swift—He keeps due distance from Rabelais—& I from him. Swift sais [*sic*] 500 things, I dare not say,—unless I was Dean of Saint Patricks" (*Letters*, 79). Tristram also asks in volume 9: "what has this book done more than the Legation of Moses [by Warburton], or the Tale of a Tub, that it may not swim down the gutter of Time along with them?" (*TS*, 9.8.754).

6. New, *A Book for Free Spirits*, 65.

7. Kathleen Williams, "Giddy Circumstance," in *Jonathan Swift: Modern Critical Views*, ed. Harold Bloom (Chelsea House Publishers, 1986), 15. As concerns Swift's satire on war, one may recall the king of Brobdingnag's dismay on hearing Gulliver's description of the engines of war commonly used in European wars: "the King was struck with horror at the description I had given of those terrible engines, and the proposal I had made. He was amazed how so impotent and grovelling an insect as I (these were his expressions) could entertain such inhuman ideas, and in so familiar a manner as to feel wholly unmoved at all the scenes of blood and desolation, which I had painted as the common effects of those destructive machines" (Jonathan Swift, *Gulliver's Travels*, ed. Peter Dixon and John Chalker [Penguin, 1967], 175).

8. Williams, 14.

9. See Richard H. Popkin, *The History of Scepticism from Erasmus to Spinoza* (California University Press, [1960], 1979).

10. "Where *is* the wise? Where *is* the scribe? Where *is* the disputer of this age? Has not God made foolish the wisdom of this world? For since, in the wisdom of God, the world through wisdom did not know God, it pleased God through the foolishness of the message preached to save those who believe" (1 Cor. 1:20–21).

11. *CH*, 140 (*Critical Review*, January 1762).

12. David McNeil, *The Grotesque Depiction of War and the Military in Eighteenth-Century Fiction* (University of Delaware Press, 1990), 163.

13. Ibid., 20.

14. Toby's speech contains several references to both Burton and Cervantes. As far as Cervantes is concerned, Toby's oration, the editors of the *Florida* observe, "owes something, perhaps, to Don Quixote's defence of knight-errantry over the profession of scholar," in which the Don later moves on to "the sufferings and hardships of the soldier" (*Notes*, 431).

15. Robert Burton, *The Anatomy of Melancholy,* 5th ed. (Oxford, 1638), 32.

16. H. J. Jackson, "Sterne, Burton, and Ferriar: Allusions to the *Anatomy of Melancholy* in Volumes Five to Nine of *Tristram Shandy,*" *Philological Quarterly,* 54 (1975), 465.

17. Richard A. Lanham, *The Games of Pleasure* (University of California Press, 1973), 82.

18. New, *A Book for Free Spirits,* 86–87.

19. Lanham, *Games of Pleasure,* 81–82.

20. Cf. his lament as a biographical writer: "I shall never overtake myself" (*TS,* 4.13.342).

21. Donald R. Wehrs, "Sterne, Cervantes, Montaigne: Fideistic Skepticism and the Rhetoric of Desire," *Comparative Literature Studies,* 25 (1988), 129.

22. John Eustace, a medical practitioner of Wilmington, Carolina, had made Sterne the gift of a "*shandean* piece of sculpture," i.e., a walking stick with several handles. "Your walking stick," Sterne observed, "is in no sense more *shandaic* than in that of its having *more handles than one*—The parallel breaks only in this, that in using the stick, every one will take the handle which suits his convenience. In *Tristram Shandy,* the handle is taken which suits their passions, their ignorance or sensibility" (*Letters,* 411). See also Arthur S. Marks, "Connections: Sterne, Shandy, and North Carolina," *Shandean,* 10 (1998), 29–44.

23. Wehrs, op. cit., 130, 139.

24. It brings to mind the trick played in volume 2, with Sterne's own sermon being reproduced to call the readers' attention to the future publication of the *Sermons of Mr. Yorick,* a rather self-seeking authorial gesture, using the seduction of fictional characters to secure money and success for their actual author. Some readers never forgave Sterne the confusion of categories. An unsigned review of the first volume of the sermons, published in the *Monthly Review,* began thus: "Before we proceed to the matter of these sermons, we think it becomes us to make some animadversions on the manner of their publication, which we consider as the greatest outrage against Sense and Decency, that has been offered since the first establishment of Christianity—an outrage which would scarce have been tolerated even in the days of paganism" (*CH,* 77).

25. Robert Alter, *Partial Magic: The Novel as a Self-Conscious Genre* (University of California Press, 1975), 55–56.

26. Swift uses analytical strategies to make his readers aware of their intellectual presumptions and relies on the combination of intellectual involvement and distance achieved by satire through the exercise of critical judgment. Sterne does the same, as well as playing with the emotional

escape and bind provided for readers by the mechanisms of identification and projection triggered by the characters. In both cases, the result is what Patricia Meyer Spacks emphasizes in her analysis of *A Modest Proposal:* "We are left in a state of profound uneasiness, recognizing our involvement in the evil to which we have earlier felt superior" (Patricia Meyer Spacks, "Some Reflections on Satire," in *Jonathan Swift: Modern Critical Views,* ed. Harold Bloom [Chelsea House Publishers, 1986], 110).

Further Reading

◆ ◆ ◆

THE STANDARD EDITION of *Tristram Shandy* is edited by Melvyn New and Joan New, with notes by Melvyn New, Richard A. Davies, and W. G. Day, 3 vols. (Gainesville: University Presses of Florida, 1978–84). Good paperback alternatives are edited by Melvyn New (London: Penguin, 2003) and Robert Folkenflik (New York: Random House, 2004). Two periodicals are invaluable: the *Shandean,* a volume devoted annually since 1989 to scholarship and criticism on Sterne, and the semi-annual *Scriblerian,* which since 1986 has carried reviews and digests of new work in the field.

Biography and Reference

Cash, Arthur H. *Laurence Sterne: The Early and Middle Years.* London: Methuen, 1975.

————. *Laurence Sterne: The Later Years.* London: Methuen, 1986.

Howes, Alan B., ed. *Sterne: The Critical Heritage.* London: Routledge, 1974.

New, Melvyn, et al. "Scholia to the Florida Edition of the Works of Sterne, from the *Scriblerian* 1986–2005." *Shandean* 15 (2004).

Parnell, J. T. *Laurence Sterne: A Literary Life.* Basingstoke: Palgrave, in press.

Patrick, Duncan. "A Chronological Table for *Tristram Shandy.*" *Shandean* 14 (2003).

Ross, Ian Campbell. *Laurence Sterne: A Life.* Oxford: Oxford University Press, 2001.

Voogd, Peter de, and John Neubauer, eds. *The Reception of Laurence Sterne in Europe.* London: Athlone, 2004.

Essay Collections

Cash, Arthur H., and John M. Stedmond, eds. *The Winged Skull: Papers from the Laurence Sterne Bicentenary Conference.* London: Methuen, 1971.

Myer, Valerie Grosvenor, ed. *Laurence Sterne: Riddles and Mysteries.* London: Vision, 1984.

New, Melvyn, ed. *Critical Essays on Laurence Sterne.* New York: G. K. Hall, 1998.

————, ed. *Tristram Shandy: Contemporary Critical Essays.* New York: St. Martin's Press, 1992.

Pierce, David, and Peter de Voogd, eds. *Laurence Sterne in Modernism and Postmodernism.* Amsterdam: Rodopi, 1996.

Traugott, John, ed. *Laurence Sterne: A Collection of Critical Essays.* Englewood Cliffs, N.J.: Prentice Hall, 1968.

Walsh, Marcus, ed. *Laurence Sterne.* Harlow: Longman, 2002.

Books

Byrd, Max. *Tristram Shandy.* London: Unwin Hyman, 1985.

Holtz, William V. *Image and Immortality: A Study of Tristram Shandy.* Providence, R.I.: Brown University Press, 1970.

Iser, Wolfgang. *Laurence Sterne: Tristram Shandy.* Cambridge: Cambridge University Press, 1988.

Keymer, Thomas. *Sterne, the Moderns, and the Novel.* Oxford: Oxford University Press, 2002.

Kraft, Elizabeth. *Laurence Sterne Revisited.* New York: Twayne, 1996.

Lamb, Jonathan. *Sterne's Fiction and the Double Principle.* Cambridge: Cambridge University Press, 1989.

Lanham, Richard A. *Tristram Shandy: The Games of Pleasure.* Berkeley: University of California Press, 1973.

Loveridge, Mark. *Laurence Sterne and the Argument about Design.* London: Macmillan, 1982.

Moglen, Helene. *The Philosophical Irony of Laurence Sterne.* Gainesville: University of Florida Press, 1975.

New, Melvyn. *Laurence Sterne as Satirist: A Reading of Tristram Shandy.* Gainesville: University of Florida Press, 1969.

————. *Tristram Shandy: A Book for Free Spirits.* New York: Twayne, 1994.

Pfister, Manfred. *Laurence Sterne.* London: Northcote House/British Council, 2001.

Stedmond, John M. *The Comic Art of Laurence Sterne: Convention and Innovation in Tristram Shandy and A Sentimental Journey.* Toronto: University of Toronto Press, 1967.

Tadié, Alexis. *Sterne's Whimsical Theatres of Language: Orality, Gesture, Literacy.* Aldershot: Ashgage, 2003.

Traugott, John. *Tristram Shandy's World: Sterne's Philosophical Rhetoric.* Berkeley: University of California Press, 1954.

Journal Articles and Chapters in Books

Allen, Dennis W. "Sexuality/Textuality in *Tristram Shandy.*" *Studies in English Literature 1500–1900* 25 (1985): 651–70.

Alter, Robert. "Sterne and the Nostalgia for Reality." In his *Partial Magic: The Novel as a Self-Conscious Genre.* Berkeley: University of California Press, 1975, pp. 30–56.

Booth, Wayne C. "Did Sterne Complete *Tristram Shandy?*" *Modern Philology* 47 (1951): 172–83.

————. "Telling as Showing: Dramatized Narrators, Reliable and Unreliable." In his *The Rhetoric of Fiction,* 2nd ed. Chicago: University of Chicago Press, 1983, pp. 211–40.

Brady, Frank. "*Tristram Shandy:* Sexuality, Morality, and Sensibility." *Eighteenth-Century Studies* 4 (1970): 41–56.

Briggs, Peter. "Locke's Essay and the Tentativeness of *Tristram Shandy.*" *Studies in Philology* 82 (1985): 494–517.

Brissenden, R. F. "The Sentimental Comedy: *Tristram Shandy.*" In his *Virtue in Distress: Studies in the Novel of Sentiment from Richardson to Sade.* London: Macmillan, 1974, pp. 187–217.

Brown, Marshall. "Sterne's Stories." In his *Preromanticism.* Stanford, Calif.: Stanford University Press, 1991, pp. 261–300.

Burckhardt, Sigurd. "*Tristram Shandy's* Law of Gravity." *ELH* 28 (1961): 70–88.

Donoghue, Frank. " 'I wrote not to be fed but to be famous': Laurence Sterne." In *The Fame Machine: Book Reviewing and Eighteenth-Century Literary Careers.* Stanford, Calif.: Stanford University Press, 1998, pp. 56–85.

Fanning, Christopher. "On Sterne's Page: Spatial Layout, Spatial Form, and Social Spaces in *Tristram Shandy.*" *Eighteenth-Century Fiction* 10 (1998): 429–50.

Gibson, Andrew. "*Tristram Shandy.*" In his *Reading Narrative Discourse: Studies in the Novel from Cervantes to Beckett.* London: Macmillan, 1990, pp. 60–77.

Ginzburg, Carlo. "A Search for Origins: Re-reading *Tristram Shandy.*" In his *No Island Is an Island: Four Glances at English Literature in a World Perspective.* New York: Columbia University Press, 2000, pp. 43–67.

Harries, Elizabeth W. "Sterne's Novels: Gathering up the Fragments." *ELH* 49 (1982): 35–49. Revised in her *The Unfinished Manner: Essays on the Fragment in the Later Eighteenth Century.* Charlottesville: University Press of Virginia, 1994, pp. 41–55.

Hawley, Judith. "The Anatomy of *Tristram Shandy.*" In Marie Mulvey Roberts and Roy Porter, eds. *Literature and Medicine During the Eighteenth Century.* London: Routledge, 1993, pp. 84–100.

Hunter, J. Paul. "Clocks, Calendars, and Names: The Troubles of Tristram and the Aesthetics of Uncertainty." In J. Douglas Canfield and J. Paul Hunter, eds. *Rhetorics of Order/Ordering Rhetorics in English Neoclassical Literature.* Newark: University of Delaware Press, 1989, pp. 173–98.

———. "From Typology to Type: Agents of Change in Eighteenth-Century English Texts." In Margaret J. M. Ezell and Katherine O'Brien O'Keeffe, eds. *Cultural Artifacts and the Production of Meaning: The Page, the Image, and the Body.* Ann Arbor: University of Michigan Press, 1994, pp. 41–69.

Jefferson, D. W. "*Tristram Shandy* and the Tradition of Learned Wit." *Essays in Criticism* 1 (1951): 225–48.

Kay, Carol. "Sterne: Scenes of Play." In her *Political Constructions: Defoe, Richardson, and Sterne in Relation to Hobbes, Hume, and Burke.* Ithaca, N.Y.: Cornell University Press, 1988, pp. 195–246.

Keymer, Thomas. "Sterne and Romantic Autobiography." In Thomas Keymer and Jon Mee, eds. *The Cambridge Companion to English Literature from 1740 to 1830.* Cambridge: Cambridge University Press, 2004, pp. 173–93.

Lamb, Jonathan. "Sterne's System of Imitation." *Modern Language Review* 76 (1981): 794–810.

————. "Sterne's Use of Montaigne." *Comparative Literature* 32 (1980): 1–41.

Loveridge, Mark. "Stories of Cocks and Bulls: The Ending of *Tristram Shandy.*" *Eighteenth-Century Fiction* 5 (1992): 35–54.

Lupton, Christina. "*Tristram Shandy,* David Hume and Epistemological Fiction." *Philosophy and Literature* 27 (2003): 98–115.

Lynch, Jack. "The Relicks of Learning: Sterne among the Renaissance Encyclopedists." *Eighteenth-Century Fiction* 13 (2000): 1–17.

McMaster, Juliet. " 'Uncrystalized flesh and blood': The Body in *Tristram Shandy.*" *Eighteenth-Century Fiction* 2 (1990): 197–214. Revised in her *Reading the Body in the Eighteenth-Century Novel.* Basingstoke: Palgrave, 2004, pp. 25–41.

Miller, J. Hillis. "Narrative Middles: A Preliminary Outline." *Genre* 11 (1978): 375–87.

Moglen, Helene, "Wholes and Noses: The Indeterminacies of *Tristram Shandy.*" *Literature and Psychology* 41 (1995): 44–79. Revised in her *The Trauma of Gender: A Feminist Theory of the English Novel.* Berkeley: University of California Press, 2001, pp. 87–108.

Moss, Roger B. "Sterne's Punctuation." *Eighteenth-Century Studies* 15 (1981): 179–200.

Mullan, John. "Laurence Sterne and the 'Sociality' of the Novel." In his *Sentiment and Sociability: The Language of Feeling in the Eighteenth Century.* Oxford: Clarendon Press, 1988, pp. 147–200.

New, Melvyn. "The Dunce Revisited: Colley Cibber and *Tristram Shandy.*" *South Atlantic Quarterly* 72 (1973): 547–59.

"Sterne, Warburton, and the Burden of Exuberant Wit." *Eighteenth-Century Studies* 15 (1982): 245–74.

Parker, Fred. "*Tristram Shandy:* Singularity and the Single Life." In his *Scepticism and Literature: An Essay on Pope, Hume, Sterne, and Johnson.* Oxford: Oxford University Press, 2003, pp. 190–231.

Porter, Roy. " 'The whole secret of health': Mind, Body, and Medicine in *Tristram Shandy.*" In John Christie and Sally Shuttleworth, eds. *Nature Transfigured: Science and Literature 1700–1900.* Manchester: Manchester University Press, 1989. 61–84.

Regan, Shaun. "Translating Rabelais: Sterne, Motteux, and the Culture of Politeness." *Translation and Literature* 10 (2001): 174–99.

Rodgers, James. "Sensibility, Sympathy, Benevolence: Physiology and Moral Philosophy in *Tristram Shandy.*" In L. J. Jordanova, ed. *Languages of Nature: Critical Essays on Science and Literature.* New Brunswick, N.J.: Rutgers University Press, 1986, pp. 117–58.

Rogers, Pat. "Ziggerzagger Shandy: Sterne and the Aesthetics of the Crooked Line." *English* 42 (1993): 97–107.

Rosenblum, Michael. "The Sermon, the King of Bohemia, and the Art of Interpolation in *Tristram Shandy*." *Studies in Philology* 75 (1978): 472–91.

Rothstein, Eric. "*Tristram Shandy*." In his *Systems of Order and Inquiry in Later Eighteenth-Century Fiction*. Berkeley: University of California Press, 1975, pp. 62–108.

Rowson, Martin. "Hyperboling Gravity's Ravelin: A Comic Book Version of *Tristram Shandy*." *Shandean* 7 (1995): 62–86.

———. "A Comic Book Version of Tristram Shandy." *Shandean* 14 (2003): 104–21.

Seelig, Sharon Cadman, "Sterne, *Tristram Shandy:* The Deconstructive Text." In her *Generating Texts: The Progeny of Seventeenth-Century Prose*. Charlottesville: University Press of Virginia, 1996, pp. 128–54.

Seidel, Michael. "Gravity's Inheritable Line: Sterne's *Tristram Shandy*." In his *Satiric Inheritance, Rabelais to Sterne*. Princeton, N.J.: Princeton University Press, 1979, pp. 250–62.

Shklovsky, Viktor. "The Novel as Parody: Sterne's *Tristram Shandy*." In his *Theory of Prose*. Elmwood Park: Dalkey Archive Press, 1991, pp. 147–70.

Spacks, Patricia Meyer. "The Beautiful Oblique: *Tristram Shandy*." In her *Imagining a Self: Autobiography and Novel in Eighteenth-Century England*. Cambridge, Mass.: Harvard University Press, 1976, pp. 127–57.

Steele, Peter. "Sterne's Script: The Performing of *Tristram Shandy*." In Douglas Lane Patey and Timothy Keegan, eds. *Augustan Studies: Essays in Honor of Irvin Ehrenpreis*. Newark: University of Delaware Press, 1985, pp. 195–204.

Thomas, Calvin. "*Tristram Shandy*'s Consent to Incompleteness: Discourse, Disavowal, Disruption." *Literature and Psychology* 36 (1990): 44–62.

Watt, Ian. "The Comic Syntax of *Tristram Shandy*." In *The Literal Imagination: Selected Essays*. Seattle: University of Washington Press, 2002, pp. 126–42.

Wehrs, Donald R. "Sterne, Cervantes, Montaigne: Fideistic Skepticism and the Rhetoric of Desire." *Comparative Literature Studies* 25 (1988): 127–51.

Zimmerman, Everett. "*Tristram Shandy* and Narrative Representation." *Eighteenth Century: Theory and Interpretation* 28 (1987): 127–47. Revised in Zimmerman, *The Boundaries of Fiction: History and the Eighteenth-Century British Novel*. Ithaca, N.Y.: Cornell University Press, 1996, pp. 179–204.